HISTORICAL ATLAS OF TEXAS

HISTORICAL ATLAS OF TEXAS

by

A. Ray Stephens and William M. Holmes

Phyllis M. McCaffree, Consultant

University of Oklahoma Press : Norman and London

By William M. Holmes

Texas: A Geography (with Terry G. Jordan and J. L. Bean)
  (Boulder, Colo., 1984)

Library of Congress Cataloging-in-Publication Data

Stephens, A. Ray.
  Historical atlas of Texas.

  Includes index.
  1. Texas—Historical geography.   2. Texas—
Maps.   I. Holmes, William M.   II. Title.
F386.S86 1988 911'.764 88-40210
ISBN 0–8061–2158–0

CONTENTS

PREFACE

STUDY OF THE HISTORY OF TEXAS is an exciting adventure. Through it we can observe the ways the native inhabitants and the later arrivals responded to each other and to the region's varied terrain. Their constant adjustment to environmental conditions and their attempts to control their surroundings led toward the era when development of the land became the equivalent of "civilization" and, even more recently, size too readily became a synonym for significance.

Over the centuries the region that is now the state developed a unique heritage, but at the same time it has remained for the most part within the mainstream of the American nation's development. We begin the study of the Texas heritage by focusing on natural resources that contributed to a favorable lifestyle and to personal gain. We then follow the various human wanderings and exploitations as different ethnic groups strove to call Texas home. You are invited to join this historical-geographical study that has become high adventure.

The purpose of this historical atlas is to illustrate particular topics in Texas history with maps accompanied by brief interpretative essays. Of course some selection was necessary, and we have sought to present those items which we feel are the most significant to the history of the entire state. At the beginning of the Atlas are maps on the geography and geology of Texas and on Texas Indians. Other maps cover topics in a chronological order, including the Spaniards and French in Texas, Anglo-American intrusion, the Texas Revolution, the Republic of Texas era, the Secession movement, the Civil War in Texas, cattle drives, and petroleum discoveries. Additional maps of special interest include hurricanes, transportation, military installations, conservation and recreational areas, educational institutions, and political and economic districts.

The essay corresponding to the concluding map 64, "Modern Texas," contains estimated population figures by county. It also provides an account of recent state population trends and explains contemporary economic activities in modern Texas.

The maps are numbered consecutively. The numbers in the index refer to the maps rather than to pages.

Our sincere appreciation is hereby extended to agencies, organizations, and individuals who provided assistance and encouragement during the preparation of this work. They include the Library of Congress Map Division, New York Public Library, University of Texas Archives, Texas State Archives, Panhandle-Plains Museum at West Texas State University, University of North Texas Library, Texas General Land Office, Texas Railroad Commission, Texas Department of Highways and Public Transportation, Coordinating Board of the Texas College and University System, Texas Legislative Reference Library, and Texas Legislative Council.

Special personal thanks go to Professor William Kamman, chairman of the University of North Texas Department of History, for his assistance in the preparation of the original base maps; Eloise Green and Betty Burch, administrative secretaries, and Kathy Henson, administrative assistant, in the University of North Texas Department of History, and their staff for their expert office assistance; the University of North Texas for a faculty development leave when the project first got under way; Fred Pass and Mike Kingston, of the *Texas Almanac,* for permission to use in this work the wealth of statistical data so vital to the study of Texas history and geography; James H. Anderson for cartographic assistance; and Phyllis McCaffree, history teacher in the Van, Texas, Junior High School, for her diligent service as consultant to the project to provide the perspective of the secondary school teacher. Her critical review of the essays and maps and her worthy suggestions on particular topics helped strengthen the historical atlas and make it more useful to secondary school classes.

And, of course, the acknowledgments would be incomplete without recognizing the many students in our respective classes with whom we have continually renewed our appreciation for the Texas heritage. They so often expressed a need for such a work as this that we teamed up to provide it.

We have endeavored to produce a historical atlas that will aid the professional scholar, provide a greater understanding of the relationship of history and geography for students in college and secondary school courses, and serve as resource material for elementary school topical studies. The general reader will find this historical atlas helpful in gaining or renewing an appreciation for the Texas heritage.

A. RAY STEPHENS
WILLIAM M. HOLMES

Denton, Texas

HISTORICAL ATLAS OF TEXAS

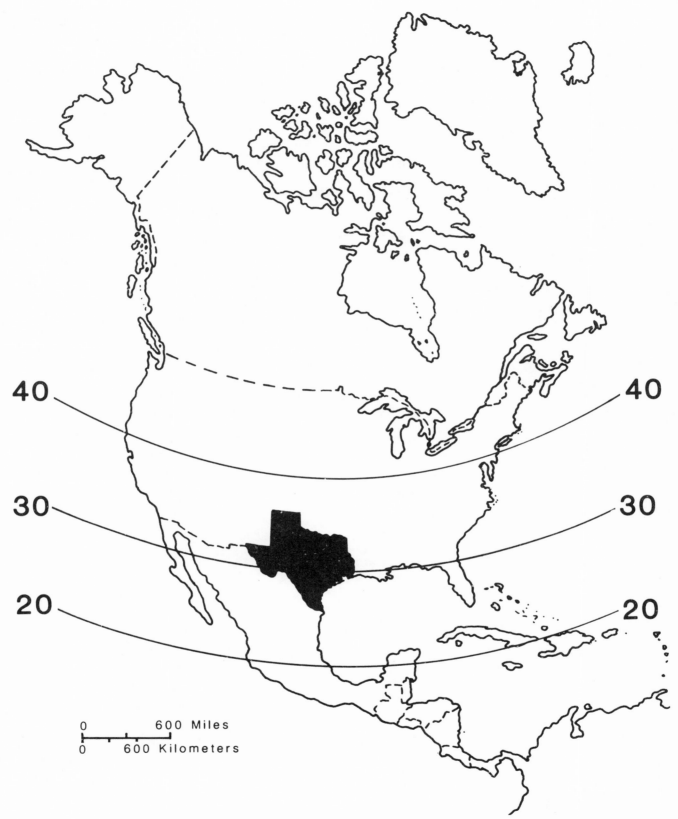

40 40

30 30

20 20

0 600 Miles
0 600 Kilometers

LOCATION WITHIN THE UNITED STATES AND IN RELATION TO MEXICO

1. LOCATION WITHIN THE UNITED STATES AND IN RELATION TO MEXICO

TEXAS, SITUATED IN THE SOUTH CENTRAL REGION OF THE UNITED STATES, became the twentieth-eighth state in the Union on December 29, 1845. Possessing common boundaries with eight American and Mexican states—New Mexico, Oklahoma, Arkansas, Louisiana, Tamaulipas, Nuevo León, Coahuila, and Chihuahua—Texas also has a lengthy tidewater coastline of 624 miles along the Gulf of Mexico.

The state's boundary is described as beginning at the mouth of the Sabine River where it flows into the Gulf of Mexico and continuing up that river through the middle of the stream to 32° north latitude, thence due north to the Red River, thence up the Red River along the south and west bank to 100° west longitude, thence due north along that meridian to 36° 30' north latitude, thence due west along that parallel to 103° west longitude, thence due south along that meridian to 32° north latitude, thence due west along that parallel to a junction with the Rio Grande at 106° 38' west longitude, thence down the Rio Grande along the middle of the stream to its mouth at 25° 50' north latitude, thence along the coastline in the Gulf of Mexico three marine leagues (10.36 miles) offshore to the place of beginning.

Distance and Texas are almost synonymous. The longest straight-line distance in a north-south direction from the northwest corner of the Panhandle to the estuary of the Rio Grande is 801 miles. In an east-west direction the greatest distance is 773 miles between a point on the Sabine River at its eastwardmost bend in Newton County at 93° 31' west longitude and a point at 106° 38' west longitude on the Rio Grande near El Paso. Texarkana is even closer to Chicago, Illinois, crossing three large states, than it is to El Paso, within the same state. El Paso is closer to Los Angeles, California, than it is to Texarkana.

At the time of its admission into the Union, Texas replaced Virginia as the largest state; it held that position until Alaska achieved statehood in 1959. The Texas land area is 262,134 square miles, or 167,765,760 acres, and the inland water area is 3,330,560 acres, for a total of 171,096,220 acres. Comparing it to other regions, one finds that Texas is larger than the combined land areas of France, Belgium, Luxembourg, the Netherlands, and Switzerland. In relation to other areas of the United States, Texas is bigger than all New England plus New York, New Jersey, Pennsylvania, Ohio, Maryland, Delaware, and Virginia.

Texas is in the transition zone between the humid Eastern Woodlands and the drier Great Plains, with portions of both regions situated in the state. Texas has forested areas in the east, a long coastline on the south, mountains in the southwest, relatively level terrain on the west and the far northwest, rolling plains in the west central area, and mildly undulating prairie country in the middle. Elevations range from sea level to 8,751 feet. Eastern and western animals and birds may be found in the same proximity, which indicates their approximate limits. Central American birds fly across the Gulf of Mexico to Texas for their northernmost migration, and Canadian waterfowl go as far south as the Texas coast during the winter. A wide variation in the growing seasons and rainfall patterns influences the life-styles of wildlife and human beings.

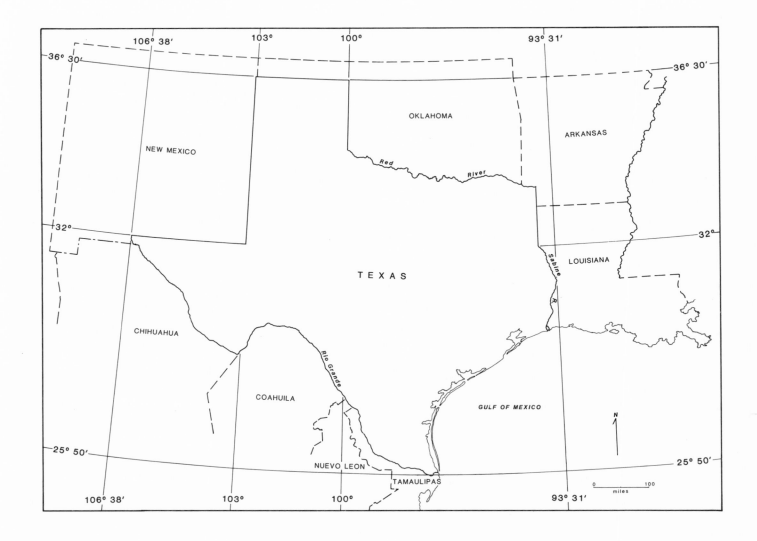

LONGITUDE AND LATITUDE

© 1988 University of Oklahoma Press

2. LONGITUDE AND LATITUDE

THE LATITUDE OF TEXAS extends from 25° 50' north, which is on the extreme southern bend of the Rio Grande in Cameron County near Brownsville, to 36° 30' north, the northern boundary of the Texas Panhandle.

The extreme eastern boundary of Texas is on the Sabine River in Newton County at longitude 93° 31' west. The westernmost point in Texas is in El Paso County on the Rio Grande at longitude 106° 38' west.

The eastern boundary of the Texas Panhandle is longitude 100° west from the Prairie Dog Town Fork of the Red River to latitude 36° 30' north. The Panhandle's western boundary extends from latitude 32° north to latitude 36° 30' north along longitude 103° west. The southern boundary of New Mexico that borders Texas begins at the intersection of longitude 103° west and latitude 32° north and extends due west to the Rio Grande near El Paso.

The eastern boundary of Texas is along the Sabine River from its mouth at Sabine Pass to latitude 32° north, and from that point due north to the Red River near Texarkana along longitude 94° 4' west.

The boundary lines were set at various times. In 1819 the Sabine and Red rivers became limits of the United States and Spain with the Adams-Onís Treaty. In 1836 the Treaties of Velasco between Texas and Mexico, and later that year by an act of the Texas Congress, established the Rio Grande as the southern limits. The northern and northwestern boundaries of present-day Texas came about as a result of the agreement between Texas and the United States known as the Compromise of 1850. The final adjustment to Texas land claims occurred when territory situated between the Prairie Dog Town Fork of the Red River (also referred to by some as the South Fork) and the North Fork of the Red River became the subject of controversy over ownership between the governments of Texas and the United States. In 1896 the U.S. Supreme Court resolved the dispute by granting exclusive jurisdiction for Greer County to the United States.

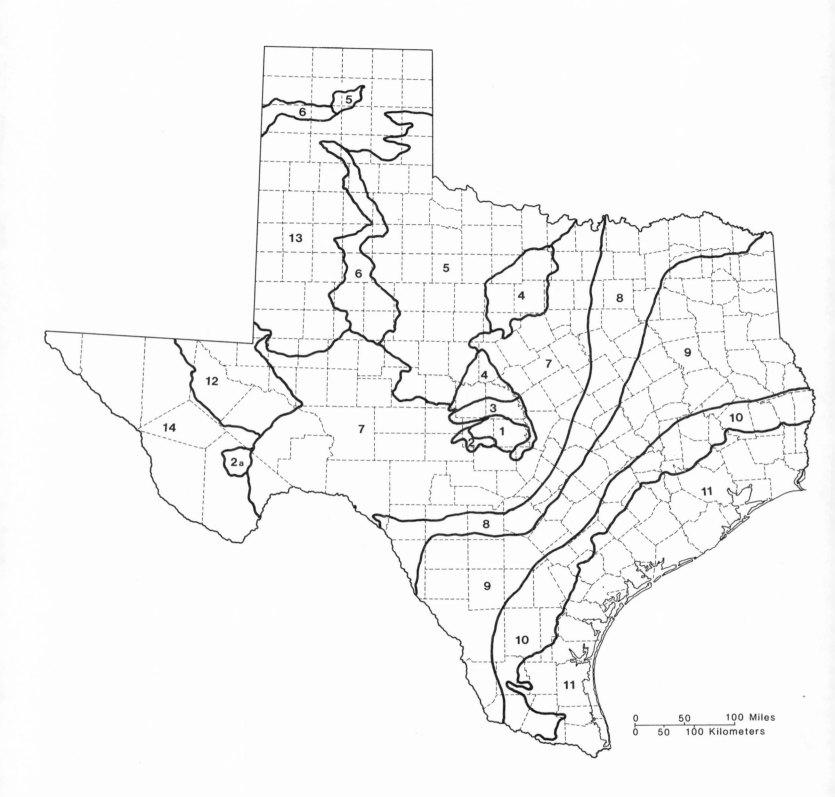

GEOLOGIC AGE OF SURFACE MATERIALS

© 1988 University of Oklahoma Press

3. GEOLOGIC AGE OF SURFACE MATERIALS

THE DIVERSITY OF GEOLOGIC MATERIALS in Texas establishes the foundation upon which other physical features have become interwoven. Landform features, soils, and vegetation are often directly related to the parent materials of the earth. The geologic map reflects a generalized distribution of surface materials of Texas as they are related to the geologic time scale. The map indicates the geologic age of surface materials in Texas as follows:

1. Precambrian of the Llano region
2. Older Paleozoics of the Llano region
2a. Marathon Basin
3. Mississippian and Ordovician of the Llano Basin
4. Pennsylvanian of the Palo Pinto Section
5. Permian of the Osage Plain
6. Triassic and Jurassic of the Cap Rock Escarpment
7. Lower Cretaceous of the Edwards Plateau, Lampasas Cut Plain, and Comanche Plateau
8. Upper Cretaceous of the Blackland Belt
9. Older Tertiary of the Gulf Coastal Plain
10. Later Tertiary of the Gulf Coastal Plain
11. Pleistocene of the Gulf Coastal Plain
12. Quaternary of the Pecos Valley
13. Late Cenozoic Alluvium of the High Plains
14. Trans-Pecos Basins and Ranges, including a confusion of occasional Precambrian outcrops interspersed with older and younger Paleozoic, Cretaceous, and undated intrusive and extrusive igneous materials making up the mountains. Desert basins consist mainly of Quaternary materials.

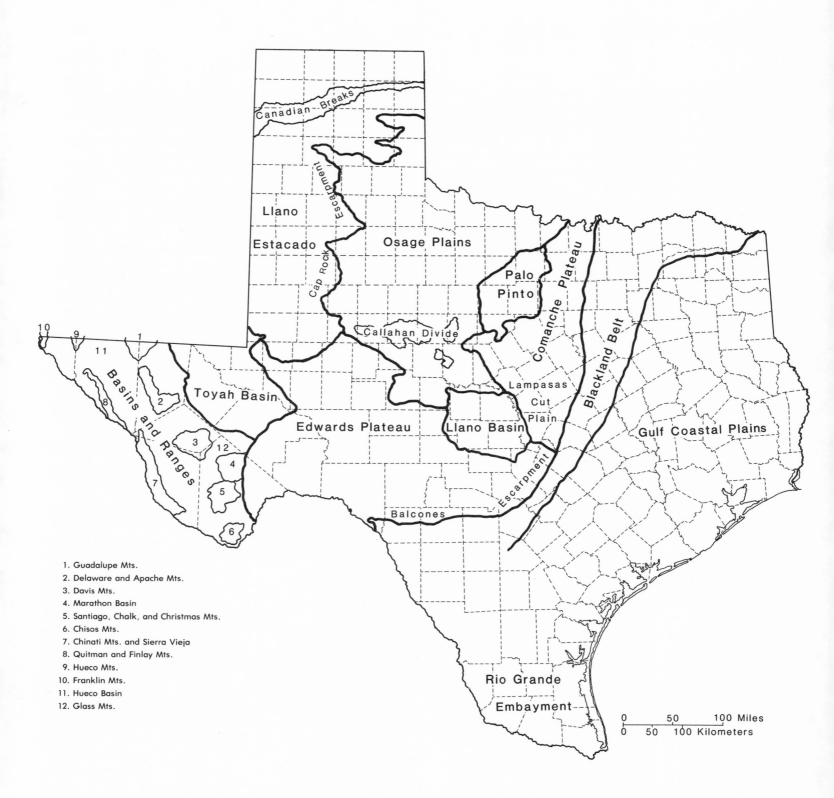

Canadian Breaks

Llano
Estacado

Cap Rock Escarpment

Osage Plains

Palo
Pinto

Comanche Plateau

Blackland Belt

Callahan Divide

Toyah Basin

Basins and Ranges

Edwards Plateau

Lampasas
Cut
Plain

Llano Basin

Gulf Coastal Plains

Escarpment

Balcones

Rio Grande
Embayment

1. Guadalupe Mts.
2. Delaware and Apache Mts.
3. Davis Mts.
4. Marathon Basin
5. Santiago, Chalk, and Christmas Mts.
6. Chisos Mts.
7. Chinati Mts. and Sierra Vieja
8. Quitman and Finlay Mts.
9. Hueco Mts.
10. Franklin Mts.
11. Hueco Basin
12. Glass Mts.

0   50   100 Miles
0   50   100 Kilometers

PHYSIOGRAPHIC REGIONS

© 1988 University of Oklahoma Press

4. PHYSIOGRAPHIC REGIONS

OF THE EIGHT MAJOR PHYSIOGRAPHIC REGIONS in the United States, five are found in Texas. Throughout its history Texas has been the crossroads of the nation in several meanings of the term. Here is where east meets west and north meets south in terms of climatic variation, vegetational striation, and wildlife diversification. Desert streams flow to humid coastal plains. Tall timber is reduced to medium-sized trees, which become stunted shrubs the farther west one travels, until even the sap of the shrubs seemingly turns into oil and the leaves are reduced to thorns. The soil substance differs markedly, also. Rich topsoil in the eastern and central portions contrasts with the shallow, rocky terrain in the far western section. Rainfall follows the same pattern of abundance in the east and scarcity in the west. Annual precipitation, adaptability of crops, available surface and subterranean water for agricultural, municipal, and industrial uses—all helped to determine the population density and life-styles of Texas and Texans. Explorers and settlers from conflicting cultures coming from opposite directions met in Texas to further complicate the existence of the native inhabitants. The story of Texas has been one of adapting to the environment and using the state's natural resources in the march to modern development.

Gulf Coastal Plains cover the eastern and southern portions of Texas. Once an ocean floor, this region extends northward to the Red River and westward to the Rio Grande. The Balcones Escarpment, running roughly in a curved line from Del Rio on the Rio Grande through San Antonio, Austin, and Temple, is the interior boundary of the Coastal Plains. North of the Brazos River that boundary is marked by the contact between the harder Lower Cretaceous rock on the west and the softer Upper Cretaceous materials on the east. The elevation varies from less than 950 feet at the extreme southwestern end of the region to sea level along the Gulf Coast. The Blackland Belt, the Eastern Cross Timbers, the Grand Prairie, and the Rio Grande Embayment are subregions in the Gulf Coastal Plains. Low barrier islands offshore form shallow bays and lagoons next to the mainland.

The *Interior or Central Lowland* is a physiographic region extending from Canada to west central Texas. Other names applied to the Texas portion of this region are Rolling Plains, Lower Plains, North Central Plains, and Osage Plains. Elevation variations in Texas range from approximately 1,000 feet on the east to 2,200 feet at the base of the Cap Rock Escarpment on the west. The relatively level prairies and undulating plains give way towards the western extremity of this region to badlands topography, sheer cliffs, and colorful canyons created by erosion of Triassic and Jurassic rocks. Subregions of the Osage Plains are the Comanche Plateau, Western Cross Timbers, Palo Pinto Basin, and Callahan Divide.

The Llano Estacado (Staked Plain), part of the *High Plains and Plateaus* region, is in West Texas. The Llano Estacado is relatively level without distinguishing landform features except where streams intersect or where playas (shallow, undrained basins) catch runoff water. Elevations there range from approximately 2,500 feet to 4,500 feet. The Edwards Plateau is on the southeastern end of this region, with the Balcones Escarpment as its eastern boundary. On the Edwards Plateau, known as the Texas Hill Country, elevations range from 850 feet on the east to 4,000 feet at the foot of the mountains west of the Pecos River. The Edwards Plateau is composed of a massive accumulation of extremely durable Lower Cretaceous limestone that is almost indestructible in that semi-arid climate. Other areas of the High Plains and Plateaus region are the Llano Basin in the center of the state and the Toyah Basin along the Pecos River.

The Great Basin, or *Basin and Range Province,* as it is known in Texas, is an extension of the terrain found in portions of the American West and northern Mexico. Extensive desert flats surround high mountains such as the Davis, Van Horn, Franklin, Glass, and Guadalupe mountains. The highest elevation in Texas, Guadalupe Peak at 8,751 feet, is in this region. The area of the Guadalupe Mountains along the Texas–New Mexico boundary is also considered to be part of the *Rocky Mountains* region, another major physiographic region of the United States.

As vast and varied as is the Texas terrain, the state has a certain cohesiveness or mystique that holds the people of the various natural regions together in unity of spirit. "Nowhere but in Texas" is an apt statement to describe the diversity that ranges from seashore to mountains, from swamps to deserts, from subtropical lands to wind-swept plains, from pine forests to short-grass country, with a variety of plant and animal life unparalleled elsewhere.

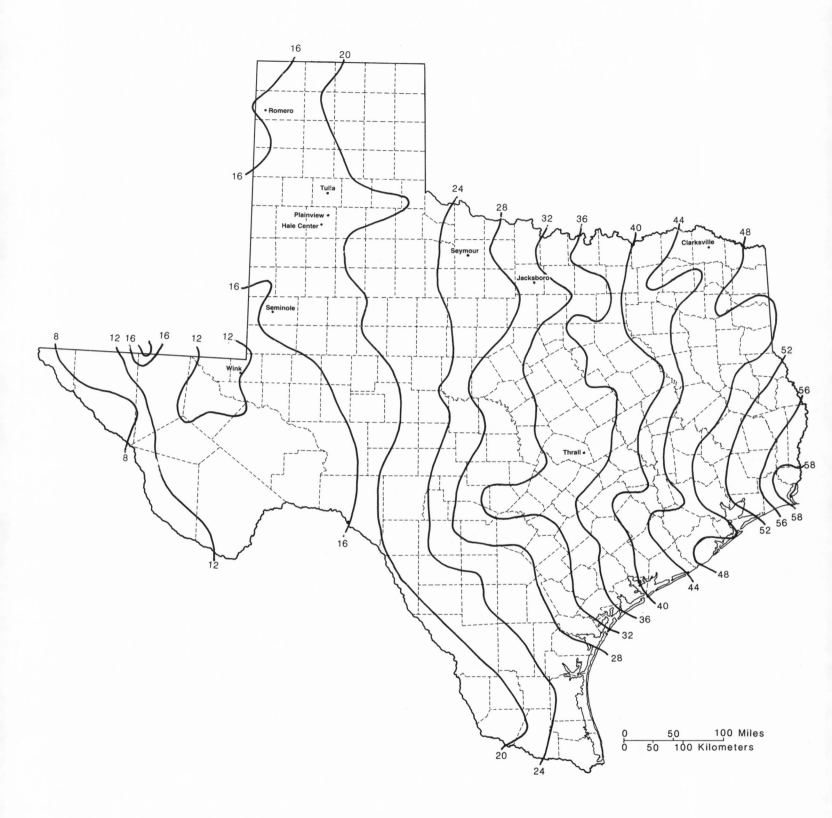

PRECIPITATION

© 1988 University of Oklahoma Press

5. PRECIPITATION

ON THE SUBJECT OF RAINFALL IN TEXAS, diversity is again the rule. While one region of the state may be experiencing excessive moisture, another may be in the clutches of a drought. The average annual precipitation ranges from over 58 inches in the Orange-Jefferson counties area to under 8 inches in El Paso. From Louisiana to New Mexico, the lines on the map depicting variation in average annual precipitation run in a northerly-southerly direction, with dryness increasing as one moves westward. Moist air from the Gulf of Mexico is a major contributing factor to rainfall in Texas.

The amount of rainfall governs the agricultural and industrial economics of Texas. Natural vegetation and cultivated crops are reflected in the rainfall pattern. Pine forests in the extreme east and short-grass plains in the far west illustrate the variation. Enough precipitation for farming falls in the eastern half of the state, but west of the ninety-eighth meridian (near Jacksboro, as a point of reference) dry-land farming practices are necessary to conserve ground moisture during the growing season. In some areas of West Texas and along the Rio Grande, irrigation from groundwater or underground sources is necessary to grow certain crops. Most precipitation in the western portion of the state falls during the warm season, while in the eastern part, east of the ninety-fifth meridian, equal amounts fall during the warm and cold seasons. Evaporation caused by summer heat frequently accounts for losses of soil moisture or water in reservoirs. The development of urban areas has been restricted to locations where water for industrial and domestic purposes is adequate. As Texas continues to grow, further restrictions are anticipated unless water in substantial quantity is imported.

Periods of abnormal moisture deficiency, or drought, have occurred frequently in various areas of the state, although usually for brief durations. During such periods, when the water table drops too low to sustain plants, dust storms have caused serious topsoil erosion. When severe thunderstorms or clouds from hurricanes produce torrential downpours on such dry soil, further erosion damage results. The worst drought in terms of intensity and length occurred in the period 1950–1956, when 244 of the 254 counties were classified as disaster areas by the end of 1956.

The two driest years on a statewide average in recorded Texas history were 1917 (14.30 inches) and 1956 (16.17) inches). The two wettest years were 1919 (42.15 inches) and 1941 (42.62 inches). The greatest annual precipitation at one location—109.38 inches—occurred at Clarksville, Red River County, in 1873. Wink, Winkler County, had the least in one year, with 1.76 inches in 1956. The most rainfall in a twenty-four-hour period—38.20 inches—occurred in Thrall, Williamson County, in 1921.

The state receives most of its snowfall during December, January, and February. Frigid northers and devastating blizzards bring polar air to mix with the warmer, wetter air off the Gulf of Mexico to produce storms that hazard the health and safety of Texans. Snowfall contributes a portion of the annual precipitation in the High Plains and the mountainous region of the Trans-Pecos, but usually no significant amount to other parts of Texas. The greatest seasonal average of snowfall was at Romero, Hartley County, with 65.0 inches in 1923–1924. The most snow in one storm was at Hale Center, Hale County, on February 2–5, 1956, when 33.0 inches fell. The most snow in a twenty-four-hour period—24.0 inches—hit Plainview, Hale County, on February 3–4, 1956.

Temperature extremes also have affected the state. The coldest recorded temperature, 23 degrees below zero, Fahrenheit, occurred at Tulia, Swisher County, on February 12, 1899, and at Seminole, Gaines County, on February 8, 1933. The hottest temperature in Texas was recorded at Seymour, Baylor County, on August 12, 1936, when the thermometer registered 120 degrees.

Although such extremes in temperature and precipitation are uncommon, climatic conditions have nevertheless played an important role in Texas history. A temperate climate, adequate moisture for the cultivation of crops during the state's formative years, and later a supply of runoff water stored in reservoirs for the development of an urban state have all contributed to produce opportunities for millions of Texans over the decades.

NATIVE PLANT–LIFE REGIONS

© 1988 University of Oklahoma Press

6. NATIVE PLANT-LIFE REGIONS

AN OUTSTANDING FEATURE OF TEXAS native plant life is the diversity of vegetation. A broad range of climatic and soil conditions influences vegetational variations. Texas is a border province between the humid lands to the east and the subhumid and semiarid lands to the west. The listing below identifies the regions on the map and explains the types of vegetation that predominate in each area.

1. Marsh and salt grasses of the Coastal Prairie.
2. Coastal Prairie. Includes andropogons and other coarse grasses. Grama grasses are found in the western portion, and panicum grasses occur on the northern margins adjacent to timbered areas.
3. Piney Woods. Shortleaf pine with scattered hardwoods, mainly oak, dominate the northern part of the region, with shortleaf, longleaf, and loblolly pines in the southern part.
4. The hardwood belts of Texas:
   4a. Post Oak Belt. Consists mainly of post oak, blackjack oak, and hickory.
   4b. Eastern Cross Timbers. Post oak, blackjack oak, and hickory are major hardwoods interspersed with occasional small prairies.
   4c. Western Cross Timbers. Post oak and hickory become more scattered than in the eastern hardwood regions and include occasional prairies with bunch, grama, and bluestem grasses.
5. The prairies of North Central Texas:
   5a. Blackland Prairie and outlying string prairies. Prairies consist of bunch grasses, mainly andropogons, grama, bluestem, and shorter buffalo grasses. Stream channels often are extensions of adjacent hardwood regions.
   5b. Grand Prairie. Grasses are essentially the same as those of the Blackland Prairie.

Conditions of growth, however, are harsher, resulting in species being more scattered and slightly shorter than their eastern counterparts.

6. South Texas Brushy Plains. The eastern portion of this region consists mainly of coarse bunch grasses and shorter grasses such as grama and curly mesquite, interspersed with occasional thickets of prickly pear and other thorny xerophytes (drought-tolerant plants). Thorny vegetation, such as mesquite, huisache, catclaw, and yucca become more abundant to the west, with scattered post oak and live oak in the east.
7. Short grass and scattered timber of the eastern Edwards Plateau and Hill Country. Trees include live oak, shinnery oak, and red oak; juniper (cedar) brakes occur in the eastern margin and extend into the southern portion of the Grand Prairie. A thin cover of such short grasses as buffalo grass and mesquite grass dominates the western half of the region.
8. Short-grass steppeland of the Osage (Lower) Plains and High Plains. Main grasses include buffalo grass, grama grass, wheat grass, and Indian grass, with scattered mesquites and xerophytes.
9. Desert vegetation with hardy bunch grasses, burro, tussock, and salt grasses interspersed with such xerophytes as yucca, mesquite, sotol, catclaw, and cenizo.
10. Mountain vegetation with xerophytic grasses and shrubs on lower slopes improving to oak, juniper, piñon pine, and ponderosa pine on higher slopes.
11. Yucca-Mesquite Steppeland of the High Plains. Vegetation includes scattered short grasses mixed with such thorny xerophytes as mesquite and yucca.

KIOWA

Kiowa–Apache

Taovaya

COMANCHE

WICHITA

Wichita

Tawakoni

Waco

LIPAN APACHE

Anadarko   Adaes

CADDO

Hasinai   Nazoni

Neche   Nacogdoche

Ais

JUMANO

ATAKAPA

KARANKAWA

COAHUILTECAN

0   50   100
miles

TEXAS INDIANS

© 1988 University of Oklahoma Press

7. TEXAS INDIANS

A CONFLICT OF CULTURES existed in Texas even before the white man came. Indians of the eastern piney Woods differed in their cultural habits from those of the Blackland and Grand prairies, the Coastal Plains, the High Plains, and the desertlike region of southwestern, Texas.

The availability of foodstuffs predetermined the quality of life for the native Americans. Those tribes living in areas where game abounded or where crops could be grown with relative ease usually had more leisure time for fellowship and social structure. Together the people could work for an advanced culture. When limited natural resources determined the necessity of a larger geographical area for living and working, Indian tribes became smaller in number and had a more constrained life-style. In such circumstances, most of the daylight hours for adults would be needed for the simple pursuits of providing a living.

Within the extension of the Eastern Woodlands area of eastern Texas and western Louisiana, the Caddo and Atakapa (Attacapa) Indians lived a sedentary life. The plentiful supply of game and the favorable growing conditions for crops meant that a sizeable population could be supported in a smaller geograpical area by people who lived in permanent villages. The Caddos were the most advanced Indians in Texas. A number of tribes within the Caddoan Confederacy had names such as Hasinai, Nazoni, Nacogdoche, Anadarko, Neches, Ais, and Adaes.

In central Texas the Wichita and Tonkawa Indian tribes roamed the prairies west of the Eastern Woodlands to the edge of the Great Plains. Seasonal hunts in addition to limited cultivation made up the year's activities. Skin tepees and pole structures covered with grass or brush provided housing. The Wichitan Confederacy included groups such as the Waco, Tawakoni, Taovaya, and Wichita.

The Karankawa Indians ranged from the Galveston area to the Nueces River along the Gulf Coastal Plains. They relied on fish and other aquatic life, hunted game, and gathered the fruit of plants.

Coahuiltecans lived in the brushy South Texas Plains below the Edwards Plateau to the Rio Grande. Their constant roaming in search of food prohibited permanent dwellings. The size of the band was limited to small groups of families or to individual families.

In southwestern Texas the Jumano Indians roamed from the San Angelo area south into Mexico and from the vicinity of Austin west to the Pecos River. In addition to following the bison, the Jumano gathered wild foods and killed small game. In the eighteenth century this once great people became absorbed into the Lipan Apache culture.

The Lipan Apache Indians lived in the Great Plains area of Texas and New Mexico. Before they obtained horses, they hunted game on foot and planted crops. When the horse came, their range increased as these people followed the bison, and their gardening efforts became more limited.

When the Comanche Indians migrated from the northern to the southern Great Plains during the eighteenth century, they forced the Lipan Apaches and the Tonkawas to move aside. From that time until 1875 the Comanches dominated the southern Great Plains. Completely nomadic, they relied on the bison for food, clothing, and shelter. Other game and wild fruits provided food for the families.

The Kiowa Indians, also formerly from the northern Great Plains, occupied the region of western Oklahoma and the High Plains of what is now the Texas Panhandle. This nomadic tribe also relied on the bison for life's basics. Associated with the Kiowas as one of their bands for purposes of protection and survival was the Kiowa–Apache tribe. These two tribes spoke unrelated langauges but communicated through the use of key words and sign language.

In time the habitat of Texas Indians became more and more confined as Anglo-American settlement expanded relentlessly westward. Tribes became restricted in their hunting and farming activities as American pioneers carved their homesteads out of the wilderness. In addition to tribes in Texas when Europeans and Americans arrived, eastern Indians also found temporary homes in Texas. Small groups of Cherokee, Kickapoo, Potawatomi, Delaware, Shawnee, Creek, Choctaw, and Chickasaw tribes lived in eastern Texas until forced to move by mid-nineteenth century. Among the emigrant Indians only the Alabama and Coushatta tribes remained.

The cultural conflict became pronounced as whites and reds vied for the same real estate. Advanced technology and social organization proved to be principal factors in determining the position of dominance.

Big Spring

El Paso

Presidio

San Marcos

San
Antonio

Galveston

Victoria

Corpus Christi

Pensacola
Tampa Bay
Presidio
Galveston
Culiacán
Havana
Santiago
Compostela
Mexico City

0   400
miles

0   50   100 Miles
0   50   100 Kilometers

CABEZA DE VACA

© 1988 University of Oklahoma Press

8. CABEZA DE VACA

FOLLOWING THE DISCOVERY of the New World, Spanish explorers actively investigated the unknown lands and sought to establish settlements. From the islands of the Caribbean and the West Indies the conquistadors sailed along the coastline of the Gulf of Mexico, stopping occasionally to take on supplies and to search for riches. Often a reception that ranged from unfriendly to hostile caused the Spanish to move on.

The name so well associated with those early explorers is Cabeza de Vaca. Alvar Núñez Cabeza de Vaca served as treasurer of the Pánfilo de Narváez expedition that sailed in 1528 from Cuba, intending to settle at the mouth of the Rio Grande after two other attempted expeditions, by Alonso Alvarez de Piñeda and Nuño de Guzmán, had failed. While en route, Narváez, Cabeza de Vaca, and a party of three hundred men landed in Florida to search for gold, then missed connections with their ships and wandered around the interior from Tampa Bay to present-day northern Florida. There they constructed five crude boats and attempted to make their way along the Gulf Coast to Mexico.

The boats separated in a storm and became shipwrecked on the Texas coast at various locations now thought to be Galveston Island, the mouth of the San Bernard River, Cavallo Pass at Matagorda Bay, and St. Joseph Island at the Aransas Pass inlet into Aransas Bay. The survivors of the shipwreck faced great misery and deprivation. Many died of hunger, exposure, and illness, or at the hands of Indians. Enslaved by Indians, the strangers became the gatherers of wood and the performers of other menial camp tasks. They also helped their Indian hosts as traders and as healers.

Of the approximately three hundred who set off afoot at Tampa Bay, only four rejoined their Spanish comrades in Mexico eight years later. These four, Cabeza de Vaca, Andrés Dorantes, Alonso del Castillo, and Dorantes's slave Esteban the Moor, who was from Azamor on the Atlantic coast of Morocco, often went with their Indian captors in search of tunas, the fruit of the prickly pear. While on such a food-hunting trip in 1535, these four survivors of the Narváez expedition escaped.

Historians differ on the route to freedom these men took. After wandering around in present south central Texas perhaps as far south as San Patricio on the Nueces River and into central Texas as far north as San Marcos, they made their way to what is now San Antonio and then headed west by northwest. They noted the abundance of water, wood, and game in the Balcones Escarpment area. The Spaniards visited with Indian tribes along the way perhaps as far northwest as Big Spring before altering their course to the southwest to the Presidio region, then up the Rio Grande to where El Paso stands today. Southwestern Borderlands historian Herbert Eugene Bolton wrote that the Indians who greeted the Coronado expedition a few years later spoke of the Cabeza de Vaca group passing not far to the south on the Great Plains. Another account holds that the survivors crossed the Rio Grande to Reynosa, traipsed around in northern Mexico by way of Monclova, and then crossed the Rio Grande again above Del Rio before skirting the northern edge of the Big Bend region. From the El Paso region they journeyed through Chihuahua, crossed the Mexican deserts south of Arizona, and went to the Pacific Coast. This foursome strongly desired to find fellow Christians and to put their captive days behind them.

The four survivors arrived at Culiacán in the spring of 1536 after their eight-month hike. Along the way they encountered many Indian tribes, served as healers to the native inhabitants, and observed carefully their surroundings as they pressed on towards the setting sun.

The legacy of Cabeza de Vaca and his companions is the first observation by Europeans of the land, people, plants, and animals from Galveston through Texas and Mexico. They also heard references to great cities of wealth in the north country, although they did not actually see them. Their stories impressed the viceroy, Antonio de Mendoza, and influenced a major expedition led by Coronado, into the interior in search of a mythical city of wealth. Cabeza de Vaca returned to Spain and later led an expedition of his own in South America. Dorantes and Castillo remained in Mexico and married rich widows. Esteban, still a slave, accompanied a Franciscan priest on an expedition into northern Mexico and the present American Southwest.

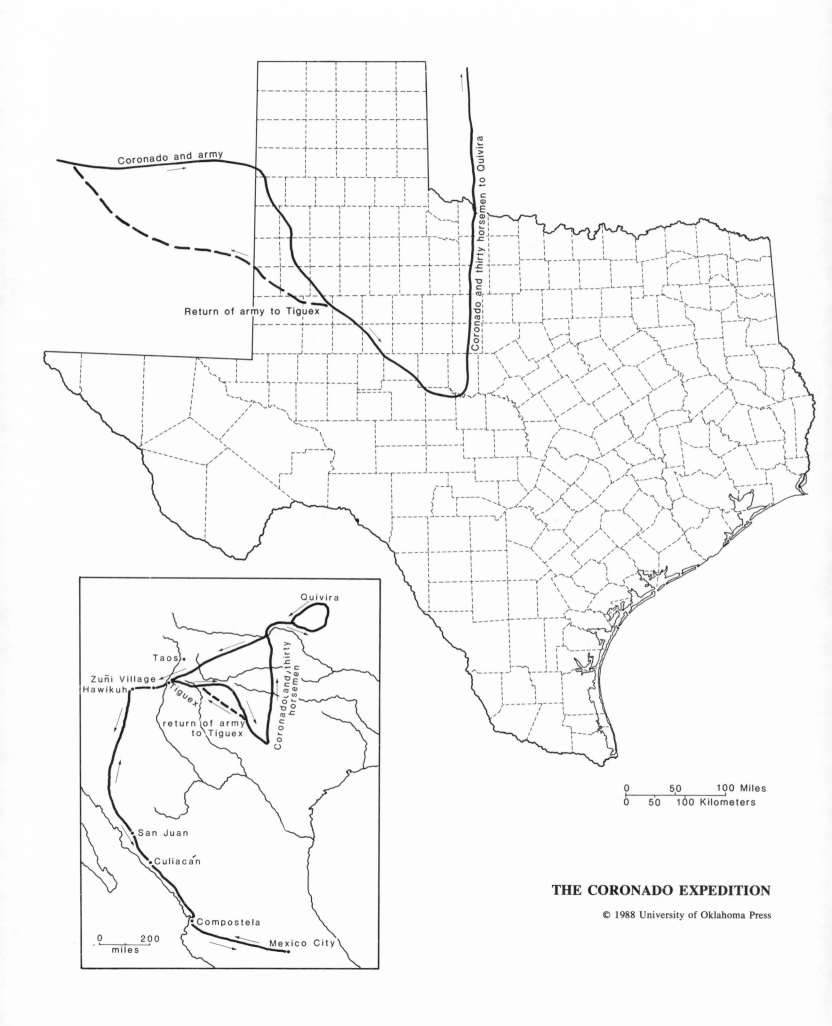

Coronado and army

Return of army to Tiguex

Coronado and thirty horsemen to Quivira

Quivira

Taos

Zuñi Village
Hawikuh

Tiguex

return of army
to Tiguex

Coronado and thirty
horsemen

San Juan

Culiacán

Compostela

Mexico City

0   200
miles

0   50   100 Miles
0   50   100 Kilometers

THE CORONADO EXPEDITION

© 1988 University of Oklahoma Press

9. THE CORONADO EXPEDITION

TALES OF THE SEVEN CITIES of Cíbola in northern New Spain had already excited the Spanish even before Cabeza de Vaca told his story. Viceroy Antonio de Mendoza at first offered the expedition's leadership to De Vaca, who declined the honor, then appointed Fray Marcos de Niza, a Franciscan priest, to head an advance party. Fray Marcos took with him Esteban the slave, survivor of the Cabeza de Vaca group, whom Mendoza had purchased from Andrés Dorantes, as a guide.

The band left Culiacán in early 1539 and moved northward. Fray Marcos sent Esteban on ahead with some Indians to observe and to report his findings. Messengers were to be sent back with a cross of sufficient size that would signify the richness of a discovery. When a messenger returned to Fray Marcos bearing a cross the size of a man, the Franciscan monk moved with haste to Cíbola.

In the meantime, Esteban had cowed local Indians along the route with his style of healing, womanizing, and boasting. He met his death at the hands of the Zuñi at the present Arizona–New Mexico state line. Apparently he came across some people who presumed by the trinkets in his possession that he was a spy for a neighboring enemy tribe.

Fray Marcos came to the death site of the bearded Moor of Azamor, stealthily peeked from a summit at Cíbola, saw the green valleys and many houses in the village, erected crosses to claim the land for Spain, and fled back to Mexico. His news encouraged Viceroy Mendoza to send forth a mighty expedition led by Francisco Vázquez de Coronado to claim the land for Spain.

In the spring of 1540, the Coronado expedition of soldiers, Indian workers, and livestock left Culiacán, journeyed through present northwestern Mexico, and arrived at a Zuñi settlement in Arizona that Fray Marcos called Cíbola. The Spanish subdued the Zuñis, explored to the north and east, and wintered at Tiguex on the Rio Grande near present-day Albuquerque. They moved to the Llano Estacado, or Staked Plains, in the spring of 1541. The Spanish acquired a guide whom they called "the Turk", who was probably a Pawnee Indian. The Turk had been captured and enslaved by Indians in New Mexico, and he looked secretly upon the Spanish as his ticket home. He offered to guide the Europeans to a fabulous place a distance away, known as Quivira, where riches abounded.

The greedy Spanish trudged along in amazement at this vast country of the Great Plains. They watched endless herds of buffalo, greeted various Indian tribes, and ate the wild fruit that grew there. Their journey seemingly became aimless because of the absence of distinctive land features to guide them in their flat High Plains country. It soon became apparent that the Turk had lied about knowing the way to Quivira, so the Spanish shackled him to the rear guard and listened to a new Indian guide.

After wandering around until they came across some sharp topographical breaks on the Cap Rock Escarpment, Coronado divided his force. He sent the army back to Tiguex while he led a contingent of thirty horsemen on to Quivira.

Historians differ on the conquistador's route from this point. He may have gone northward through the Tule and Palo Duro canyons on his way to the Arkansas River. Then again, in order to pass through the country where the types of vegetation his chronicler mentioned are abundant, he may have continued to the southeast for a distance, then cut back north. The more likely course, since Coronado's group traveled "by the needle" as they moved northward, probably beginning this phase of their trip from present-day Coleman County, was to cross the Red River near the mouth of the Salt Fork north of present-day Vernon and then proceed through western Oklahoma and Kansas to the Arkansas River.

Coronado reached his destination in the summer of 1541. The villages of Quivira were in south central Kansas near the great bend of the Arkansas River. The Spanish, extremely disappointed at their descovery of villages with grass-thatched roofs instead of cities of gold, explored a little beyond before deciding to return to Tiguex. Before they left Quivira, they repaid the Turk for his lies and misleading directions and for fomenting attacks on the Spanish by garroting him with a rope.

Coronado's quest for riches now vanished, the expedition turned southwestward to Tiguex for the winter of 1541–42. His force returned to Mexico in 1542 by retracing their earlier route. After two years on the trail and at considerable expenditure of the Crown's treasury and manpower, the Coronado expedition limped home. They left an excellent account of the land and its people, but also left the notion that the Great Plains and the Texas area were not worth the further attention of Spain. This notion prevailed for the next one and one-half centuries.

Guasco

Daycao River Village

Daycao village

DeSoto's death place

Pánuco

Havana

Santiago

0   400
miles

0   50   100 Miles
0   50   100 Kilometers

THE DE SOTO–MOSCOSO EXPEDITION

© 1988 University of Oklahoma Press

10. THE DE SOTO–MOSCOSO EXPEDITION

WHILE SPANISH SOLDIERS MARCHED to the Great Plains from the southwest, other agents of Spain approached Texas from the east. Spanish authorities sought precious metals in the interior as they made a long trek through the wilderness of present-day Florida, Georgia, South Carolina, North Carolina, Tennessee, Alabama, Mississippi, Arkansas, Missouri, Oklahoma, and Texas. Hernando de Soto, who had developed wealth and a reputation in Peru with Pizarro, led the explorers as they recorded their impressions of this vast land new to Europeans.

De Soto had received a commission from Emperor Charles V as governor of Cuba and *adelantado* of Florida. After attempting unsuccessfully to persuade Cabeza de Vaca to accompany his expedition, De Soto set out in April, 1538, with six hundred men on nine ships. They crossed the Atlantic Ocean, stopped briefly in Cuba, then went on to Tampa Bay. For the next three years this group experienced occasional military victories, misfortunes, hunger, and discoveries. They left a record of courage, improvisation, and frequent cruelty towards the native inhabitants, in addition to lengthy descriptions of the country they traversed. But they found no treasure in the form they sought.

From mid-1539 to early 1542 the expedition explored the present southeastern United States. The trek took its toll on the Europeans. Lost, reduced in force in men and animals by more than half, and short of supplies, the Spaniards' hardships increased in 1542 when their commander became terminally ill with fever. As he lay dying, De Soto named Luis de Moscoso as his successor.

Upon assuming command, Moscoso conferred with officers about the best course to leave from this spot where the Arkansas River flowed into the Mississippi River. The leadership collectively agreed to head west in order to reach Mexico and salvation by land. The De Soto–Moscoso expedition moved across southern Arkansas to Hot Springs and then across the Red River probably near present Texarkana. Where the Spaniards entered Texas and their route within Texas are in dispute. The written account mentions rivers, villages, the abundance or scarcity of food, disposition of Indians, and terrain.

In general the group of Spaniards with their Indian retinue traveled in a westwardly direction for 150 leagues (approximately 425 miles) from the Mississippi River. Presuming they did not stray too far from such a course, and supported by a modern understanding of the terrain as well as animal and plant life, we may reasonably assume the Moscoso party moved along the higher ground that divides the natural drainage between the Red and Sulphur rivers to the Bonham-Sherman area and on to Gainesville. Dipping to the southwest slightly, the Spanish went through the Eastern Cross Timbers, crossed the Grand Prairie, and entered the Western Cross Timbers. They probably made camp on the Brazos in the general region of Young County at a place they called Guasco.

The Spanish learned from Indian captives that other white men had been seen farther to the west. Moscoso did not know about the Coronado expedition and must have been most curious about this information. Perhaps Mexico was closer than he knew. If these travelers the Indians mentioned could be found, then he and his men could soon get back to civilization and leave this deprived area and their hardships behind. The Spanish experienced a scarcity of game and corn the farther west they went. They gave up on finding precious metal and now worried about survival in a hostile environment.

Scouting parties going out from Guasco in various directions found nothing of interest to the Spanish. Moscoso then led his men on a journey of ten days to the sunset on the advice of Guasco natives. The local inhabitants oftentimes went to the suggested location in pursuit of deer. The trip was through an area covered by trees. When they reached the river they named Daycao, which may be the Double Mountain Fork of the Brazos River in northwestern Fisher County, the Spanish turned back to their headquarters in Guasco. They discovered that the farther west they went, the more inhospitable the country became. Already the summer was getting away. To spend a winter in such an area was not even considered.

Hastily, the Spaniards retraced their steps to the Mississippi River, built boats, and floated to the sea. They traveled along the Texas coast to Pánuco, where they arrived on July 2, 1543. This ill-fated expedition journeyed thousands of miles through the humid woodlands to the semiarid Great Plains but found no great riches in the forms expected. Their contribution to our heritage is our first recorded glimpse of the interior from Florida to Texas.

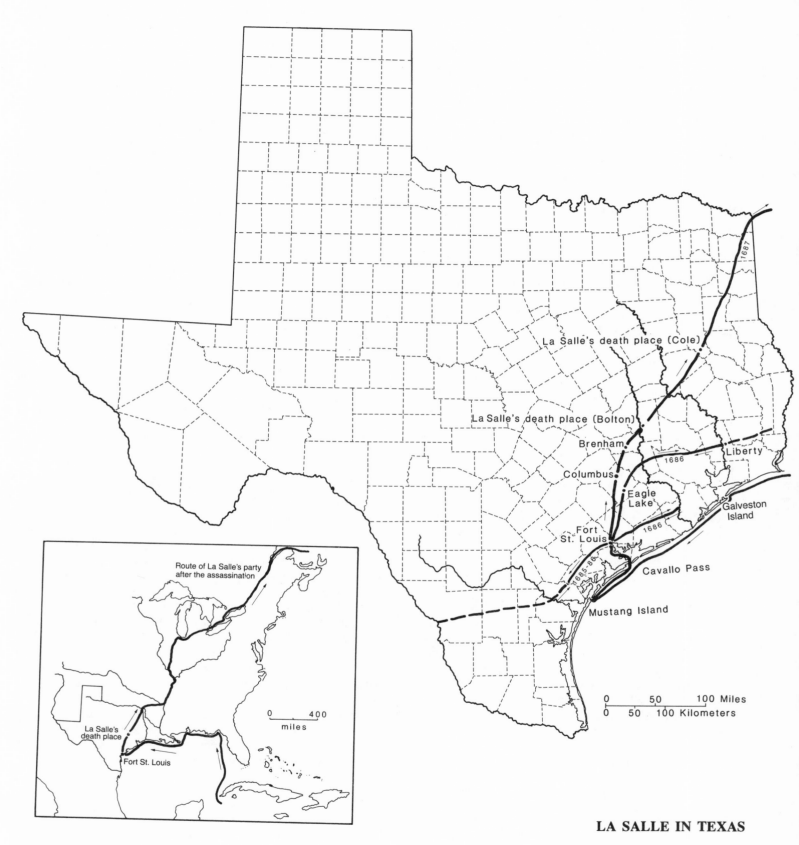

La Salle's death place (Cole)

La Salle's death place (Bolton)

Brenham

1686

Liberty

Columbus

Eagle
Lake

Fort
St. Louis

1686

Galveston
Island

1685-86

Cavallo Pass

Mustang Island

1687

0   50   100 Miles
0   50   100 Kilometers

Route of La Salle's party
after the assassination

La Salle's
death place

Fort St. Louis

0   400
miles

LA SALLE IN TEXAS

© 1988 University of Oklahoma Press

11. LA SALLE IN TEXAS

ONE OF THE GREATEST FRENCH ADVENTURERS in North America was René Robert Cavelier, Sieur de la Salle. During the seventeenth century, French explorers penetrated the wilderness from the St. Lawrence River to the Great Lakes and eventually to the Mississippi River. In 1682, La Salle led an expedition to the mouth of the Mississippi. He retraced his steps to the Great Lakes and then returned to France, where he received permission to establish a colony in the New World.

The entourage of four ships with crew, soldiers, mechanics and laborers, civilian volunteers, several families, and some single girls looking for husbands sailed from Rochelle, France, in July, 1684. La Salle's official destination was the mouth of the Mississippi River, but he may have intended to land farther west in order to mount attacks on the internal provinces of New Spain. Along the way the enterprise lost to Spanish buccaneers one ship loaded with the provisions and tools necessary for colonization. Missing the mouth of the Mississippi because of fog, or by intent, the expedition went as far west as Mustang Island before doubling back to Matagorda Bay. After they went through Cavallo Pass into Matagorda Bay, another ship, which carried weapons, tools, medicine, and most of the baggage, was lost by grounding. The fleet's flagship returned to France with essential cannon and balls because the captain, with whom La Salle was at odds, claimed the sea was too rough to remove the iron being used as ballast.

La Salle located his permanent camp, Fort St. Louis, on a high point where Garcitas Creek flows into Lavaca Bay. Some authorities contend that the fort was located on the Lavaca River nearby. The struggling colonists constructed buildings, planted crops, and raised livestock they brought with them. Plagued by Indians, illness, and drought, the French began to waver in their resolve. La Salle began a series of explorations in late 1685. He went westward to the Nueces and possibly to the Rio Grande perhaps to scout out Spanish defenses in the internal provinces before returning to Fort St. Louis in March, 1686. The leader became despondent when he learned that in his absence his remaining ship had been wrecked near the inlet to Matagorda Bay. Stranded, short of supplies, and desperate, La Salle now attempted to find the Mississippi.

The party crossed the Colorado and Brazos rivers and eventually reached the Trinity River. Some historians suggest La Salle went as far east as present De Soto Parish, Louisiana, before returning to the main camp on Lavaca Bay, where desertion, Indian attack, illness, and death had greatly reduced the number of inhabitants. Despair gripped these lost Frenchmen in a strange land.

In January, 1687, La Salle set out to find his way back to the Great Lakes. He took nineteen men with him and left twenty men, women, and children behind at the settlement. After crossing the Colorado River near present-day Columbus, the party continued on to the Brazos River, where they camped. La Salle became concerned when some of his men who had crossed the Brazos did not return immediately, so he searched for them. Dissatisfaction over the leader's sternness now led some of the men to violence. The dissidents killed La Salle's nephew, La Salle's personal servant, and a Shawnee Indian hunter, and when La Salle came upon the scene, they killed him, also. To add further insult, the murderers stripped his body, dragged it into nearby undergrowth, and left it there for wild animals to devour. On March 19, 1687, at the age of forty-three, this great explorer lay dead far from home in an inhospitable land he did not know and one he had tried unsuccessfully on several occasions to leave.

A dispute exists concerning the exact place of La Salle's death. Some authorities contend he was killed on the east side of the Brazos near the confluence of the Navasota River. Others locate the death site farther east on a branch of the Trinity. Still others believe La Salle died on the east bank of Larrison Creek in the southern part of Cherokee County. But regardless of the site on modern maps, the survivors continued a northeastward trek until they reached the land of the Caddo Indians in present-day northeast Texas, and then on to the Red River before turning east to the mouth of the Arkansas River. The wandering Frenchmen found their way to the Great Lakes and then home.

A smallpox outbreak and additional Indian attacks wiped out the remnant left at Fort St. Louis. The only French citizens left in Texas by 1689 when the Spanish found the fort were a few French deserters living as members of some Indian tribes. The great attempt to plant a French colony along the Gulf Coast and possibly a place to mount attacks against Spanish defenses in northern New Spain came to a tragic end.

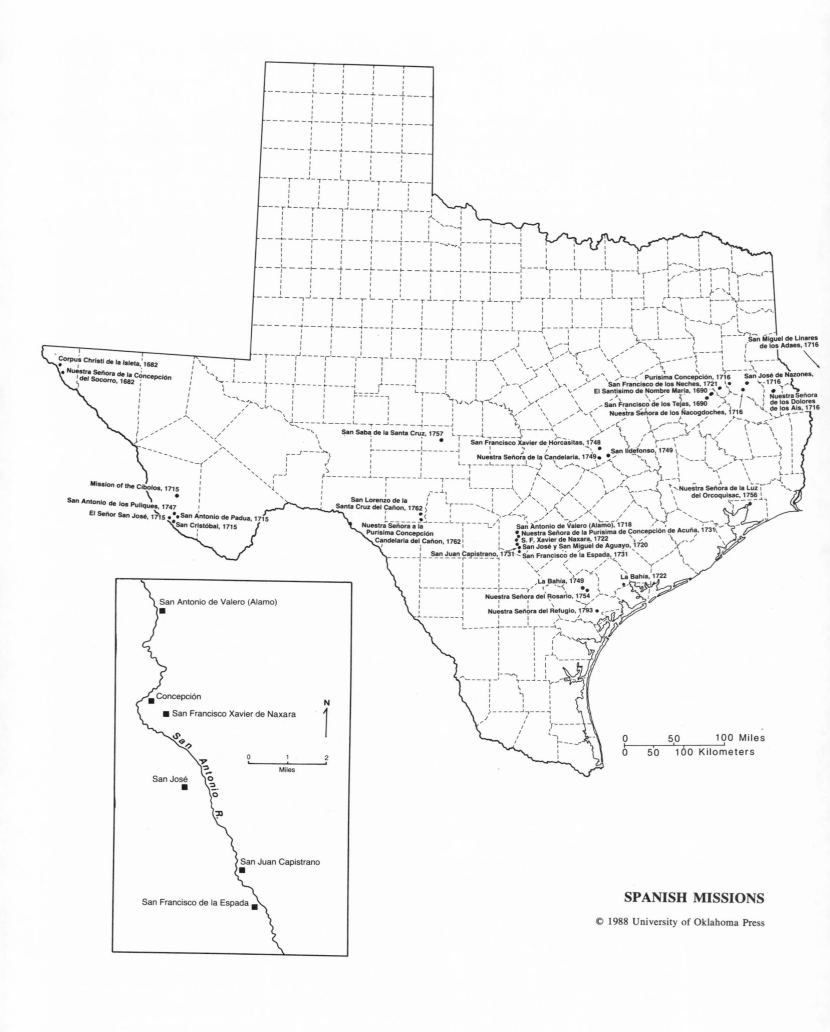

Corpus Christi de la Isleta, 1682
Nuestra Señora de la Concepción del Socorro, 1682

San Miguel de Linares de los Adaes, 1716

Purísima Concepción, 1716
San Francisco de los Neches, 1721
El Santísimo de Nombre María, 1690
San José de Nazones, 1716
San Francisco de los Tejas, 1690
Nuestra Señora de los Nacogdoches, 1716
Nuestra Señora de los Dolores de los Ais, 1716

San Saba de la Santa Cruz, 1757
San Francisco Xavier de Horcasitas, 1748
Nuestra Señora de la Candelaria, 1749
San Ildefonso, 1749

Nuestra Señora de la Luz del Orcoquisac, 1756

Mission of the Cíbolos, 1715
San Antonio de los Puliques, 1747
El Señor San José, 1715
San Antonio de Padua, 1715
San Cristóbal, 1715

San Lorenzo de la Santa Cruz del Cañon, 1762
Nuestra Señora a la Purísima Concepción Candelaria del Cañon, 1762

San Antonio de Valero (Alamo), 1718
Nuestra Señora de la Purísima de Concepción de Acuña, 1731
S. F. Xavier de Naxara, 1722
San José y San Miguel de Aguayo, 1720
San Juan Capistrano, 1731
San Francisco de la Espada, 1731

La Bahía, 1749
La Bahía, 1722
Nuestra Señora del Rosario, 1754
Nuestra Señora del Refugio, 1793

0   50   100 Miles
0   50   100 Kilometers

Inset map:
San Antonio de Valero (Alamo)
Concepción
San Francisco Xavier de Naxara
San Antonio R.
N
0   1   2
Miles
San José
San Juan Capistrano
San Francisco de la Espada

SPANISH MISSIONS

© 1988 University of Oklahoma Press

12. SPANISH MISSIONS

THE SPANISH MISSION SYSTEM IN TEXAS operated as a political arm of New Spain as it expanded into the frontier. Although Spanish explorers traveled across portions of the present state, they did not attempt to establish missions except along the Rio Grande until they learned of the presumed French threat led by La Salle in the 1680s.

Spanish authorities sent out expeditions by land and by sea to counteract the French presence but found only an abandoned fort in ruins. Alarmed that the French might try again, in 1690 New Spain sent soldiers and missionaries to eastern Texas. A short time later, this time reacting to the French lack of thrust, the Spanish retreated back to present Mexico. They realized the excessive expense of establishing and equipping new outposts. It is with this fact in mind that one understands the reluctance of Spain to expend the means necessary to hold the vast lands on the fringe of empire. Additional reactions to French expansion in Louisiana brought renewed mission efforts in 1716 and 1721.

Religious and economic reasons also prompted Spanish expansion. The salvation of the aborigine's soul and the support of his overlords who taught and supported him served as important considerations. In the extensions of the kingdom, Spanish officials sent soldiers to act as a safeguard against foreign encroachment and hostile Indians, missionaries to convert the unenlightened, and economic agents to exploit the labor of the local inhabitants.

Franciscan colleges at Zacatecas and Querétaro sponsored the friars who ventured into the Texas wilderness. Rather than having the missionaries learn the various Indian languages, the Spanish chose the much more expeditious way of teaching the Indians the Spanish language so that any new priest could enter the mission field and begin his work without a language-learning delay.

The work of the Spanish consisted of erecting missions, constructing forts, and establishing agriculture and local industry, all with Indian labor. Instruction in religion, language, and life-styles promoted European civilization in Texas. The general plan called for a self-supporting mission, with the new converts assuming control after a ten-year period, but the theory had to be adjusted in Texas when a longer period of tutelage proved necessary. The degree of success varied from region to region, depending on political imperatives, financial backing, and the receptivity of the Indians.

Although the Spanish planted missions in several locations in Texas, the main areas of importance were in eastern Texas, along the Gulf Coast, and at San Antonio. The eastern Texas episode reached as far east as Los Adaes near present Robeline, Louisiana, a short distance from the French settlement at Natchitoches, but the majority of the Spanish energy concentrated around Nacogdoches and San Augustine. Along the coast, authorities at first established the La Bahía mission at Garcitas Creek on the site of La Salle's Fort St. Louis then moved it to the Guadalupe River and finally to present Goliad on the San Antonio River. At San Antonio de Bexar several efforts succeeded with the establishment of a series of missions on the San Antonio River downstream from the present-day central city. Less successful attempts occurred in the Milam County area in central Texas, at Anahuac in southeastern Texas, and in Menard and Edwards counties in western Texas.

Spain reexamined its purpose in Texas when France abandoned its North American claims following the French and Indian War of 1756–63. In recognition of their real frontier versus their imaginery frontier, the Spanish pulled back to the Rio Grande except for outposts at present-day Goliad and San Antonio. Some of the evacuees returned soon to the Nacogdoches area without official permission and remained. The last mission attempt in Texas occurred on the Gulf Coast in 1793 at Goff Bayou in Calhoun County, but the mission was moved to Refugio shortly thereafter. In 1794, Spanish officials began a program of secularization whereby the secular clergy replaced the missionaries.

Spanish priests worked in another mission field in present Texas not directly related to those already discussed. In 1682, missionaries fleeing the revolt of the New Mexico pueblos constructed churches in the El Paso area for the converts they brought with them in their retreat. Other missions were established along the Rio Grande, particularly in present-day El Paso and Presidio counties.

The missionaries learned to love and appreciate their charges, but purposes of state often overrode their plans. Overall, the clergy mapped places and streams, recorded events, and instituted the first vestiges of outside influences that in time overpowered the Indians of Texas.

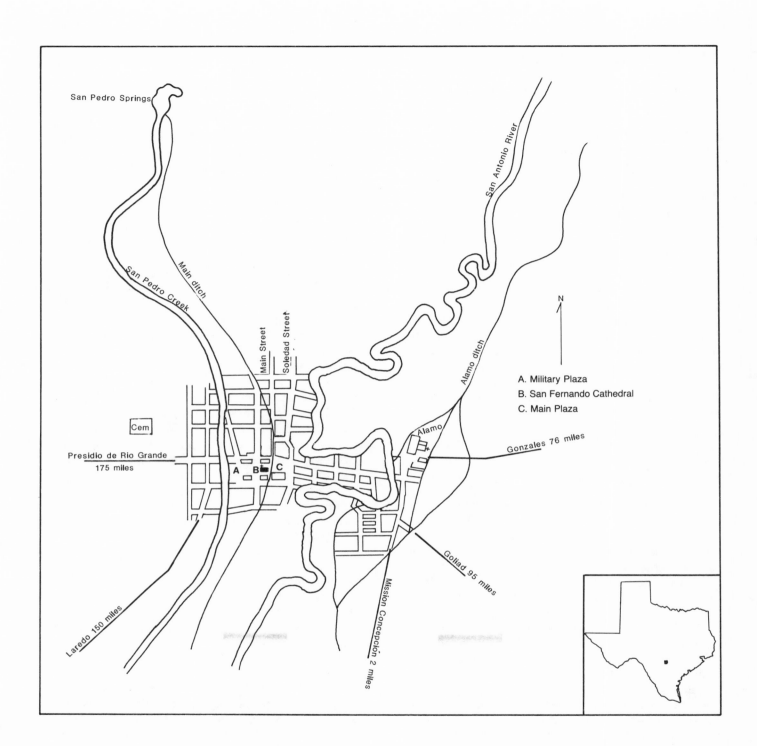

San Pedro Springs

San Antonio River

San Pedro Creek

Main ditch

Main Street

Soledad Street

N

Alamo ditch

A. Military Plaza
B. San Fernando Cathedral
C. Main Plaza

Cem

Presidio de Rio Grande
175 miles

A B C

Alamo

Gonzales 76 miles

Goliad 95 miles

Laredo 150 miles

Mission Concepción 2 miles

SAN ANTONIO DE BEXAR

© 1988 University of Oklahoma Press

13. SAN ANTONIO DE BEXAR

THE SPANISH ATTEMPTED to establish missions in East Texas after they learned of the French presence under La Salle. The mission effort, 1690–93, failed. As the Spanish continued their northward extension in Mexico up to San Juan Bautista on the Rio Grande, the French established an outpost on the Red River at Natchitoches. Louis Juchereau de St. Denis, a Canadian-born French official in Louisiana, appeared at San Juan Bautista in 1714 on a trading venture which alarmed the Spanish officials. If French traders could cross Texas without challenge, then it would be easy for French civil authorities to extend jurisdiction over territory claimed by Spain.

In order to meet this presumed threat, the viceroy sent Captain Domingo Ramón to reestablish missions in East Texas. Along the way in 1716, the assembly of soldiers, missionaries, and settlers stopped at San Pedro Springs in present-day San Antonio, where they noticed the abundance of wood, water, and building stone. Later, when the suggestion was made for a supply station between the Rio Grande and the East Texas missions, this site was selected. In 1718, Martín de Alarcón, governor of Coahuila, established a mission on the San Antonio River. The mission was San Antonio de Valero (the Alamo). A settlement known as Villa de Bexar sprang up nearby.

Settlers from Mexico and mission Indians developed an irrigation system for their fields, cultivated crops, planted fruit trees, and raised livestock. In 1719, when the Marqués de Aguayo replaced Alarcón as governor, he permitted the establishment of a new mission in Bexar that would be named for him. In 1720, missionaries began their program at the San José y San Miguel de Aguayo Mission.

After leaving San Antonio, Governor Aguayo journeyed to East Texas, where he strengthened the Spanish position so thoroughly with new presidios and missions that the French threat diminished. Upon his return to San Antonio de Bexar, the governor approved the location for a new mission, San Francisco Xavier de Naxera, adjoining on the south the grant of the San Antonio de Valero Mission. Before he left Texas, Aguayo recommended the settlement of several hundred families between San Antonio and the East Texas missions.

His health broken because of the rigorous expedition, Aguayo resigned as governor. His successors soon began to reduce the numbers of East Texas missions and presidios in the interest of economy. The weakened defenses in East Texas alarmed the clergy, causing them to relocate three missions in present-day Houston and Nacogdoches counties to the San Antonio River near Bexar. They were Nuestra Señora de la Purísima Concepción de Acuña, San Juan Capistrano, and San Francisco de la Espada missions.

Life for the Indian residents at the missions in Texas consisted of religious instruction, agricultural work, and agriculture-related industry. Conversion of the native inhabitants served as a main purpose of the Spanish missionaries' presence on the frontier. The stationing of troops to protect the missionaries and the converts also provided a buffer against hostile Indians and foreign government intrusion onto territory the Spanish claimed. Missionaries went among the various tribes making friends, offering gifts, and establishing missions as they also served as diplomatic agents of the Crown, which supported them financially. The missions at Bexar remained under the charge of the priests until the secularization movement began. San Antonio de Valero was secularized in 1793, and the other four missions in 1794.

In an effort to provide Spanish settlers on the Texas frontier when he was governor, Aguayo recommended the recruiting of two hundred families from the Canary Islands. The king increased the goal to four hundred, but only ten families made the intitial journey to Veracruz by way of Havana before the economy-minded Brigadier Pedro de Rivera persuaded the viceroy to halt further immigration. The Canary Islanders made their way to Mexico City and on to Cuatitlán, where they prepared for the long journey to Texas. Through marriage the number of families increased to fifteen, for a total of fifty-six persons of various ages who started north. One died along the way. In March, 1731, the new settlers arrived at Bexar, then laid out plans for a church, city lots, streets, and common lands for farming. They established the first civil government in Texas in the community known as San Fernando de Bexar near the presidio of San Antonio de Bexar. When the Spanish inhabitants in other parts of Texas retreated from East Texas under government orders following the French withdrawal from the North American mainland, the population along the San Antonio River increased. In 1772 San Antonio de Bexar became the capital city of Texas upon the abandonment of Los Adaes, and it remained such until 1824, when Coahuila and Texas became united as a state under the Mexican constitution. Although Saltillo served as the state capital, San Antonio remained the principal Texas municipality under Mexican rule during the Anglo-American colonization period until shortly before the Texas Revolution.

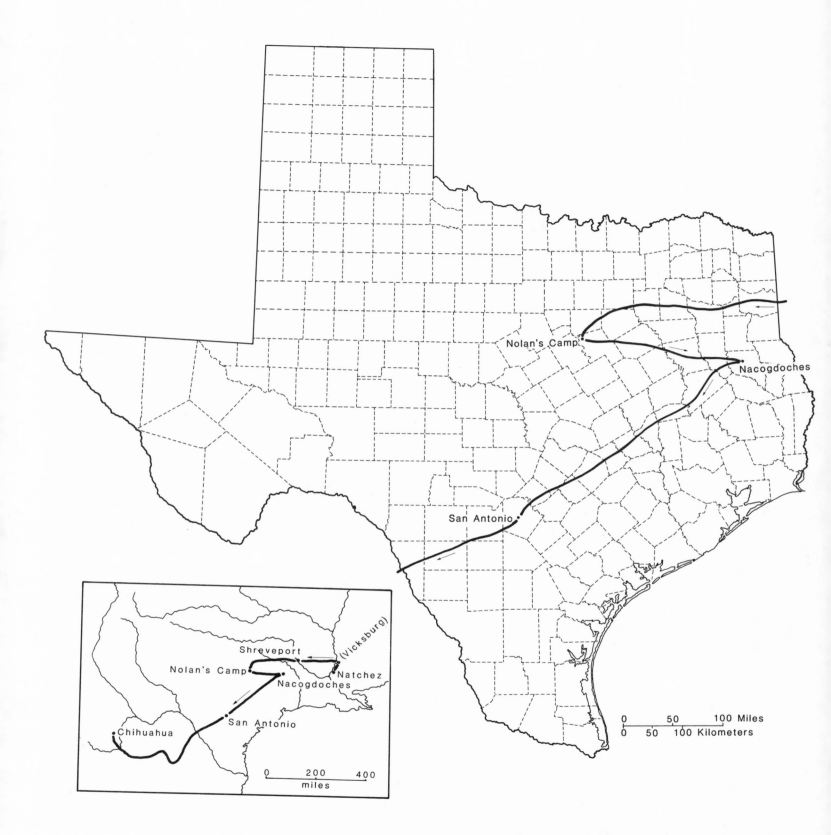

Nolan's Camp

Nacogdoches

San Antonio

0   50   100 Miles
0   50   100 Kilometers

Shreveport
(Vicksburg)
Nolan's Camp
Natchez
Nacogdoches
San Antonio
Chihuahua

0   200   400
miles

THE PHILIP NOLAN EXPEDITION, 1800–1801

© 1988 University of Oklahoma Press

14. THE PHILIP NOLAN EXPEDITION, 1800–1801

OF THE FILIBUSTERS who entered Spanish Texas illegally to exploit its natural resources, none was more colorful than Philip Nolan. In 1791 this native son of Ireland began capturing wild horses in Texas to sell to the Spanish military garrisons in Louisiana and to southern planters. Nolan posed as a friend of the Spanish while telling friends secretly that he longed for the day when the United States would expand into the American Southwest.

In 1800, Nolan visited Vice-President Thomas Jefferson in Philadelphia, then returned to his Natchez home. That fall, Nolan led a party of twenty-eight heavily armed men from Natchez up the Mississippi River to the vicinity of present-day Vicksburg. On November 1 the group crossed the river and headed west. They took a route farther north than usual to evade Spanish officers. Dodging Spanish soldiers seeking their arrest for trespassing, Nolan and his men crossed the Ouachita and Red rivers, moved into Texas, and pressed on westward through the eastern woodlands and central Texas prairies to the Cross Timbers. The mustangers constructed a log fort and log corrals at a site near the Brazos River. The exact location has been disputed by local historians, but in 1936 the state of Texas placed a granite historical marker to designate Nolan's camp at the intersection of State Highway 174 and Nolan River near the town of Blum in northwestern Hill County.

At the camp, Nolan's party rounded up wild horses that roamed in immense herds. They kept the better animals for riding and draft purposes and slaughtered the remainder primarily for manes and tails, which would be used for making horse-hair ropes. Some of the men scouted a distance farther west to get a look at the country before returning to the camp.

On March 21, 1801, a company of 120 Spanish soldiers surprised the eighteen horse traders in the stockage, and a battle commenced. When the skirmish stopped, Nolan lay dead. As a final insult to the adventurer, William Barr, a Nacogdoches trader who was a personal enemy of Nolan's, cut off the mustanger's ears as a gift to the Spanish governor at San Antonio.

The survivors were marched under guard first to Nacogdoches and later to San Antonio. These men had come to Texas for wealth but instead found extreme misfortune. Eventually they were taken to Mexico to be imprisoned while their captors considered proper punishment. On November 9, 1807, the men, by now in Chihuahua, learned the king had decreed that for each five who had fired on Spanish troops at Nolan's camp, one would be executed. Since only nine prisoners fitted that category, one person must die.

On the appointed day, the mustangers were assembled in the plaza at Chihuahua. One by one the blindfolded prisoners rolled dice from a crystal cup onto a drum. Ephraim Blackburn's four proved to be the lowest. On November 11, 1807, as the survivors were forced to watch, Blackburn was hanged. The other men spent the remainder of their lives in Mexico at hard labor. Only one, Ellis Peter Bean, eventually escaped.

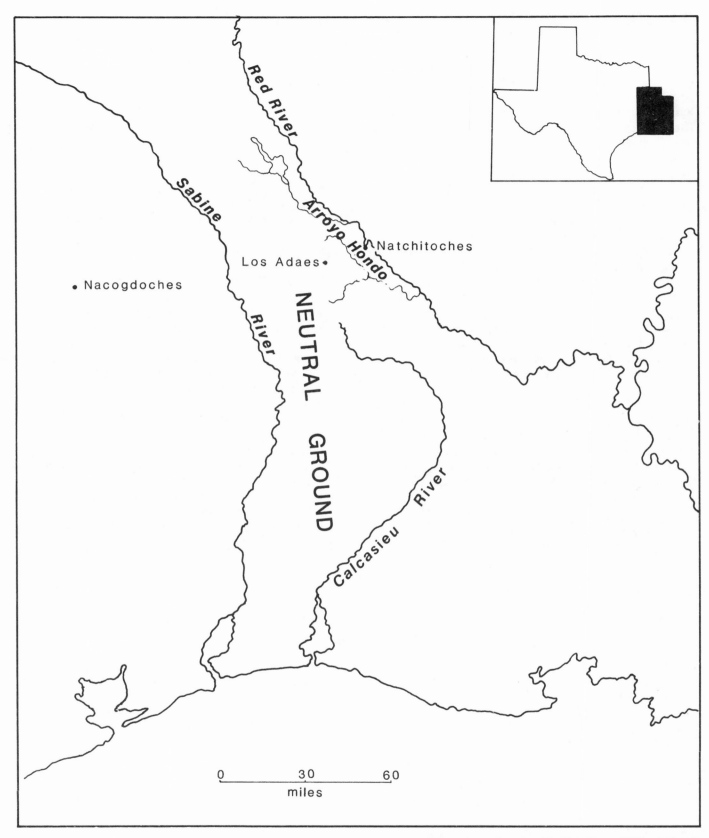

THE NEUTRAL GROUND AGREEMENT

© 1988 University of Oklahoma Press

15. THE NEUTRAL GROUND AGREEMENT

THE LONG, NARROW STRIP OF LAND between Louisiana and Texas was the subject of a dispute between the United States and Spain from 1806 to 1821. Beginning in the late seventeenth century, Spain had established missions in East Texas to counter a recent French colonization attempt along the Gulf Coast. Fearful that the French explorers might encroach on their territory, the Spanish extended mission activities to the Arroyo Hondo east of the Sabine River in the vicinity of present-day Robeline, Louisiana. Spain's influence in that region waned with the passage of time, as did that of France. With the acquisition of Louisiana by the United States in 1803, the question of jurisdictional boundaries was again raised.

President Thomas Jefferson and a number of prominent Americans interpreted available documents to mean that the French claims thus transfered in 1803 included land westward to the Rio Grande from its mouth to its source. Spanish authorities countered with a claim that Texas extended eastward to Natchitoches on the Red River and then by a line southward to the Gulf of Mexico along the Calcasieu River.

Diplomatic negotiations between the two powers failed to resolve their difference. In 1805, Spain rejected the American claim to the Rio Grande and also the subsequent American suggestion that a neutral ground be established where neither would recognize land claims between the Sabine and the Colorado rivers.

Where the diplomats failed, the military field commanders succeeded. Spanish officals feared an American invasion into Texas and sent a sizeable military force to strengthen their frontier posts east of the Sabine River. A clash almost resulted from this action when American officers, mistaking this move to be an invasion of Louisiana, mobilized their forces in western Louisiana. After some maneuvering and power demonstrations with only the river separating the two armies, conflict seemed likely to occur. But common sense prevailed, and the two field commanders, Spanish Lieutenant Colonel Don Simón de Herrera and American General James Wilkinson, agreed on November 6, 1806, to withdraw their troops from the disputed territory to let the question of boundaries be settled by their respective governments. Until those governments acted, the land between the Arroyo Hondo and the Sabine River, the primary area in question, would be a "neutral ground" and would not be subject to either authority. Southward to the Gulf Coast, the territory between the Calcasieu and Sabine rivers also became a part of the Neutral Ground.

Hunters, trappers, Indians, and persons fleeing jurisdiction of the United States or Spain lived in this lawless area without external restraint except for two occasions when both governments cooperated in joint expeditions to expel outlaws. The Adams-Onís Treaty of 1819, which became effective upon ratification by both governments in 1821, solved the boundary controversy by extending American control to the Sabine River. The region that comprised the so-called Neutral Ground remained a problem in law enforcement for American officials for several decades afterward.

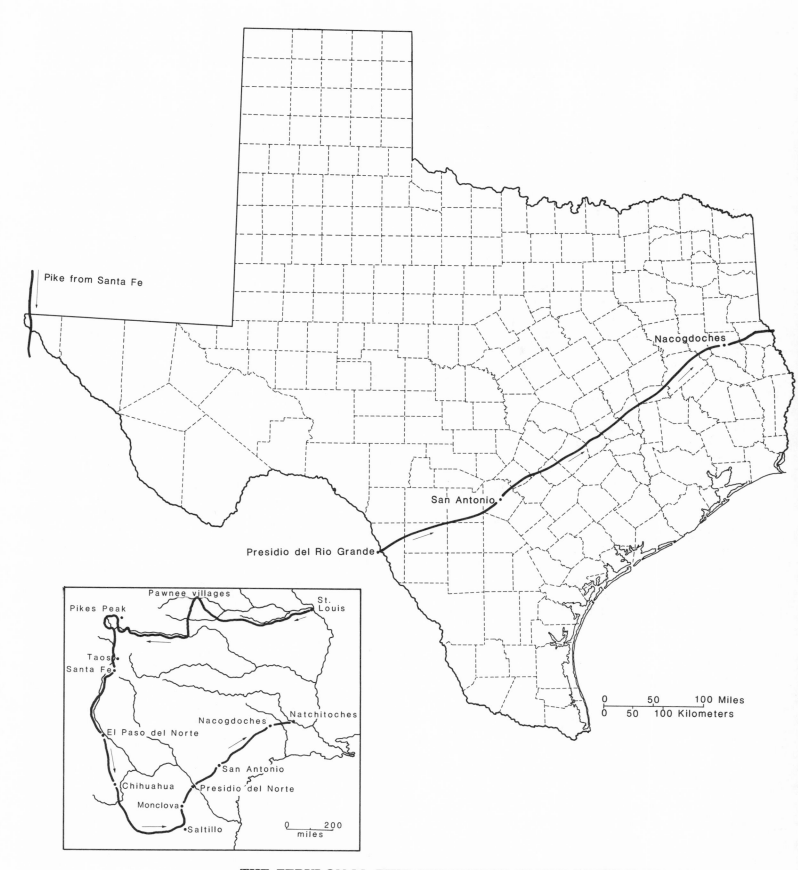

Pike from Santa Fe

Nacogdoches

San Antonio

Presidio del Rio Grande

0   50   100 Miles
0 50   100 Kilometers

Pawnee villages
Pikes Peak
Taos
Santa Fe
St. Louis
Natchitoches
Nacogdoches
El Paso del Norte
San Antonio
Chihuahua
Presidio del Norte
Monclova
Saltillo

0   200
miles

THE ZEBULON M. PIKE EXPEDITION IN THE SOUTHWEST, 1806–1807

© 1988 University of Oklahoma Press

16. THE ZEBULON M. PIKE EXPEDITION IN THE SOUTHWEST, 1806–1807

FOLLOWING A TOUR OF DUTY in 1805–1806 to investigate the upper reaches of the Mississippi River, Lieutenant Zebulon Montgomery Pike, U.S. Army, received orders from General James Wilkinson to explore westward from St. Louis across the Great Plains. Pike and his detachment left St. Louis on July 15, 1806, with instructions to observe the geographical and scientific features of the land and establish friendly relations with the native inhabitants of the American Southwest. After reaching the Arkansas River, Pike was to ascend that stream to the Rocky Mountains and in time return to the settled area of the United States by way of the Red River.

When he reached the Rocky Mountains, Pike explored along the front range, then journeyed west to the Rio Grande in present-day Colorado, where he became lost in a snowstorm. Spanish soldiers captured the Americans and took them to Santa Fe. Uncertain what to do with the intruders, the New Mexican officials escorted Pike and his men as prisoner-guests southward. Spanish soldiers took them to El Paso del Norte (now Juárez, Mexico), then to Chihuahua, and on June 1, 1807, they reached the Presidio del Rio Grande near modern-day Eagle Pass, Texas.

Their journey across Texas was accomplished in four weeks, with several days of partying in San Antonio as guests of local officials. The Americans, under constant Spanish military escort, continued along the Camino Real, the Old San Antonio Road, past the locales of the present-day communities of New Braunfels, Lockhart, Bastrop, Bryan, Madisonville, Crockett, Nacogdoches, and San Augustine. On July 1, 1807, after a year's absence from the United States, Pike and his men arrived at Natchitoches in present-day Louisiana, then the westernmost U.S. military outpost.

Pike's papers and baggage had been confiscated by the Spanish. When he left Chihuahua, Pike had been ordered not to take notes. But he soon developed the technique of excusing himself frequently for privacy in the bushes, where he would record his observations about the people and terrain of northern Mexico and Texas. To avoid detection of his notes, he rolled them and stuffed them down the barrels of the rifles of his men. Following his arrival in the United States, Pike retrieved the notes and, with additional observations from memory, published his memoirs.

His description of Texas as a good place to farm excited many Americans. Pike wrote about well-watered, well-wooded fertile soil for farming, grassy meadows for grazing, immense herds of wild horses, and abundant game. He claimed that Texas had one of the most delightful climates in the world. The Pike report contributed to the land hunger and profit seeking for which Americans were noted. These scientific and geographical observations made the Pike expedition second only to the Lewis and Clark expedition in contributing to the knowledge of the American frontier.

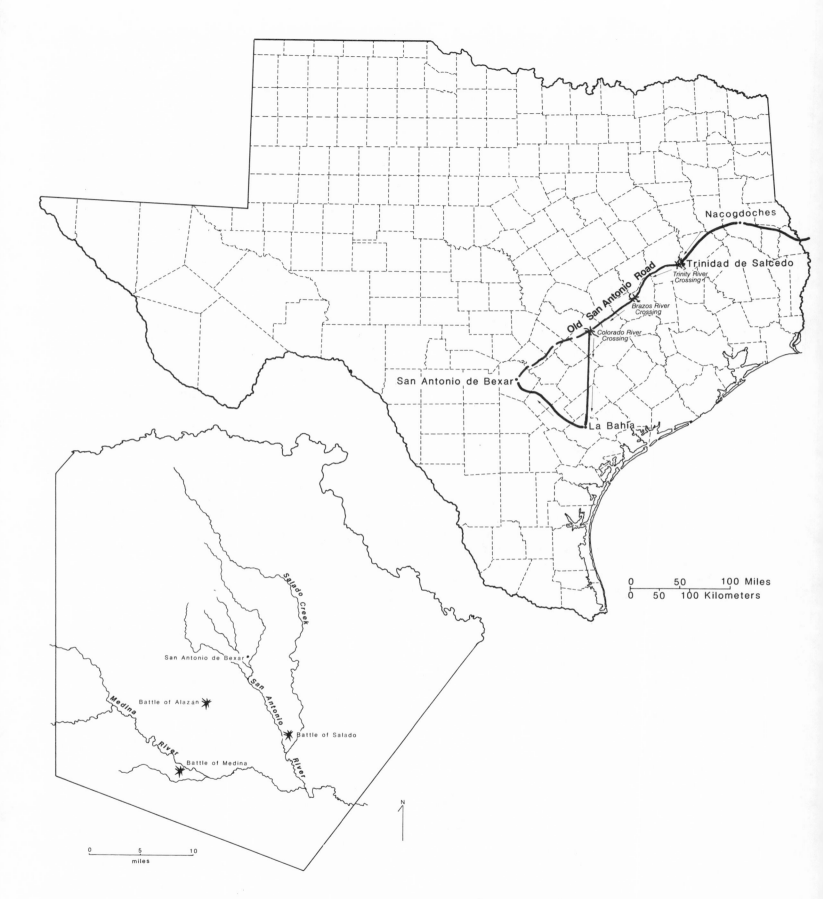

THE GUTIÉRREZ–MAGEE EXPEDITION, 1812–1813

© 1988 University of Oklahoma Press

17. THE GUTIÉRREZ–MAGEE EXPEDITION, 1812–1813

DURING THE SECOND DECADE of the nineteenth century, several filibuster expeditions attempted to wrest Texas from Spanish control. The most noteworthy, although it failed, was the Gutiérrez-Magee Expedition of 1812–13.

Spanish interest in the Interior Provinces waned in the early nineteenth century partly because of events in Europe. In 1810, when Spain became controlled by a puppet regime influenced by the French emperor, Napoleon Bonaparte, affairs in the Spanish American colonies became chaotic. Independence became a goal of some Mexicans. When Father Miguel Hidalgo y Costilla gave the cry for Mexican independence on September 16, 1810, at the village of Dolores, a movement began that within a decade swept across Spanish America.

Among the leaders of the subsequent movement in northern Mexico was José Bernardo Maximiliano Gutiérrez de Lara, who fled to Louisiana to avoid prosecution. He then journeyed to Washington, meeting along the way many prominent public figures interested in the possibility of land speculation and profitable free trade in Texas. Gutiérrez struck a responsive chord in the United States when he proposed that a republican form of government be established in Texas. Many U.S. citizens, already believing that all or part of Texas was American territory because of the Louisiana Purchase, enthusiastically received Gutiérrez.

Back in Natchitoches, Gutiérrez aligned with Augustus Magee, a young U.S. Army officer, who resigned his commission to be the leader of the Republican Army of the North. Successful recruiting in Louisiana and in the Neutral Ground swelled the filibusters' ranks to approximately five hundred men. In August, 1812, the Republican Army crossed the Sabine River and captured Nacogdoches without a fight. Although Magee served as the supreme commander of the military force, Gutiérrez held the title of commander-in-chief in order to give the liberating operation a Mexican flavor.

The filibusters advanced along the Old San Antonio Road from Nacogdoches toward San Antonio de Bexar, the political capital of Texas. When they got to the Colorado River, they met a loyalist deserter who informed them that Texas Governor Manuel María de Salcedo and military commandant Simón de Herrera had concentrated forces at Bexar, but that the garrison at La Bahía, weakly defended, could be taken easily.

Redirecting their path, the Republican Army marched to La Bahía and took it easily in October. Considerable amounts of much-needed supplies and munitions fell into their hands. Meanwhile, Salcedo and Herrera, learning of the invaders' presence at La Bahía, laid a siege against that fortress that lasted four months before the loyalists retreated to Bexar. Magee had become ill while enroute and died at La Bahía. His place as commander was taken by Samuel Kemper, a participant in the successful 1810 revolt against Spanish authority by Americans in the West Florida region around Baton Rouge.

By late February, 1813, the invading army of fourteen thousand Americans, Mexicans, and Indians moved against Bexar. On March 29 the filibusters defeated a Spanish force near the capital city at the Battle of Salado, which convinced the inhabitants of Bexar that resistance was hopeless. Defenders now became greeters as the Republican Army rode triumphantly into Bexar.

United in the march across Texas, the army of freebooters soon became quarrelsome. Harsh, cruel, and barbaric treatment against Spanish officials and townspeople by persons under the orders of Gutiérrez caused many American volunteers to lose interest in further cooperation with him.

On April 6, 1813, the conquerors proclaimed a declaration of independence from Spain. A ruling council controlled by Gutiérrez assumed full command. Prominent Anglo-Americans in the revolution, such as Samuel Kemper, were excluded from the junta. Many of them left for Louisiana. As discord became general among the victors, discipline declined, and disorder became prevalent.

On June 20, 1813, the Republicans repelled a small royalist force near Bexar at the Battle of Alazán. Even in victory the intrigues of the ambitious never ceased. The excessive arrogance and brutal treatment of local inhabitants turned some prominent supporters in the United States against Gutiérrez, and they encouraged José Álvarez de Toledo to journey to Texas. Within a short time the ruling council deposed Gutiérrez, exiled him to the United States, and made Toledo the new leader.

Meanwhile, Colonel José Joaquín de Arredondo, commandant of the eastern division of the Provincias Internas, moved northward into Texas and marched against the Republicans. By clever deployment of his troops, Arredondo overwhelmed the revolutionaries at the Battle of Medina on August 13, 1813, and took control of Bexar. Within a short time the Spanish military brutally swept Texas clean of insurgents. Texas was once again in Spanish hands.

Nacogdoches•

Champ d'Asile•

San Antonio•

Campeche
Galveston
Island

0   50   100 Miles
0   50   100 Kilometers

CHAMP D'ASILE, 1818

© 1988 University of Oklahoma Press

18. CHAMP D'ASILE, 1818

OTHER FILIBUSTERING ATTEMPTS had the same degree of failure in early Texas. In 1816, a number of French exiles who had fled post-Napoleon France were living in the Philadelphia, Pennsylvania, area, but, they desired a permanent location on the American frontier. The group became known as the French Agricultural and Manufacturing Society and also as the Society for the Cultivation of the Vine and the Olive. Congress granted the group's request for land in the wilderness and awarded them title to approximately 23,000 acres at $2.00 per acre, on a fourteen-year deferred payment plan, on the Tombigbee River in Mississippi Territory, later a part of Alabama.

General Charles Lallemand was chosen as president of the society. In late 1817 and early 1818 the French colonists traveled from Philadelphia to the Tombigbee with their vines, olive trees, and farming equipment. Lack of knowledge about American cultural techniques and the desire of the men for military drills rather than farm work caused the experiment to fail. Within a short time most of the Tombigbee settlers returned to Philadelphia.

The Spanish minister to the United States, Luis de Onís, suggested to Lallemand that the viceroy might permit these former supporters of Napoleon to settle in Texas. In December, 1817, General Lallemand left for New Orleans, intending to go on to Mexico City to plead his case before the viceroy, but that official stated that only the king could grant permission to settlers and ordered port officials to refuse Lallemand's admission to any place in New Spain.

Lallemand made preparations to send colonists and supplies from New Orleans to a temporary base on Galveston Island while he investigated the coastal plains between the Sabine and Trinity rivers. In the meantime, another group of French exiles under the leadership of General Antoine Rigaud, Lallemand's second-in-command, sailed from Philadelphia to New Orleans, then on to Galveston, where they waited for General Lallemand to bring supplies. Lallemand arrived at Galveston in early March, 1818, with the provisions and more colonists. The Texas group now numbered approximately four hundred. In addition to the French exiles, the membership consisted of Tombigbee refugees, French nationals who had fled earlier from slave uprisings in the French West Indies, Spaniards, Poles, Mexicans, and Anglo-Americans.

With the aid of the renowned pirate Jean Lafitte, Lallemand sent supplies by ships up Galveston Bay and the Trinity River while he led most of the colonists overland to their new home, which he located on the Trinity River in the vicinity of present-day Liberty. At this site, which took the name of Champ d'Asile, the people constructed fortifications and houses, then began the tedious work of farming. All the land was held in common, as all persons labored for the common good. With gardens for table vegetables, game from the woods, and fish from the streams, the colonists seemed to be on the way to prosperity after several years of wandering. In addition to military drills, they interspersed their work schedules with social and literary activities while they dreamed of life back in France. Lallemand issued a manifesto to the world that despite the Spanish demand that they leave, these French settlers intended to remain, because they had a God-given right to establish homes in the wilderness and prosper through their labor.

The U.S. government became apprehensive about the French settlement in Texas because the Monroe administration held that the Louisiana Purchase gave to the United States all the territory to the Rio Grande. Secretary of State John Quincy Adams sent a confidential agent, George Graham, to confer with the French in the summer of 1818.

Paradise was soon lost when in July, 1818, the Champ d'Asile colonists learned that a Spanish military force was marching from San Antonio to dislodge them from Spanish Texas as hostile intruders. Lallemand and his followers fled to Galveston Island. To compound their problems, the French were attacked by supposedly friendly Indians as they left. Spanish troops destroyed the village, attempted to attack the exiles at Galveston, then returned to San Antonio. The Champ d'Asile refugees lacked supplies. Their suffering became more intense when a major hurricane flooded the island, destroying the small amount of foodstock on hand. Some survivors fled overland to Nacogdoches or to New Orleans, while others took ship passage to New Orleans, thus putting to a dramatic end the utopian experiment of French exiles in Texas.

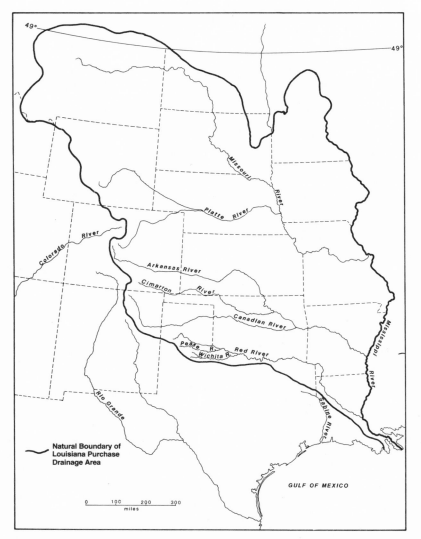

Natural Boundary of
Louisiana Purchase
Drainage Area

GULF OF MEXICO

0   100   200   300
miles

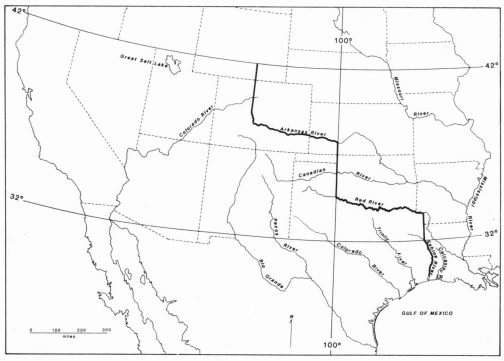

0   100   200   300
miles

GULF OF MEXICO

**ADAMS–ONÍS
TREATY, 1819**

© 1988 University of Oklahoma Press

19. ADAMS-ONÍS TREATY, 1819

UPON THE PURCHASE of Louisiana from France by the United States in 1803, the official boundaries of the American nation were extended westward to enclose a wilderness approximately the same size as the existing Union. Authorities conducting the cession of Louisiana noted in the treaty that the original boundaries of French Louisiana at the time of transfer to Spain at the conclusion of the French and Indian War in 1763 would be recognized as the boundaries of this transfer. Spain had controlled the area by treaty from 1763 to 1800, when ownership of Louisiana returned to France. Some notable Americans, including President Thomas Jefferson, argued that the French Southwest extended to the Rio Grande because of La Salle's activities in Texas.

Since the exact boundary lines were indefinite, disputes soon arose between Americans in western Louisiana and Spanish in eastern Texas. A respite occurred in 1806 when opposing military commanders in the field established a neutral ground between the Sabine River on the west and the Arroyo Hondo on the east. The area of neutrality on the east was soon extended southward to the Gulf of Mexico, with the Calcasieu River as the line of demarcation.

Another controversy arose when the U.S. government claimed the area drained by waters flowing into the Mississippi River as a part of the Louisiana Territory. Such streams as the Wichita and Pease rivers head south of the Red River in the area Spain regarded as its own. The headwaters of the several branches of the Red River, as well as those of the Canadian and Cimarron rivers, rise in territory Spain traditionally had claimed.

The question of the exact international boundaries between Spanish Texas and the United States became a part of the diplomatic negotiations conducted by the American secretary of state, John Quincy Adams, and the Spanish minister to the United States, Don Luis de Onís y Gonzales, over Florida during the administration of President James Monroe. The United States desired Florida as a place for expansion by American pioneers and to quiet Indian raids emanating from the area. Adams wanted to claim to the Rio Grande but offered first the Colorado River and later the Trinity River as the boundary of the Louisiana Purchase. Onís contended the Arroyo Hondo and the Calcasieu River formed Spain's eastern limits.

The diplomatic wrangling lasted several months until on February 22, 1819, both parties agreed on the western extent of the United States. By using the 1818 edition of John Melish's "Map of the United States and the Contiguous British and Spanish Possessions," the diplomats listed the definite boundaries. The line began at the mouth of the Sabine River and moved upstream along the west bank to the thirty-second parallel. From there the boundary went due north to the Red River. With this treaty the Neutral Ground established in 1806 ceased to exist.

From the Red River, the boundary continued upstream along the south and west bank to the one hundredth meridian, thence due north to the Arkansas River, and then upstream along the south and west bank of the Arkansas to its headwaters. From those headwaters a line would be drawn due north or south, as the case may be, to the forty-second parallel, thence due west along that parallel to the Pacific Ocean. In return for establishing the exact boundary limits and for surrendering its claim to Florida, Spain received five million dollars to satisfy American claims against Spain in the Southeast.

The U.S. Senate ratified this transcontinental treaty immediately, but the Spanish sovereign, beset as he was with problems of home and empire, stalled his approval until October 24, 1820. In February, 1821, two years after preliminary approval by the Senate, both nations exchanged ratifications and declared the treaty in effect. Adams lauded his own efforts in establishing a mutually recognized boundary, but some Americans believed that with a bit more pressure Adams could have acquired Texas as well. The "reoccupation" of Texas became a rallying cry for expansion and a national political issue in the United States for several decades following.

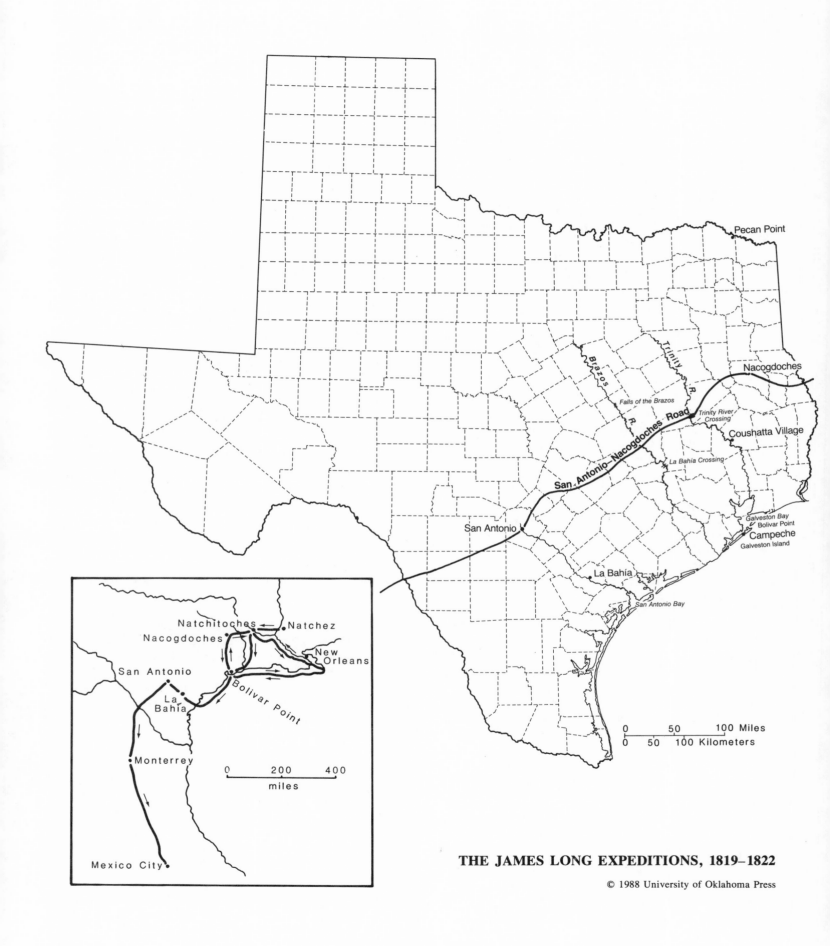

Pecan Point

Nacogdoches

Brazos R.

Trinity R.

Falls of the Brazos

Trinity River Crossing

Coushatta Village

San Antonio–Nacogdoches Road

La Bahía Crossing

San Antonio

Galveston Bay
Bolivar Point

Campeche

Galveston Island

La Bahía

San Antonio Bay

Natchitoches ← Natchez

Nacogdoches

New Orleans

San Antonio

La Bahía

Bolivar Point

Monterrey

0   200   400
miles

Mexico City

0   50   100 Miles
0   50   100 Kilometers

THE JAMES LONG EXPEDITIONS, 1819–1822

© 1988 University of Oklahoma Press

20. THE JAMES LONG EXPEDITIONS, 1819–1822

THE LAST OF THE MAJOR FILIBUSTERS in Spanish Texas was Dr. James Long. Born of a frontier family, Long drifted from place to place holding various jobs, including that of an army post surgeon although he had no formal medical training. With the signing of the Adams–Onís Treaty in 1819 between the United States and Spain, many Americans became agitated about the alleged surrender of American claims to Texas. That treaty established an international boundary at the Sabine River between Texas and Louisiana.

Long became the leader of a plot to retake Texas from Spain. One of the instigators in this scheme was Bernardo Gutiérrez, who had attempted unsuccessfully to establish a stronghold in Texas several years earlier. The expedition had the financial support of influential American merchants and public figures who hoped for riches by speculating in Texas real estate.

In June, 1819, the freebooters went from Natchez to Nacogdoches. While crossing the Neutral Ground, Long's force expanded from the original seventy-five to approximately three hundred men because of the attraction of financial gain through land acquisition. After creating an independent republic, the filibusters established a supreme council, named Long as the president, and organized an army with Long as the commanding general.

Long attempted to consolidate control of the surrounding country in the likely event the Spanish would seek to dislodge him. He sent men to establish trading posts for Indian commerce at the Trinity River Crossing, the Falls of the Brazos, and Pecan Point on the Red River. Detachments went to the Coushatta Village on the Trinity River and to La Bahía Crossing on the Brazos River near present Washington.

With these plans laid, the leader went to Galveston Island to enlist the support of Jean and Pierre Lafitte at Campeche, present-day Galveston. Long dreamed of having Galveston as the port of entry into this new Texas republic, which would give his organizational efforts a considerable boost, since the land under his presumed jurisdiction would be more valuable if he could establish a supply line by sea. The filibuster's plan did not succeed. Those infamous pirates received Long graciously but refused to scheme with him. Long started back home and had gotten no farther than the Coushatta Village when he learned that a strong Spanish military force from San Antonio was marching rapidly against the Anglo-Americans in East Texas.

Colonel Ignacio Pérez took the outposts at the Falls of Brazos and at La Bahía Crossing, then attacked the trading post on the Trinity and continued on to Nacogdoches by mid-October, 1819. In the meantime, James Long hurriedly returned to Nacogdoches, but soon fled with his family to Natchitoches as his dream for a republic faded. Pérez sent troops to chase the Anglo-Americans across the Sabine while he led the main body to the Coushatta Village in order to sweep Texas clean of those who trespassed on Spanish soil. An international crisis almost occurred when American troops from Fort Jesup near Natchitoches occupied the east bank of the Sabine River and faced the Spanish army on the west bank. The Spanish remained in East Texas for several weeks, burning homes to discourage outsiders from settling in Texas. Long joined the remnants of his force at Bolivar Point on Galveston Bay, where they built a fort. Then the general continued on to New Orleans and Natchitoches to obtain recruits and provisions for another expedition.

In a second attempt at conquest and colonization, James Long returned to Bolivar Point, where he convened the supreme council in April, 1820. José Felix Trespalacios became the president of the Republic of Texas, with Bernardo Gutiérrez as vice-president.

Events in Mexico altered Long's plans. Mexico declared its independence from Spain in 1821 under the leadership of Augustín de Iturbide. Long supported that political action and wanted to help drive the Spanish out of Texas. With some of his men he sailed from Bolivar Point to San Antonio Bay, then moved inland to capture the Spanish fort at La Bahía. A superior force from San Antonio under Colonel Pérez soon overpowered them. Long, now a prisoner, was escorted to San Antonio and eventually to Mexico City, where he visited with Iturbide. In April, 1822, the leader of the final attempt to take Texas by force was killed by a guard.

An era of social unrest, political intrigue, and intermittent filibustering operations came to an end. Soon Anglo-Americans entered Texas by invitation through the efforts of empresarios who contracted with the Mexican government to bring in settlers.

100°

42°

TERRITORIO DE ALTA CALIFORNIA

• Santa Fé

TERRITORIO DE SANTA FE DE
NUEVO MEXICO

SONORA Y SINALOA

TERR. DE BAJA CALIFORNIA

Gulf of California

COAHUILA Y TEXAS

1. Monterrey
2. Ciudad Victoria
3. Zacatecas
4. San Luis Potosí
5. Guanajuato
6. (GUANAJUATO)
7. (QUERÉTARO)
8. Querétaro
9. Puebla
10. Veracruz
11. San Juan Batista
12. San Cristóbal
13. (TLAXCALA)

CHIHUAHUA

San Felipe de Austin

San Antonio de Bexar

• Chihuahua

El Fuerto

NUEVO
LEON

DURANGO

Saltillo • • 1

• Durango

ZACATECAS

• 2

Gulf of Mexico

TAMAULIPAS

• 3

• 4
SAN
LUIS POTOSI

• 5
6 • 8 7

Guadalajara

JALISCO

Mérida •

YUCATAN

Valledolid

13
• 9

Colima •
COLIMA

MICHOACAN

MEXICO

México •

10

PUEBLA

TABASCO
• 11
VERACRUZ

Oaxáca •

OAXÁCA

12 • CHIAPAS

SOCÓNUSCO

100°

0   300
Miles

TEXAS AS A PART OF MEXICO IN 1824

© 1988 University of Oklahoma Press

21. TEXAS AS A PART OF MEXICO IN 1824

TEXAS CONTINUED AS A FRONTIER REGION of an independent Mexico in 1821 as it had existed earlier under the rule of Spain. The absence of precious-metal mining produced a lack of direct economic interest in Texas by Spanish and Mexican authorities, but people from the United States saw a different kind of wealth to lure them to Texas. The rich prairies and river-bottom lands at first beckoned a trickle of settlers that within a short time became a flood of immigrants. Political instability in the halls of state in Mexico City shortly after independence brought about the establishment of a dictatorship by Augustín de Iturbide in 1822. That emperor was desposed within a year. Politicians then drafted a plan of government patterned closely after the system in use in the United States, and in 1824, Mexico adopted a federal constitution to create a democratic republic consisting of nineteen states and four territories.

What had been the province of Texas now became consolidated with Coahuila as the state of Coahuila y Texas. The northern boundaries of the states of Tamaulipas and Nuevo León and the northeastern boundary of the state of Chihuahua stopped at the Rio Grande, while the territory of New Mexico extended southward to the present El Paso region and eastward roughly to the one hundredth meridian. Texas would remain a part of this consolidation until it warranted a separate government. The federal constitution ceded to the states the legal right to dispose of public lands and provide for colonization in order to remove these matters from national politics. A limited number of delegates from Texas would be elected to participate in the state legislature of Coahuila y Texas.

Approximately 500 miles separated the towns of San Felipe de Austin, the principal settlement of Stephen F. Austin's colony, and Saltillo, the state capital. Mexico City, the national seat of government, lay another 550 miles to the south. The extreme distance, with accompanying hardships for travellers, quite obviously deterred communication, supply, and political contact. As a consequence, the Anglo-American settlement of Texas developed an economic system that did not rely on Mexico. Its trade lines extended to New Orleans and other places in the United States, although the political allegiance to Mexico continued until the Texas Declaration of Independence on March 2, 1836, instituted local self-government for Texans.

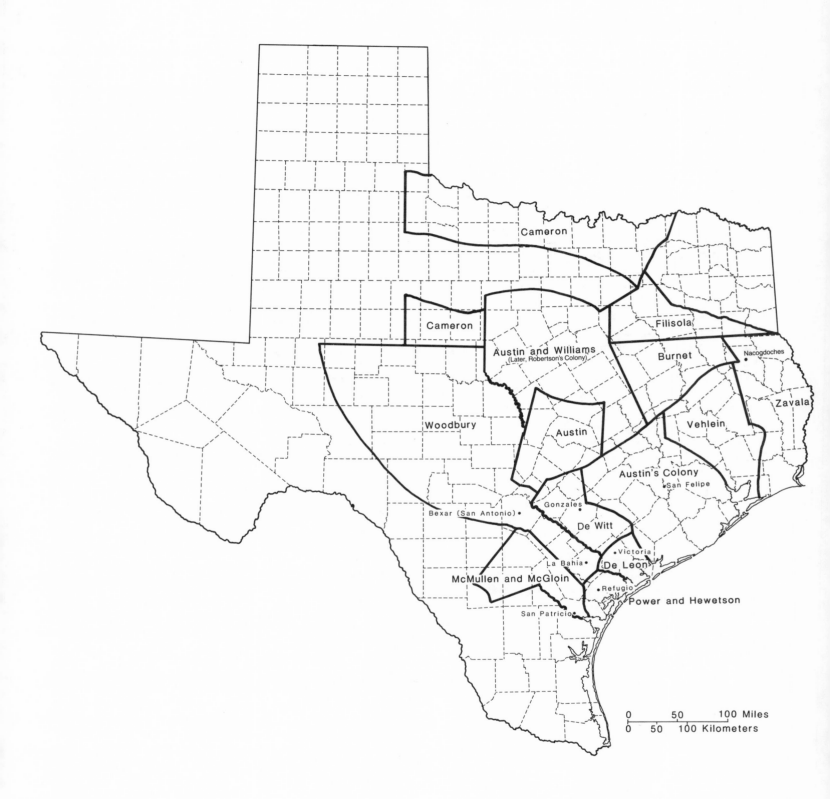

Cameron

Cameron

Austin and Williams
(Later, Robertson's Colony)

Filisola

Burnet

Nacogdoches•

Woodbury

Zavala

Austin

Vehlein

Austin's Colony

•San Felipe

Bexar (San Antonio) •

Gonzales
•

De Witt

•Victoria

La Bahia •

De Leon

McMullen and McGloin

•Refugio

Power and Hewetson

San Patricio•

0   50   100 Miles
0   50   100 Kilometers

EMPRESARIO GRANTS

© 1988 University of Oklahoma Press

22. EMPRESARIO GRANTS

ANGLO-AMERICAN COLONIZATION in Texas developed during the initial period of Mexican independence when a flood of contractors, or empresarios, sought land on which to locate families. Moses Austin, a former Spanish citizen and the first person to receive such authorization, died before he could carry out his plans. Upon his death, Mexico City authorities awarded the contract to his son, Stephen Fuller Austin. When Augustín de Iturbide became emperor of Mexico, Austin received permission to bring three hundred families into Texas under the Imperial Colonization Law of 1823. A short time later, when Iturbide was overthrown by revolution, the newly created Mexican Republic repealed the 1823 colonization law but permitted Austin to keep his contract.

The government then approved a national colonization law in 1824 but left to the states the task of colonization in their own boundaries, subject to a few general regulations applicable to all the states and the persons subsequently admitted. The national government reserved for itself the right to grant land within twenty leagues of foreign boundaries and ten leagues of the seacoast. Among other provisions, Mexico claimed the option of prohibiting the entrance of foreigners if circumstances in the national interest required it. The legislature of the state of Coahuila y Texas passed its colonization law on March 24, 1825. General provisions called for the settlers to be Catholic with written evidence of good standing in their home communities, to be law abiding, and to protect Mexico against its enemies.

In his new homeland a married man could receive as much as 4,428 acres if he chose to farm and to raise livestock. The unmarried man could receive one-fourth that amount. Both types could take up to six years to pay for their land, with payments beginning the fourth year. In order to have a system for colonization, the law authorized state officials to enter contracts with individuals known as empresarios who would be granted a colony for the introduction of an established number of families. The empresario would receive a premium of five leagues and five *labors* for each hundred families he brought in, provided he did not retain more than eleven leagues for his personal use.

Just as soon as the Coahuila y Texas legislature enacted its colonization law, empresarios began applying for grants. In the following years the map of Texas was plastered over with claims for land by em-

presarios, but only those contracts made to Austin and Green De Witt were completed. Under the state colonization law, Austin received additional land grants. The Haden Edwards contract for the region around Nacogdoches was canceled by the Mexican government after a civil disturbance in which Edwards created a Republic of Fredonia, only to have it crushed by armed force. Edward's land then went to other empresarios. David G. Burnet, Joseph Vehlein, and Lorenzo de Zavala received individual grants but consolidated them into the Galveston Bay and Texas Land Company, which brought in settlers. The Robertson Colony, also known as the Austin and Williams Colony, Leftwich Colony, Upper Colony, or Nashville Colony, established some persons in Texas. The colony of Martín De León introduced a number of Mexican families, while two others, McMullen and McGloin, and Power and Hewetson, brought in Irish nationals. Thirteen grantees failed to meet any of the obligations of their contracts (Wavell, Wilson, Wilson and Exeter, Woodbury, Cameron, Dominguez, Filisola, Padilla and Chambers, Thorn, Purnell and Lovell, Beales and Royuela, Campos, and Beales and Grant).

Changes in the central government of Mexico and gnawing fear of American intentions toward Texas brought about a harsh reaction to the empresario system. Article 11 of the national law of April 6, 1830, halted all further Anglo-American immigration into Texas. Although the national government had reserved the right for this action in its law of August 18, 1824, many Texans and Americans loudly protested. The restriction against Anglo-American colonization in Texas was lifted in 1834.

In 1834 and 1835, a complex series of laws was passed which brought on a great amount of speculation in Texas lands. The Mexican government forsook the empresario system to sell land directly to individuals so that profits which once went to the contractors in premiums should now go to the government. Considerable confusion resulted over legal titles to land. Further complications came when in November, 1835, the provisional government of Texas assumed the issuing of land titles. After the creation of the Republic of Texas, the Texas Congress on June 12, 1837, claimed all contracts had ceased when Texas declared its independence. The Congress allowed persons to file suits against the republic to settle claims to land.

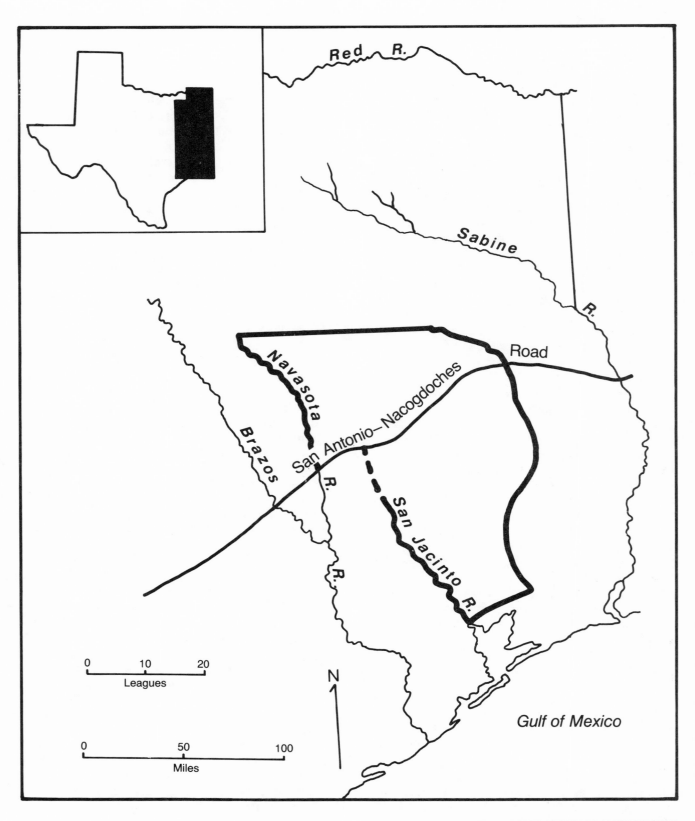

Red R.

Sabine

R.

Navasota

Brazos

San Antonio–Nacogdoches

Road

R.

R.

San Jacinto R.

0   10   20
Leagues

0   50   100
Miles

N

Gulf of Mexico

THE FREDONIAN REPUBLIC

© 1988 University of Oklahoma Press

23. THE FREDONIAN REPUBLIC

THE FREDONIAN REPUBLIC AROSE from a conflict between Anglo-Americans newly arrived in the Nacogdoches area and people who had lived in that region for some time, including both Hispanics and other Anglo-Americans. The results of this uprising cast a long shadow on American-Mexican relations in the late 1820s.

Haden Edwards, a native of Virginia, early developed an interest in land speculation. After lobbying with Mexican officials for three years, he received permission in 1825 to settle eight hundred families in East Texas. The usual conditions had to be met: remain loyal to the government of Mexico, be or become Catholic, produce written evidence of good character, and bear arms in defense of the Republic of Mexico if necessary. The colonists would be exempt from general taxes for a ten-year period.

Boundaries of the Edwards grant extended from a point on the San Jacinto River ten leagues from the Gulf of Mexico eastward parallel with the coast to a point twenty leagues from the Sabine River, thence northward to a point fifteen leagues above Nacogdoches, thence due west to the Navasota River. Turning southward, the boundary ran downstream until it reached the San Antonio–Nacogdoches Road, along that road to a point north of the headwaters of the San Jacinto River, and then along the San Jacinto to the point of beginning ten leagues from the coast.

While in Mexico seeking his grant, Edwards had expended approximately fifty thousand dollars, and now he wanted to recover quickly from his financial strain by selling land. He sought to charge more than the usual sum of one bit (twelve and one-half cents) per acre, which caused some grumbling. One of the terms of his grant was to respect the titles to land of existing settlers but Edwards notified persons residing within his colony that they must produce the necessary documents to their land, move, or buy their land back from him. Disgruntled settlers protested to the political chief of Texas in San Antonio.

Political problems, chiefly Edwards's becoming actively involved in the election of his son-in-law as alcalde, added to the volatile situation. The complaints to José Antonio Saucedo, the political chief, convinced that official that the situation was getting out of hand. Even though he lacked the authority, Saucedo decreed that empresarios could not contract for land with colonists and could not collect the twelve and one-half cents per acre; their reward would come with the premium land allotments of five leagues and five *labors* for each one hundred families settled. After further complaints, Saucedo prohibited additional settlements in the Edwards grant after November 1, 1826. Edwards objected to the procedure in a letter to Governor Rafael Gonzales of Coahuila y Texas. In December, 1826, Gonzales canceled the empresarial grant.

Haden Edwards and his brother, Benjamin Edwards, then organized resistance to Mexican authority with plans to create an independent republic. They discussed the endeavor with local Indians, principally Cherokees, who had been promised land by Spain and by Mexico without result. The Edwards brothers then gathered other like-minded men around them and marched on Nacogdoches. Along the way the group designed a flag with a red stripe and a white stripe to symbolize the union of Anglos and Indians. They inscribed the words "Independence, Liberty, and Justice" on the cloth and then placed their names on the banner.

The rebel group arrived in Nacogdoches on December 16, 1826, reoccupied the Old Stone Fort, and formed a Council of Independence. They formed a treaty of alliance with approximately two dozen Indian tribes, encouraged the Anglo residents around Nacogdoches to join the rebellion, and then proclaimed their independence from Mexico as the Republic of Fredonia. Tension mounted as a loyalist group attempted to retake Nacogdoches. On January 4, 1827, street fighting erupted around the Old Stone Fort. Mexican soldiers from San Antonio, together with the militia from Austin's Colony, marched on Nacogdoches, causing the Fredonians to flee beyond the Sabine for safety in Louisiana. By the end of March, 1827, the rebellion was completely suppressed.

Haden Edwards and other rebel leaders eventually returned to Texas, but in the meantime the Mexicans became increasingly suspicious of Anglo-Americans entering Texas. What the government leaders saw as a possible plot—Americans entering Texas in increasing numbers to rise up on command from Washington City in revolt against the host country—was nothing more than land-hungry individualists seeking to improve their lot in life by moving to the fertile soils of Texas without regard for authority or boundary. The Mexican government divided the Edwards empresarial grant and awarded it to other empresarios.

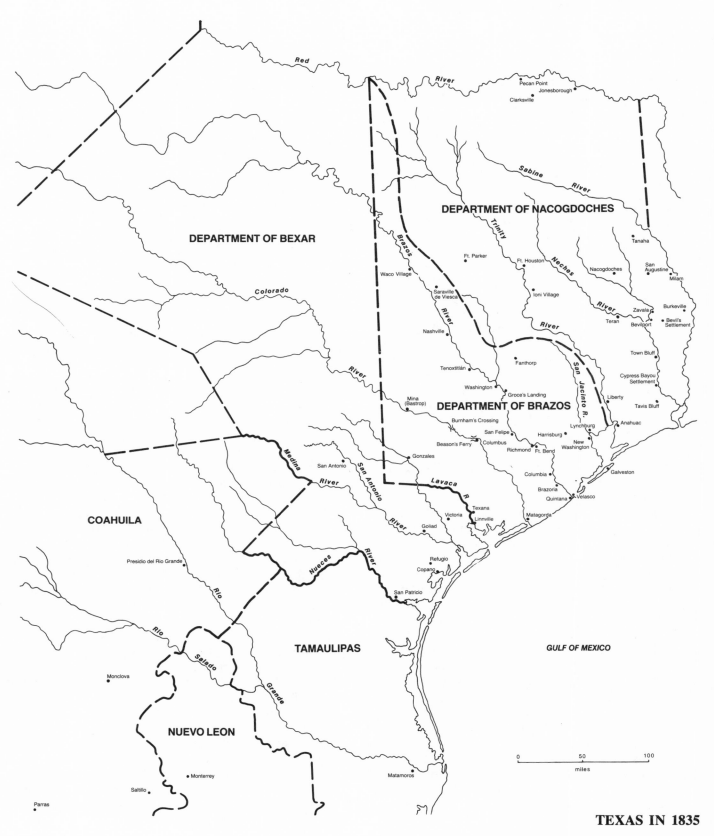

Red River

DEPARTMENT OF NACOGDOCHES

DEPARTMENT OF BEXAR

Pecan Point
Jonesborough
Clarksville

Sabine River

Trinity
Ft. Parker
Ft. Houston
Neches
Tanaha
Nacogdoches
San Augustine
Milam

Colorado

Waco Village
Saraville de Viesca
Ioni Village
Burkeville
Zavala
Teran
Bevilport
Bevil's Settlement

Nashville
Town Bluff

Tenoxtitlán
Fanthorp
San Jacinto R.
Cypress Bayou Settlement

Washington
Groce's Landing
DEPARTMENT OF BRAZOS
Liberty
Tavis Bluff

Mina (Bastrop)

Burnham's Crossing
Lynchburg
Anahuac

San Felipe
Harrisburg
New Washington

Beason's Ferry
Columbus
Richmond
Ft. Bend

Gonzales
Columbia
Galveston

Medina River
San Antonio River
Lavaca R.
Brazoria

San Antonio
Quintana
Velasco

Nueces River
Texana
Victoria
Linnville

COAHUILA
Goliad
Matagorda

Presidio del Rio Grande
Refugio
Copano

GULF OF MEXICO

Rio
San Patricio

Rio
Salado
TAMAULIPAS

Monclova
Grande

NUEVO LEON

Monterrey

Saltillo
Matamoros

Parras

0   50   100
miles

TEXAS IN 1835

© 1988 University of Oklahoma Press

24. TEXAS IN 1835

BY THE YEAR 1835, events had reached crisis proportions in the relationship between the people of Texas and the Mexican government. What had begun as friendly cooperation over a decade earlier now became militant antagonism. During the period of colonization, Americans entered Texas in increasing numbers. Alarmed about the rapid influx, Mexican officials in 1830 sought to prohibit further immigration. Their efforts did not stop the flow, but instead angered Anglo-Texans who desired friends and relatives to join them. Texans met in convention in 1832 and 1833 to express their desires for a separate state government, laws printed in both Spanish and English, right of trial by jury, and certain other liberties and freedoms they felt due them. Their efforts did not succeed.

Texas had existed as a separate province from 1727 to 1824, when it was united with Coahuila. Before 1831, Texas consisted of one department, with headquarters first at Los Adaes and later at San Antonio de Bexar. In 1831 the Department of Texas was divided into two parts: the Department of Bexar, with San Antonio as the capital city, and the Department of Nacogdoches, with Nacogdoches as the capital city. A further division in 1834 created the Department of Brazos, with San Felipe de Austin as the captial city. Within each department a *jefe politico* (political chief) served as the administrative head of government. A local community, called a *villa* (village) or *ciudad* (city), served as the administrative center for a district, which was known as a municipality. The legislative arm of a local government was called the *ayuntamiento* (city council), and its members were *regidores* (city council members). An *alcalde* (judge, mayor, and policeman combined) presided over the *ayuntamiento*. Except in San Antonio de Bexar, local officials in the municipalities by 1835 were mostly Anglo-Texans.

Immigrants entered Texas principally by way of coastal towns such as Galveston, Matagorda, and Copano and across the Sabine River at Pendleton's Crossing (or Gaines's Ferry) north of Milam. Ineffective enforcement of the decree of April 6, 1830, failed to halt the flow of unauthorized Americans from entering Texas. Some people developed farms in the prohibited strip within twenty leagues of the Sabine River and ten leagues of the coast, as well as in existing neighborhoods from the coast in the south to the Old San Antonio Road on the north. The settled portion of Texas extended as far west as the Nueces River. The extreme northeast corner along the Red River was sparsely inhabited by people who at first thought they were in Miller County, Arkansas. The population of Texas increased from approximately twenty thousand in 1830 to approximately thirty thousand by the time of independence. New residents became the primary proponents for direct action against the centralized Mexican government.

In late September, 1835, Mexican officials became alarmed at the reports of increasing militancy among Texans. A military force from San Antonio marched to Gonzales to take back a cannon given to the citizens there four years earlier for defense against Indian attacks. On October 2 a battle occurred in which citizens of Gonzales forced the soldiers to retreat back to San Antonio without the artillery piece. On October 5 the municipalities elected delegates to attend a convention called the Consultation of All Texans, which finally began on November 3 at San Felipe.

In the meantime, armed Texans captured Goliad where there was a store of much-needed supplies and munitions. Another volunteer group advanced to San Antonio, where they took the Espada, San Juan, and San José missions and then engaged in a battle with Mexican soldiers at Concepción Mission on October 28.

At San Felipe, the Consultation delegates met and heatedly debated the issue of a declaration of independence versus continued loyalty to the Mexican Constitution of 1824. They struck a middle ground by creating a provisional state government as a part of Mexico to better enable them to work out their differences with the national government. The delegates selected a governor, Henry Smith; a lieutenant governor, James W. Robinson; a commander of the Texas army, Sam Houston; and certain other officials and provided for a council consisting of one member from each municipality. The convention sent Stephen F. Austin, Branch T. Archer, and William H. Wharton to seek aid for their cause in the United States. Before adjourning on November 14, the delegates set a meeting for March 1, 1836, to examine at that time their next course of action.

The armed group in San Antonio, meanwhile, had laid seige against the Mexican army there. On December 11 the Mexican army under the command of General Martín Perfecto de Cós surrendered and agreed to leave Texas under the condition they never return north of the Rio Grande. By New Year's Day, 1836, no Mexican soldier was in Texas.

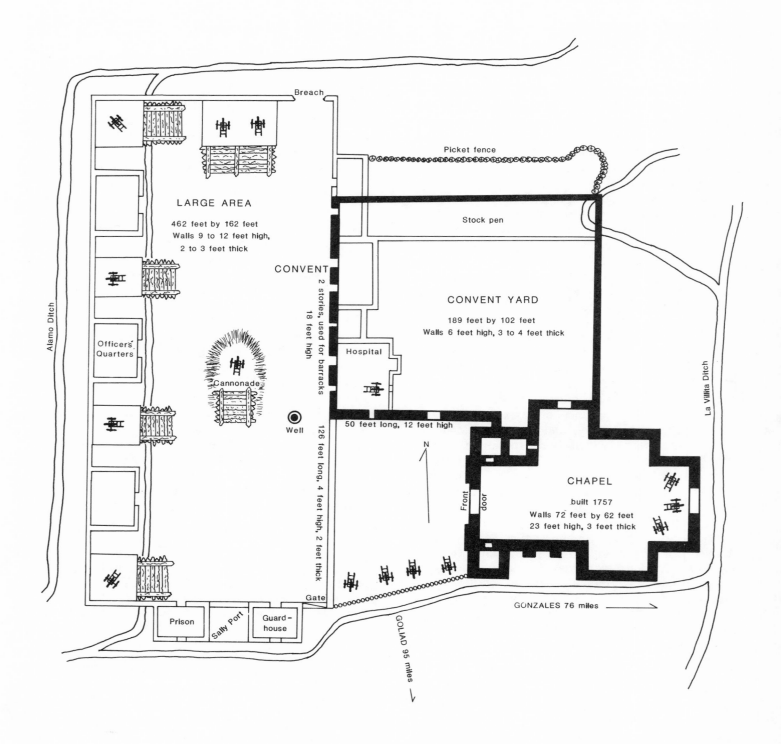

Breach

LARGE AREA

462 feet by 162 feet
Walls 9 to 12 feet high,
2 to 3 feet thick

Alamo Ditch

CONVENT

2 stories, used for barracks

18 feet high

Officers'
Quarters

Cannonade

Well

126 feet long, 4 feet high, 2 feet thick

50 feet long, 12 feet high

Prison

Sally Port

Guard-house

Gate

Picket fence

Stock pen

CONVENT YARD

189 feet by 102 feet
Walls 6 feet high, 3 to 4 feet thick

Hospital

La Villita Ditch

N

Front
door

CHAPEL

built 1757

Walls 72 feet by 62 feet
23 feet high, 3 feet thick

GONZALES 76 miles

GOLIAD 95 miles

THE ALAMO

© 1988 University of Oklahoma Press

25. THE ALAMO

NO NAME STANDS HIGHER in the esteem of Texans who are conscious of their heritage than that of the Alamo. Called the "Cradle of Texas Liberty" because of the events of 1836, the mission-fortress located in San Antonio is the symbol of Texas for tourists and residents alike. During the course of its existence the buildings housed missionaries, Indians, Spanish soldiers, Mexican soldiers, and Texas patriots long before it became a museum commemorating the disaster that befell it during the Texas Revolution.

Spanish authorities established the Mission San Antonio de Valero in 1718. Construction of permanent facilities continued over the next several decades to provide a chapel, a *convento* (monastery), workrooms, a granary, corrals for work animals, and housing for neophytes. Pastures, fields, and irrigation canals were located nearby. Following secularization in 1793, a company of Spanish soldiers from San Carlos del Alamo de Parras in Coahuila used the buildings as its headquarters. The soldiers had referred to their previous post as the Alamo and now applied that name to their new assignment.

In November, 1835, delegates from communities in Texas met as the Consultation of All Texans, declared their loyalty to the Mexican Constitution of 1824, created a provisional state government, and sent a military expedition to expel units of the Mexican dictator's army at San Antonio. After a successful siege, the Texans forced General Martín Perfecto de Cós to retreat beyond the Rio Grande. The Consultation appointed General Sam Houston as the commanding officer of the Texas army. Houston attempted unsuccessfully to consolidate the army into a single unit of resistance closer to the interior and ordered the outlying posts abandoned. By early February, 1836, Colonel James Bowie commanded the volunteers at the Alamo, and Colonel William Barrett Travis commanded the regulars. They decided to defend the Alamo and called upon Texans to come to their aid.

General Antonio López de Santa Anna, the Mexican dictator-president, marched to Texas after suppressing revolts in northern Mexico. He split his army and led the central force from Guerrero, across the Rio Grande from present-day Eagle Pass, Texas. When Santa Anna arrived in San Antonio on February 23 and demanded the surrender of the Alamo garrison, Travis answered by firing a cannon. The Mexican commander's response was to raise a red flag over San Fernando Church to signify no quarter would be given in the battle. The church lay approximately eight hundred yards from the west wall of the Alamo fortress.

Bowie became ill on February 24, and Travis assumed command of both the regulars and the volunteers. Even though Travis repeatedly sent calls for reinforcements, only thirty-two men from Gonzales responded. The Alamo defenders contended with inadequate food and munitions, a frigid norther, and constant nightly bombardments.

On the evening of March 5, after twelve days of siege, Santa Anna ordered his men to move quietly near the outer walls of the Alamo. There they remained all night without coats or blankets even though a fresh norther blew in. In the light of a full moon in the pre-dawn cold on March 6, the Mexican soldiers were signaled to their feet by the short, shrill blasts of a bugle as it sounded *el Deguello* and sent them forward against the Alamo. That particular call meant no mercy would be given to the enemy. On the third assault the attackers breached the north wall and rushed into the compound, where they engaged in hand-to-hand combat with the defenders using knives, swords, tomahawks, and bayonets. Within two hours after the battle commenced, an eerie quiet hung over the devastated fortress. A search of the rooms revealed that not all the defending combatants died in battle. Some participants and observers mentioned five, while others stated six or seven survived. One unresolved controversy is whether Davy Crockett, the legendary Tennessean, was among the survivors. A Mexican officer at the scene wrote that Crockett died by execution after the battle, while Mrs. Susanna Dickinson, wife of Travis's artillery officer, claimed she saw Crockett dead among his fellow Tennesseans in their place of defense. The survivors were summarily slain by being run through with swords. Santa Anna ordered his own dead buried but denied that custom to the Texans except one, Gregorio Esparza, whose body was released to his family after their personal petition to Santa Anna. The Texan corpses were placed in three stacks interspersed with wood soaked with grease and oil and set aflame. Their ashes were later buried at San Fernando Church.

Santa Anna's army of over 5,000 suffered approximately 1,600 killed and wounded. All 187 Texan combatants died. Of those Texans who perished, seven were of Mexican ancestry. Approximately thirty women, children, and slaves survived the siege and fall of the Alamo. Santa Anna met with Susanna Dickinson, then sent her eastward to tell the other Texans what they could expect from continued rebellion.

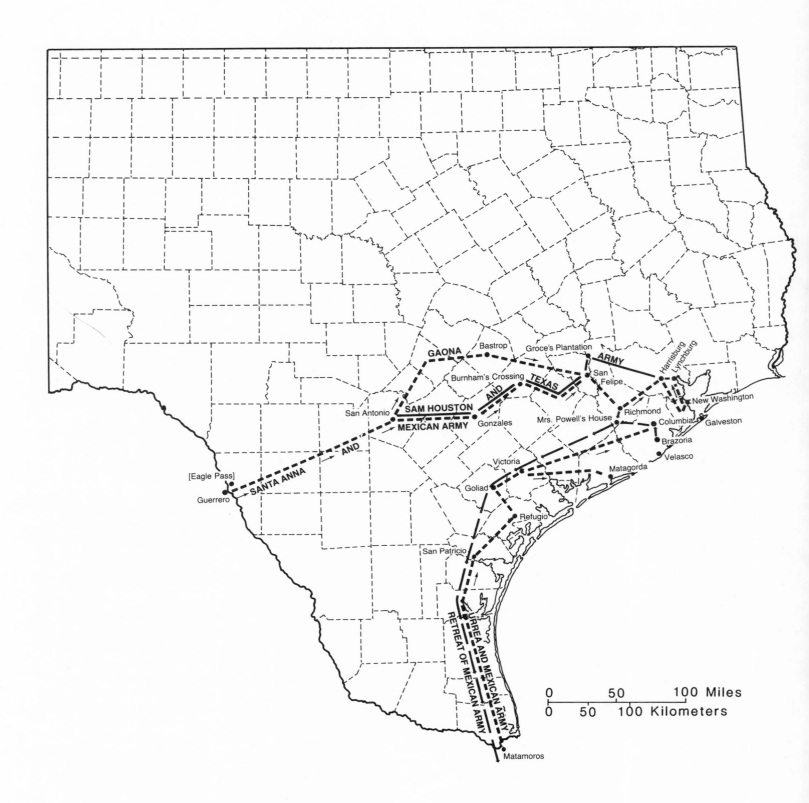

GAONA Bastrop Groce's Plantation ARMY
Burnham's Crossing TEXAS Harrisburg Lynchburg
San Felipe
SAM HOUSTON AND
San Antonio MEXICAN ARMY New Washington
Gonzales Mrs. Powell's House Richmond
AND Columbia Galveston
Brazoria
[Eagle Pass] Victoria Velasco
SANTA ANNA Matagorda
Guerrero Goliad
Refugio
San Patricio

URREA AND MEXICAN ARMY
RETREAT OF MEXICAN ARMY

0   50   100 Miles
0   50   100 Kilometers

Matamoros

THE TEXAS REVOLUTION

© 1988 University of Oklahoma Press

26. THE TEXAS REVOLUTION

WHILE THE MEXICAN ARMY besieged the Alamo, Texans met as previously arranged on March 1, 1836, at Washington-on-the-Brazos. The following day, the delegates approved a Declaration of Independence to inform the world that usurpations of power by the government of General Antonio López de Santa Anna ended any hopes of reconciliation between Texas and Mexico. Therefore, self-preservation of Texas could be secured only by independence. The convention appointed Sam Houston as commander-in-chief of the Texas army and began work on a constitution for the Republic of Texas.

General Houston went immediately to Gonzales, where he learned from Mrs. Susanna Dickinson, a survivor of the Alamo affair, the fate of the Alamo's defenders and the intentions of Santa Anna toward all Texans. Houston needed time to enlist and train an army for the coming struggle. With his men he fell back to Burnham's Crossing (La Grange), Beason's Crossing (Columbus), San Felipe, and Groce's Plantation (near Hempstead). The news of Mexican atrocities at San Antonio, San Patricio, Refugio, and Goliad spread rapidly that spring. The horror stories multiplied with subsequent tellings. Fear stalked the land. Families hastily gathered necessities of food and clothing, hid personal treasured possessions, turned out livestock to forage for themselves, and began a trek eastward to the Sabine and safety. This rush eastward later became known as the "Runaway Scrape." Although men knew they were needed for the Texas army, most of them escorted their families toward Louisiana.

Santa Anna went eastward to Gonzales, San Felipe, Harrisburg, and New Washington on Galveston Bay as he unsuccessfully pursued Texas government officials. He turned back toward Harrisburg when he learned that Houston had begun a march in his direction. Both opposing commanders knew of the other's movements as they maneuvered for position between Harrisburg and New Washington. They eventually met for battle near the confluence of Buffalo Bayou with the San Jacinto River, where on April 21, 1836, the Texas army attacked the Mexican camp with remarkable results.

Following the battlefield carnage, the victorious Texans rounded up the Mexican army survivors. Among them was the president of Mexico himself. Despite demands by Texans to hang Santa Anna forthwith, Houston refused to comply because he knew that a live Santa Anna could assist in getting Texas independence recognized by Mexico, whereas a dead Santa Anna would be just another enemy casualty. Houston had been wounded during the battle, so he soon left for New Orleans to seek medical treatment. Texas *ad interim* president David G. Burnet negotiated with Santa Anna, and they agreed on terms. On May 14 at Velasco, both presidents signed a public agreement and a secret agreement. By the public agreement Santa Anna would cease hostilities and direct his remaining force to evacuate the territory of Texas, passing to the other side of the Rio Grande. Further, all private property belonging to Texans captured during the war would be restored, an equal number of prisoners would be exchanged, and neither the Texan nor the Mexican armies would come in contact with the other. Santa Anna would receive safe passage to Veracruz in time. The secret agreement called for Santa Anna to order his government to receive a Texas delegation to negotiate all differences, establish a trade treaty with Texas, acknowledge Texas independence, and set the international boundary at the Rio Grande.

A force of approximately 5,000 enemy soldiers then within easy striking range of San Jacinto could have overcome the Texans had General Vicente Filisola, now in command of the Mexican army, been willing to disobey Santa Anna's order to withdraw. The nearby commanders with their well-equipped units were Filisola at Richmond, General Joaquín Ramírez y Sesma at Richmond, General José Urrea at Brazoria, Colonel Mariano Salas at Columbia, and Colonel Augustín Alcerrica at Matagorda. In addition, General Antonio Gaona with 725 men was marching in that direction but was lost temporarily between Bastrop and San Felipe.

Filisola complied with his captured commander's request. He assembled the Mexican combined forces at Mrs. Powell's house at Thompson's Crossing halfway between Richmond and Columbia approximately fifteen miles west of the Brazos River, and began the homeward retreat. Gaona returned to Mexico by retracing his route. By early summer, all enemy soldiers had evacuated Texas.

The two months between the siege of the Alamo and the Battle of San Jacinto had been a time of anxiety. Texas was born in a dream, nurtured in despair, and matured in victory. No longer fearing an organized assault from Mexico, the people of Texas returned to their homes. Ahead lay the awesome task of forging a republic that would endure.

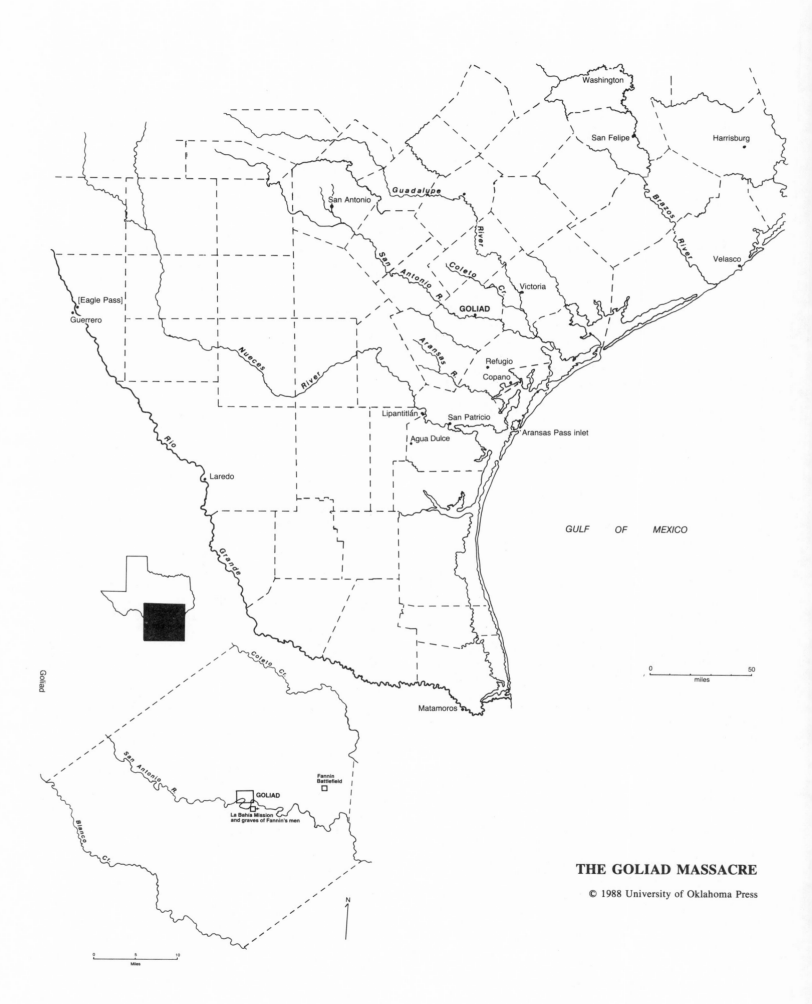

Washington

San Felipe

Harrisburg

Guadalupe

San Antonio

River

Velasco

Coleto

Victoria

San

GOLIAD

[Eagle Pass]

Guerrero

Aransas R.

Antonio R.

Refugio

Copano

Nueces

River

Lipantitlán

San Patricio

Agua Dulce

Aransas Pass inlet

Rio

GULF   OF   MEXICO

Laredo

Grande

0   50
miles

Goliad

Coleto Cr.

Matamoros

San Antonio R.

Fannin
Battlefield

GOLIAD

La Bahía Mission
and graves of Fannin's men

Blanco

Cr.

N

THE GOLIAD MASSACRE

© 1988 University of Oklahoma Press

0   5   10
Miles

27. THE GOLIAD MASSACRE

TEXAS STOOD AGHAST at the atrocities of Santa Anna but took pride in the heroism of the Alamo's defenders. Those men fought bravely to the end and asked for and received no quarter. Later in that month of March, 1836, however, an event at Goliad stirred the emotions of Texans against the government of Mexico so greatly that hatred turned into a burning desire for revenge. In the United States the aftermath of Goliad turned the interests of a few in the Texas cause into a celebrated rush to aid their beleaguered kinsmen against the publicized barbarity of the Mexican army.

The story of Goliad in the Texas Revolution began with plans of the Provisional State of Texas to launch an expedition against Matamoros. Texans believed that the capture of Matamoros would bring support of Mexican liberals and provide much-needed funds for the state's treasury. Attempts to launch the Matamoros expedition became confused when officials could not agree upon who should be in charge or even that the campaign should be undertaken. The power play between General Sam Houston, Governor Henry Smith, and the Provisional Legislative Council disrupted the state's activities so thoroughly that in the critical period from mid-January to early March the public affairs of Texas became chaotic. The governor dismissed the council, the council deposed the governor and installed an acting governor, the council did not meet quorum requirements for official business, and the commanding general took a furlough to negotiate with the Texas Cherokee Indians.

In early January, Colonel Francis W. Johnson and Colonel James W. Fannin, Jr., each claimed authority to lead the expedition to Matamoros. They issued calls for volunteers to meet at San Patricio for the march to the Rio Grande. Santa Anna learned of the Texans' plans while at Saltillo and dispatched General José Urrea to Matamoros to begin operations along the coast to Lipantitlán, sweeping Texas clean of dissidents.

Volunteers under Colonel James Grant and Colonel Johnson began arriving in early January at Copano, Refugio, and Goliad. They went to San Patricio to await reinforcements and to obtain horses for the expedition. Colonel Fannin left Velasco for Copano by way of Aransas Pass in early February. Upon arriving at Refugio and learning the Mexican army intended to strike simultaneously the posts at Goliad and San Antonio, Fannin retreated to Goliad to prepare a proper defense at the old Spanish presidio. On February 27, Urrea surprised Johnson's camp at San Patricio and executed the survivors. On March 2 the same fate befell Grant's men when they were attacked twenty-five miles away at Agua Dulce. Urrea obeyed the decree of Santa Anna issued December 30, 1835, that all prisoners taken in arms against the government should be regarded as pirates and shot.

After Texas declared its independence, General Houston ordered Fannin to fall back to Victoria. When the men of Goliad finally got started on March 19 after too long a delay for an unsuccessful evacuation of families from Refugio, they soon became surrounded by Urrea's forces on a prairie approximately ten miles from Goliad and two miles from Coleto Creek. Fannin's men formed a hollow square for defense and repulsed attack after attack from three o'clock until dusk, but the shortage of water, provisions, and ammunition forced them to consider the folly of continued resistance. At the Battle of Coleto the Mexicans had approximately thirteen hundred soldiers to the Texans' four hundred.

Early on the morning of March 20, Fannin signed surrender terms that placed the Texans at the discretion of the supreme government. Urrea promised to use his influence to secure their parole to New Orleans, then marched the survivors back to Goliad. Other Texans under Colonel William Ward, who had escaped Urrea at Refugio, were captured at Victoria and sent to Goliad.

Upon being informed of the victory at Coleto, Santa Anna ordered the execution of the Texan survivors. The onerous duty fell to Colonel José Nicolás de la Portilla in the absence of Urrea, who at the time was at Victoria. On Palm Sunday, March 27, 1836, the Texans arose at dawn, fell into three ranks, and marched off in different directions under guard for what they supposed would be work details. At a given signal, the Mexican soldiers opened fire at the sitting and kneeling prisoners. A total of 352 Texans were slaughtered in cold blood. Only 28 escaped from the Goliad Massacre. The Mexicans spared an additional 98 men because of illness or their absence for work detail or because they were not directly involved in the Battle of Coleto. Still another 80 men from Nashville who arrived too late for the conflict were exempted. Bodies of the slain Texans were piled and burned. Dogs and vultures finished what the fire did not consume.

The fate of the men of Goliad and the perfidious manner in which they were killed shocked and alarmed the people of Texas. Revenge came on the San Jacinto battlefield three weeks later when the charging Texas soldiers put action to their words—"Remember Goliad!"

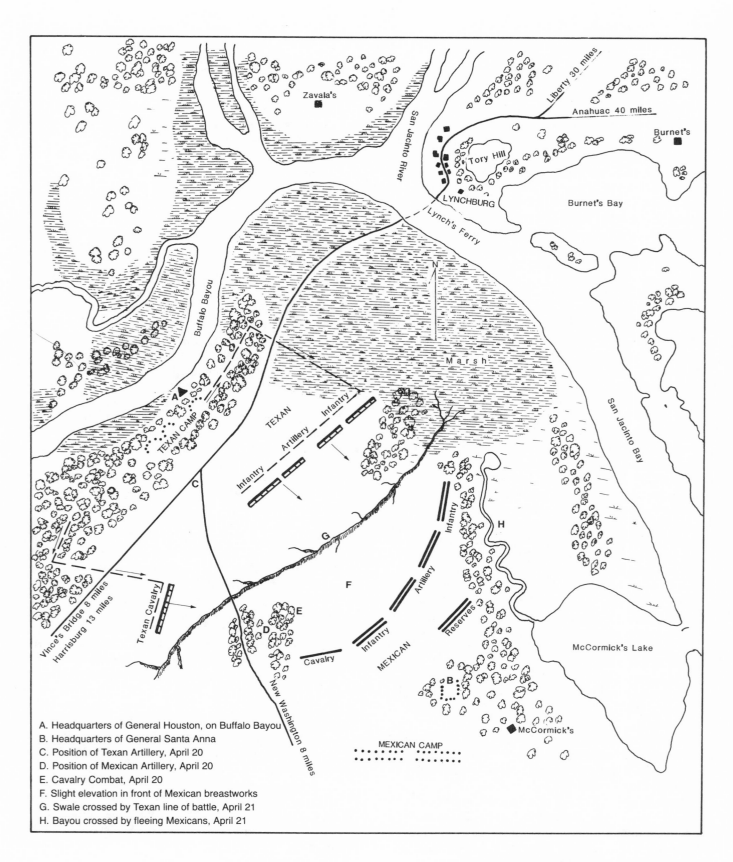

A. Headquarters of General Houston, on Buffalo Bayou
B. Headquarters of General Santa Anna
C. Position of Texan Artillery, April 20
D. Position of Mexican Artillery, April 20
E. Cavalry Combat, April 20
F. Slight elevation in front of Mexican breastworks
G. Swale crossed by Texan line of battle, April 21
H. Bayou crossed by fleeing Mexicans, April 21

THE BATTLE OF SAN JACINTO

© 1988 University of Oklahoma Press

28. THE BATTLE OF SAN JACINTO

THE TEXAN ARMY under the command of General Sam Houston had only a limited amount of military training before its direct encounter with Mexican forces at the San Jacinto battlefield. But what the men lacked in formal instruction they more than made up by a fierce determination to protect their homeland and provide for a democratic government.

Good fortune befell the Texans on April 18 as they camped near the burned-out town of Harrisburg when they learned from captured Mexican couriers that General Antonio López de Santa Anna left his main army near Richmond while he led an advance party then at New Washington. The Texas commander became convinced that the Texan army, by moving quickly against Santa Anna, had a better than even chance of success on the battlefield. After a stirring speech in which he indicated the battle would soon be joined, Houston gave the order to march. In a sense, the hunted now became the hunter.

The Texans continued on to Lynch's Ferry at the junction of Buffalo Bayou and the San Jacinto River. Santa Anna learned of the Texan army behind him as he burned New Washington, and he turned to meet Houston's army. After brief sorties on April 20, both armies withdrew to their camps.

When April 21 dawned, the two forces faced each other across a prairie approximately three-fourths of a mile distant. A rise in the land between them prevented a direct sight of the other camp, but scouts on both sides kept their commanders informed. Santa Anna received reinforcements during the night when approximately four hundred men arrived after an exhausting march from Harrisburg. Since his own men also needed rest after several days of rapid marches across the muddy Texas countryside, Santa Anna permitted his entire camp to relax. The Mexican force, numbering now approximately fourteen hundred men, felt so secure that the soldiers slept, ate, or played cards without posting sentries to watch the supposedly trapped Texans.

About noon on April 21, Houston called his first council of war since he assumed command of the army, listened to his commanders, and dismissed them without stating his intentions. He then sent Deaf Smith and Henry Karnes to destroy the bridge across Vince's Bayou. The downed bridge would obstruct any Mexican reinforcements coming up behind the Texans to create a vise between the two enemy divisions.

At 3:30 that afternoon, General Houston ordered the army to prepare for an attack. Infantry, cavalry, and artillery units, assembled in a two-man-deep formation nine hundred yards wide, with Houston in front, advanced rapidly across the open prairie. About the time the Texans reached the enemy camp, Deaf Smith rode up to announce, "Vince's Bridge is down!" The advancing Texans were not discovered until they got within approximately two hundred yards of the enemy. Pandemonium broke loose, however, when the Texans scaled the enemy's breastworks shouting,"Remember the Alamo! Remember Goliad!" Mexican officers unsuccessfully attempted to rally their soldiers for defense as disorder turned to rout.

In the carnage that followed, Mexican soldiers attempting to flee were pursued and slain without mercy on the open prairie and in nearby marshes. Some Mexican soldiers, seeing escape was impossible, fell to their knees calling out "Me no Alamo! Me no Goliad!" but to no avail; they were slaughtered on the spot. Houston's officers attempted without success to stem the terrible vengence when they saw the battle had been won. Houston knew that if his men exhausted their ammunition and ruined their weapons using them as clubs, he would have no means to face enemy reinforcements coming from encampments on the Brazos. Although Houston in his official report stated that the main battle lasted only eighteen minutes after the two lines first joined in combat, the furious search and destroy activities continued until nightfall. A roundup of prisoners continued for several days.

The Texans had 783 fighting effectives and lost 2 killed and 23 wounded. Six of the wounded later died. Houston reported that the Mexican losses numbered 630 killed and 730 captured, of whom 280 were wounded. Only approximately 40 Mexican soldiers escaped.

With a stroke of daring favored by good luck, the Texan army seized the initiative, took the battle to the enemy, and triumphed on the prairie of San Jacinto. This battle shaped the course of Texas history as no other single event. Among other things, it brought about the withdrawal of the remaining Mexican army beyond the Rio Grande and obtained Santa Anna's promise to work for the recognition of Texas independence by Mexico. In the crucible of San Jacinto, political fortunes were made. In addition to serving as republic and state officials, many of the combatants have been memorialized with the naming of cities, counties, and schools as a lasting reminder of this aspect of the Texas heritage.

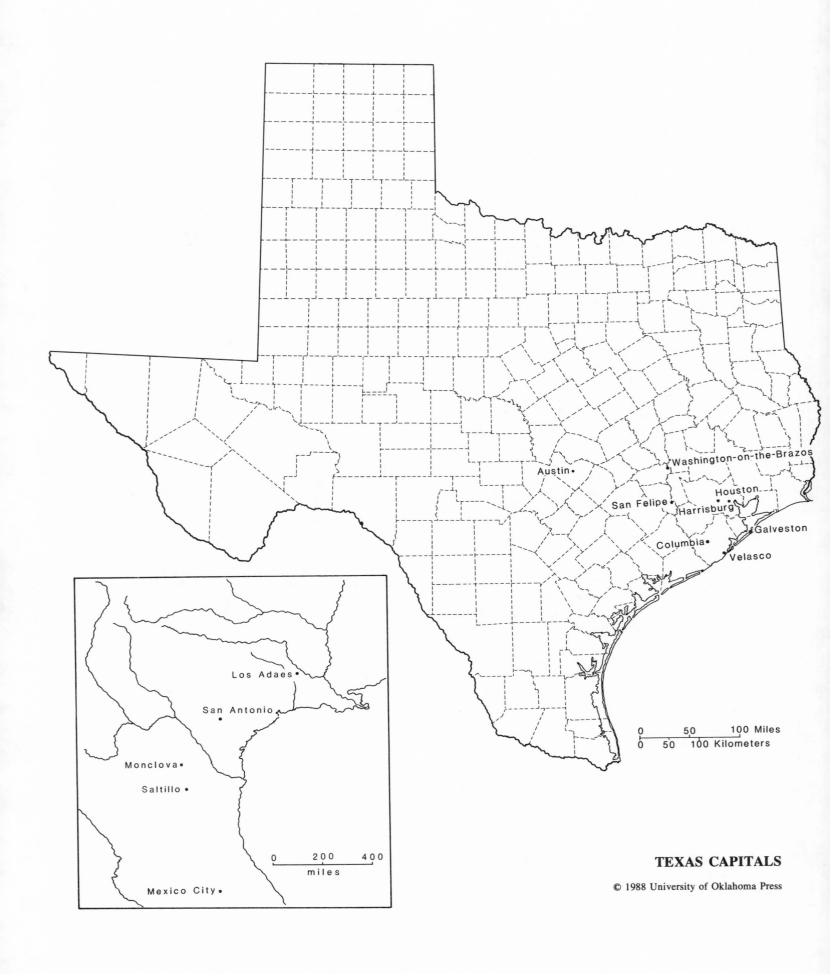

Austin •

Washington-on-the-Brazos •

Houston •

San Felipe •

Harrisburg •

Columbia •

Galveston •

Velasco •

Los Adaes •

San Antonio •

Monclova •

Saltillo •

Mexico City •

0   200   400
miles

0   50   100 Miles
0   50   100 Kilometers

TEXAS CAPITALS

© 1988 University of Oklahoma Press

29. TEXAS CAPITALS

OVER THE CENTURIES Texas has had more than a dozen capitals. Political control over what is now the state of Texas was first centered in Mexico City as the Spanish explored and extended settlements northward. The furthermost mission site of the Spanish, established to meet a constant French threat from settlements on the Red River in Louisiana, and serving the Adaes Indians, was at present-day Robeline, Louisiana, on the Arroyo Hondo. This community of Los Adaes became the capital of Texas in 1722 and remained as such until after the French gave up all claims to the North American mainland. In 1772, Spanish officials shifted the seat of government to San Antonio de Bexar, where it remained until 1824. During the infant years of the Republic of Mexico, political dominance over Texas was directed from Saltillo (1824–33) and Monclova (1833–36). Even before Texans severed ties with Mexico, however, a demand for local control brought about action.

In November, 1835, the Consultation of All Texans met at San Felipe de Austin and created a provisional state government within the Mexican republic. The delegates adjourned on November 14 to meet again on March 1, 1836, at Washington-on-the-Brazos. During the interim, conditions between Texas and the Mexican government deteriorated to the point of invasion by the Mexican army led by President Antonio López de Santa Anna. While the village of San Antonio de Bexar was under siege, the delegates met on schedule and considered two choices: servile submission or active resistance. The Texas representatives quickly chose to go alone by declaring independence from Mexico on March 2.

Washington-on-the-Brazos became the first capital town of this fledgling republic. Within a short time, however, the *ad interim* government relocated at Harrisburg and then at Galveston Island to escape capture by Santa Anna. Following the victory at San Jacinto, President David G. Burnet moved the temporary capital from Galveston to the mainland at Velasco, a summer resort for inland colonists, where Texan and Mexican authorities signed the treaties that ended the Texas Revolution.

A search for a more central location with adequate accommodations resulted in the relocation in October, 1836, to Columbia. An even more important consideration was that the only real newspaper in Texas at the time, the *Telegraph and Texas Register,* had moved to Columbia from San Felipe during the recent crisis. Officials moved again in April, 1837, to the new town of Houston after a congressional committee selected that site.

Apparent dissatisfaction with the town on Buffalo Bayou caused congressional committees to look toward the interior of Texas. More than a dozen offers by individuals and communities were received and investigated. Under President Mirabeau B. Lamar, the government was relocated in October, 1839, to the community of Waterloo, which was renamed Austin, on the Colorado River. Sam Houston, incensed over this action, attempted to change the government's headquarters back to his namesake city when he resumed the office of president in late 1841. Adamant Austinites, however, thwarted the president's plans to remove the government's official papers in an event called the "Archive War." But Houston used his executive powers to convene Congress first at the town of Houston in 1842, after the Mexican invasion of Texas that spring, and then at Washington-on-the-Brazos. The latter location served as the republic's principal town from 1842 to 1845.

When annexation became an issue in 1845, President Anson Jones convened the Texas Congress at Austin to deal officially with the American offer. After the U.S. Congress admitted Texas to the Union, Texas President Jones on February 19, 1846, presided over ceremonies in Austin that transferred Texas from independence to statehood. Finally, to settle the matter where the permanent capital would be located, Texans voted in 1850 in favor of the city of Austin.

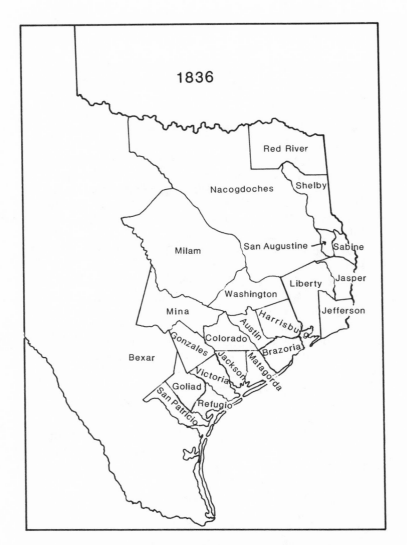

1836

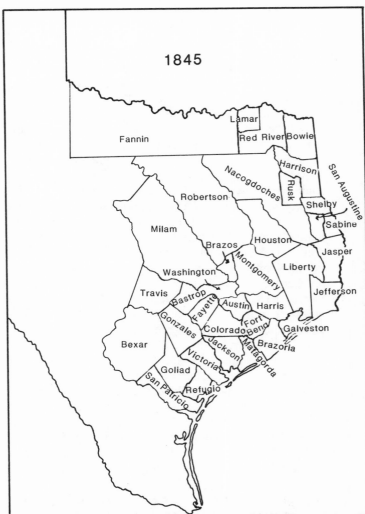

1845

TEXAS COUNTIES, 1836 AND 1845

© 1988 University of Oklahoma Press

30. TEXAS COUNTIES, 1836 and 1845

THE REPUBLIC OF TEXAS existed for almost a decade after the Battle of San Jacinto. During the period 1836–45 this independent nation struggled with tough problems of organizing a stable government, coping with inadequate finances, meeting attacks on the Indian and Mexican frontiers, and quelling domestic violence. Yet through it all, the resourceful people continued cultivating crops, raising families, laying out towns, improving transportation facilities, and building a better future for themselves.

Texas leaders hoped to attract a large number of people from the United States to purchase land. The republic had approximately 250,000 square miles, or four times the area of Virginia, then the largest state in the United States. At first, efforts to sell land met with little success because of the American depression that began in 1837. Sales picked up with the recovery of the American economy, and during the early 1840s a stream of settlers entered Texas. The 1836 population of 30,000 increased to 55,000 by 1840 and to 145,000 by 1845.

Texas lost potential revenue in land sales to its citizens when it began a liberal land distribution program by means of headright certificates. The government issued such permits to persons living in Texas before and immediately after the March 2, 1836, Declaration of Independence. A first-class certificate entitled the head of a family to one league (4,428 acres) and one *labor* (177 acres) of land. A single man received one-third of a league. A second class certificate entitled the head of a family to 1,280 acres and a single man to 640 acres. The third- and fourth-class certificate holders who were heads of families received 640 acres, and single men received 320 acres. Special headright certificates, also known as bounty or donation awards, went to survivors and heirs of the men who fell at Goliad, the Alamo, and other battles of the Texas Revolution. Approximately 37 million acres were granted under the various headright and bounty certificates.

During the summer of 1836, Texas voters approved the constitution drafted at Washington-on-the-Brazos the previous March. When the permanent government began in October, 1836, the Congress created twenty-three counties based on the twenty-three municipalities in existence at the time of Texas independence. The republic organized the current and future counties according to the system used in the southern United States.

Each county had as its governing body a county board made up by elected justices of the peace and an appointed chief justice of the county court. In 1845, four elected commissioners replaced the justices of the peace as county governing officials. Other county officers were sheriff, coroner, clerk, tax assessor, and surveyor.

As the population increased, the Republic of Texas Congress created new counties in order for the people to be better served. Counties with large land areas were divided in order to place a county seat of government closer to existing communities. By 1845, Texas had a total of thirty-six counties.

Original Counties	Year Created
Austin	1836
Bexar	1836
Brazoria	1836
Colorado	1836
Goliad	1836
Gonzâles	1836
Harrisburg	1836
Jackson	1836
Jasper	1836
Jefferson	1836
Liberty	1836
Matagorda	1836
Milam	1836
Mina	1836
Nacogdoches	1836
Red River	1836
Refugio	1836
Sabine	1836
San Augustine	1836
San Patricio	1836
Shelby	1836
Victoria	1836
Washington	1836

Counties Added During the Republic Era	Year Created
Fannin	1837
Fayette	1837
Fort Bend	1837
Houston	1837
Montgomery	1837
Robertson	1837
Galveston	1838
Harrison	1839
Bowie	1840
Lamar	1840
Travis	1840
Brazos	1841
Rusk	1843

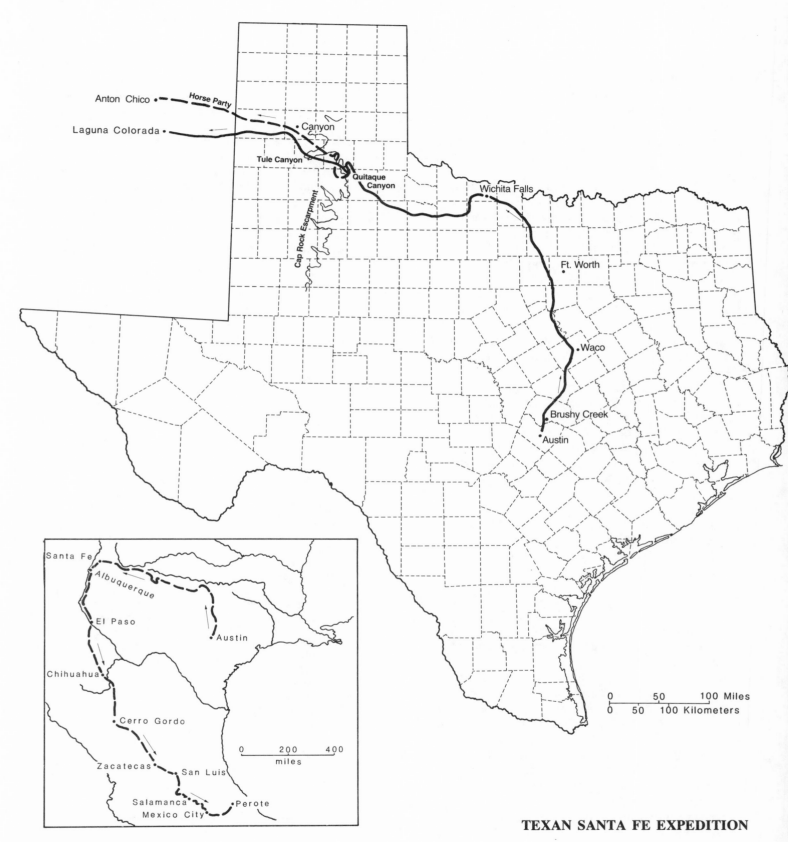

Anton Chico •—— *Horse Party*

Laguna Colorada •

• Canyon

Tule Canyon

Quitaque Canyon

Cap Rock Escarpment

Wichita Falls

• Ft. Worth

• Waco

Brushy Creek •
• Austin

Santa Fe
Albuquerque
El Paso
• Austin
Chihuahua
Cerro Gordo
Zacatecas • • San Luis
Salamanca • • Perote
Mexico City

0   200   400
miles

0   50   100 Miles
0   50   100 Kilometers

TEXAN SANTA FE EXPEDITION

© 1988 University of Oklahoma Press

31. TEXAN SANTA FE EXPEDITION

IN AN EFFORT to bolster the weak financial resources of the republic, Texas President Mirabeau B. Lamar in 1841 attempted to establish trade with Santa Fe. A supply of mercantile goods had been flowing from Missouri to Mexico's northern provinces for almost two decades, with substantial profits for Missouri citizens. Lamar wanted to redirect that commerce to benefit Texas. In addition, the Texas government hoped to expand political control over the region it claimed by persuading New Mexico residents to cast their lot with the Texans against the usurpations of power by the central government of Mexico.

Lamar twice attempted unsuccessfully to have the Texas Congress appropriate funds for an expedition. When these measures failed, the president ordered his treasury secretary to withdraw $89,000 of public funds to outfit the expedition, which became known as the Santa Fe Pioneers. On June 20, 1841, a total of 321 men set out on the journey to Santa Fe from an encampment on Brushy Creek, approximately twenty miles northeast of Austin. The group consisted of civil commissioners, military officers and soldiers, merchants, teamsters, and visitors. Lamar appointed General Hugh McLeod to command the military. The civil commissioners were Colonel William D. Cooke, Dr. Richard F. Brenham, and José Antonio Navarro, with George Van Ness as secretary. The military contingent consisted of five companies of infantry and one of artillery. Lamar's stated reason for sending troops was to protect the caravan, since it would be traveling through hostile Indian country.

The group traveled northward then turned westward in the vicinity of present-day Wichita Falls. For a time the trip was exciting. Exploring previously unknown country, hunting buffalo, and furthering the cause of the Republic of Texas kept the men's spirits high. Gradually, dry summer weather, shortages of food, parched grass that failed to strengthen the draft and riding animals, lack of knowledge of waterholes, and harassment by Comanches and Kiowas wore down the travelers. They became hopelessly lost. An advance party of approximately one hundred men went forward by horseback to find a way across the Cap Rock Escarpment and the Llano Estacado, while the main group made their way slowly with the wagons through the broken terrain of the Quitaque and Tule canyons. Once the advance party arrived at a New Mexico settlement, they would send guides to direct the way for the main party.

When New Mexico Governor Manuel Armijo learned of the expedition, he sent a detachment of his soldiers to intercept the Texans. On September 15 those troops captured a party of five Texans, and they then forced the surrender of the entire advance group on September 17 at Anton Chico. In the meantime, Mexican guides found the main camp of the Santa Fe Pioneers on September 17 and led McLeod's party through the canyons and across the Staked Plains. The main command arrived on October 4 at Laguna Colorada near the headwaters of Tucumcari Creek, a tributary of the Canadian River. The following day McLeod surrendered his exhausted force without any resistance. The captors promised good treatment to the starving and weakened Texans.

Instead of receiving humane treatment as promised, the Texans were marched under considerable hardship, with demonstrated barbarity by their captors, through Albuquerque, El Paso, Chihuahua, San Luis Potosí, and Mexico City. Many died along the way. While some prisoners remained in the capital city, others became imprisoned at Puebla and Perote Castle. Not all persons on the expedition were Texans by nationality. Two noted visitors were George Wilkins Kendall, editor of the *New Orleans Picayune,* and Thomas Falconer, a British attorney. Both of them wrote accounts of their experiences as members of the Texan Santa Fe Expedition.

The episode caused a great anti-Mexico feeling in the United States. Some members of the American Congress spoke of punitive action against Mexico if all the prisoners with their belongings were not immediately released. Speeches from politicians and editorials from newspaper publishers flowed freely. Even though most of the prisoners were released by April, 1842, an unfavorable attitude toward Mexico persisted.

The Texan Santa Fe Expedition indicated that the people of New Mexico were not dissatisfied enough to revolt against Mexico City's control. The episode also indicated a serious lack of knowledge about the Texas frontier. Had the caravan left earlier and journeyed northward with the spring green-up, the men and animals might have been stronger by the time they reached New Mexico, and events might have turned out differently. What did occur, however, served to strengthen the friendship between Texas and the United States and to increase hostile feelings between Texas and Mexico.

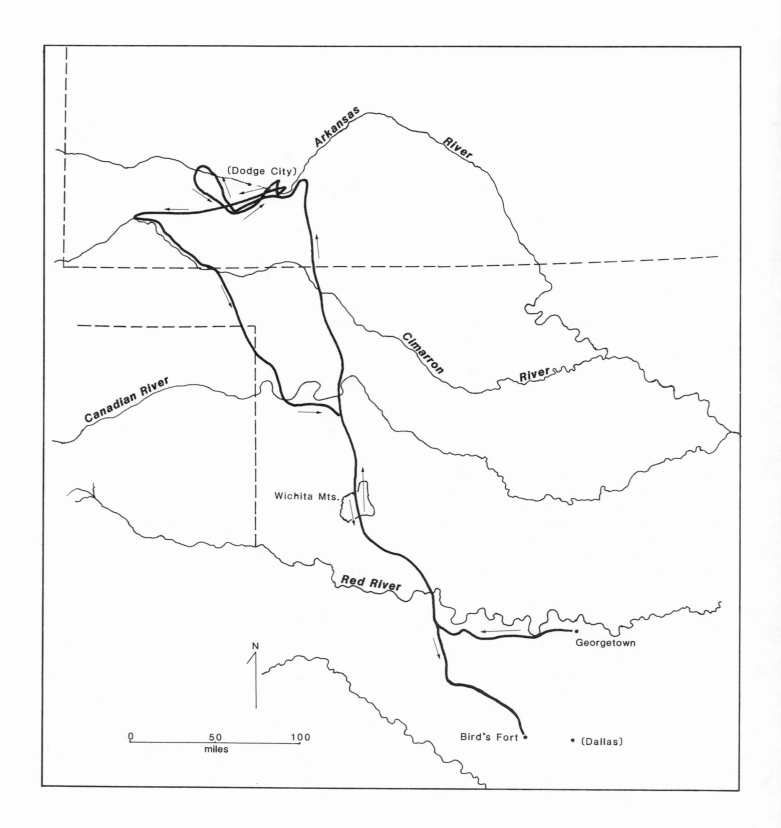

Arkansas River

(Dodge City)

Cimarron River

Canadian River

Wichita Mts.

Red River

Georgetown

N

| 0 | 50 | 100 |

miles

Bird's Fort •   • (Dallas)

THE SNIVELY EXPEDITION

32. THE SNIVELY EXPEDITION

IN AN ATTEMPT to retaliate against Mexico for the indignities committed against Texas in the Mexican raids on San Antonio in 1842 and the capture of Texans in the Mier Expedition, Jacob Snively petitioned the Republic of Texas government on January 28, 1843, to raid Mexican caravans as they passed through Texas territory on the Santa Fe Trail between Missouri and New Mexico. Snively was the adjutant and inspector general of the Republic of Texas. His plan was to organize a force, travel through Texas west of the one hundredth meridian to the Arkansas River, and waylay Mexican wagons loaded with trade goods. The government granted authority on the condition that the spoils would be divided equally between the republic and the men on the expedition.

Snively organized his force of 177 men into three companies on April 24, 1843, at the settlement of Georgetown in present Grayson County. The next day the party left and moved westward until Snively believed he was beyond the hundredth meridian. Actually he had gone no further than present Clay County where the main Wichita River flows into the Red River. There the expedition crossed the Red River.

The self-styled "Battalion of Invincibles" went north by northwest through the Wichita Mountains and onto the plains of present Oklahoma and Kansas. On May 27 they reached the Arkansas River at the southwest corner of present Edwards County, Kansas, approximately twenty-six miles east of present-day Dodge City. The group scouted the area. They met traders from Bent's Fort who told the Texans that a Mexican caravan was coming. While they waited for their target to arrive, Snively's force skirmished with a detachment of Mexican troops sent to intercept them. The battalion killed or captured almost all of the Mexican soldiers and took their supplies and weapons.

Bickering developed in the ranks while the men waited on the Mexican caravan. Some desired to go home. The Snively expedition became divided. One group, the "home boys," elected Eli Chandler to guide them back to Texas. The other group, the "mountaineers," elected Snively as commander.

While on the north side of the Arkansas River on a hunt on June 30, the mountaineers were surprised by U.S. Army dragoons commanded by Captain Philip St. George Cooke. After discussion between the opposing commanders, Cooke crossed to the south side of the Arkansas to surround the Texan camp at Ferguson Grove on the Arkansas River ten miles downstream east of Dodge City. Since the Texans had no chance against such a superior force, they surrendered. Cooke offered to escort those who wanted to accompany him back to the Missouri River, where they could get river and ocean passage to Texas. For those who desired a more direct route home, Cooke permitted the Texans to keep ten rifles for hunting. Snively's men hid their own weapons and surrendered the rifles recently captured from the defeated Mexican force.

A controversy developed over the location of the Texan camp. Was it within U.S. territory or Texas territory? According to the best authority of the day, the Melish Map, Snively was fifty miles west of the hundredth meridian and therefore well within the territorial claims of Texas. Later determinations of the boundary line placed it at the eastern edge of Dodge City, Kansas, which meant Snively was ten miles east of the true one hundredth meridian as understood now and therefore barely within the territorial claims of the United States.

After leaving Cooke's dragoons, the Texans recovered their weapons and attempted to overtake the Mexican caravan. The "Invincibles" became panic-stricken when they suspected a strong Mexican force now guarded the wagons.

Turning homeward, the combined Snively and Chandler forces skirmished with Comanches, retraced their path in Oklahoma, and on August 6, 1843, arrived at Bird's Fort in North Texas, where they disbanded.

The Texas government lodged an official protest against Captain Cooke's action. A court of inquiry at Fort Leavenworth found that Cooke had acted properly. Nevertheless, the U.S. Congress must have felt that Cooke had violated the international boundary, because it made a token appropriation to the Texans engaged in the expedition.

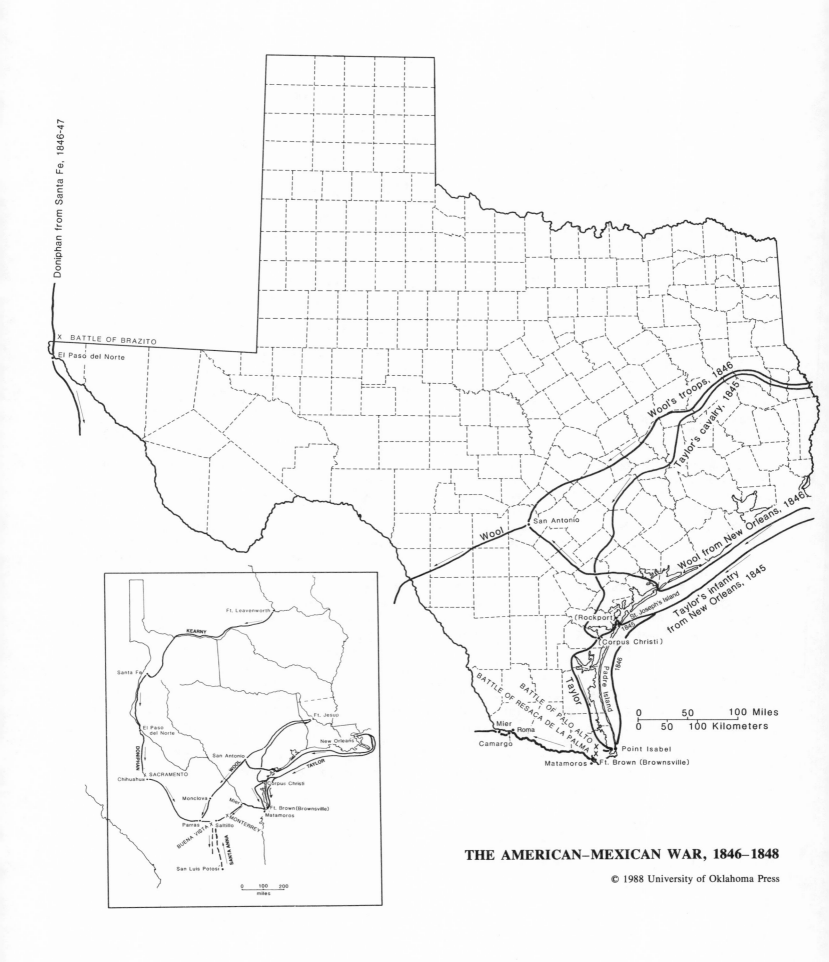

Doniphan from Santa Fe, 1846-47

X BATTLE OF BRAZITO

El Paso del Norte

Wool's troops, 1846

Taylor's cavalry, 1845

Wool

San Antonio

Wool from New Orleans, 1846

Taylor's infantry from New Orleans, 1845

St. Joseph's Island

(Rockport)
1845

(Corpus Christi)

Padre Island

1846

Taylor

BATTLE OF RESACA DE LA PALMA

BATTLE OF PALO ALTO

Mier

Roma

Camargo

Point Isabel

Matamoros • Ft. Brown (Brownsville)

0   50   100 Miles
0   50   100 Kilometers

Ft. Leavenworth

KEARNY

Santa Fe

El Paso del Norte

Ft. Jesup

DONIPHAN

New Orleans

San Antonio

WOOL

TAYLOR

X SACRAMENTO

Chihuahua

Monclova

Corpus Christi

Mier

Ft. Brown (Brownsville)

Matamoros

Parras

X MONTERREY

BUENA VISTA X   Saltillo

SANTA ANNA

San Luis Potosi

0   100   200
miles

THE AMERICAN–MEXICAN WAR, 1846–1848

© 1988 University of Oklahoma Press

33. THE AMERICAN-MEXICAN WAR, 1846-1848

THE SETTLEMENT OF AMERICAN FAMILIES in Texas beginning in the 1820s became a major factor in the relations between the United States and Mexico. Following the acquisition of independence, Texans experienced difficult times as an independent nation, and soon sought annexation to the U.S. In 1844 the U.S. Senate defeated ratification of a treaty of annexation, but after the election of expansionist-minded James K. Polk, outgoing president John Tyler on March 1, 1845, signed a joint resolution of Congress extending statehood to Texas pending submission of an acceptable constitution by the end of the year. On December 29, 1845, Congress admitted Texas as the twenty-eighth state in the union.

When American officials approved the joint resolution, Mexico broke off diplomatic relations with the United States. Conditions deteriorated during that year, with the talk of war becoming common. President Polk ordered General Zachary Taylor to take his army to Texas to provide security while Texans debated the annexation offer. Taylor sent some troops overland to the vicinity of present-day Corpus Christi while supplies came by ship from New Orleans. Those vessels unloaded their cargo on St. Joseph Island before taking the supplies to Rockport and then on to Corpus Christi, where the troops remained until early 1846.

When scouting reports reached General Taylor about the massing of Mexican troops at Matamoros for a punitive expedition against Texas, Taylor relayed this information to the president. In March, 1846, Polk ordered Taylor's army to go to the Rio Grande opposite Matamoros to offset any Mexican military move across the river. Texas claimed, and the United States accepted, the international boundary as the Rio Grande.

While American troops marched through the sandy brush country between the Nueces River and the Rio Grande, American ships transported supplies to Point Isabel at the southern tip of Padre Island. Reconnaissance patrols scouted along the left (Texas) bank of the Rio Grande looking for activity of the Mexican army in Texas. On April 25, 1846, a conflict occurred. The report of the skirmish reached President Polk on May 9. With the assistance of his cabinet, the president drafted a war message to Congress in which he stated that the conflict occurred because Mexico had "invaded our territory and shed American blood upon the American soil. She has proclaimed that hostilities have commenced, and that the two nations are now at war." The message went to Congress on May 11, and Congress responded for war on May 13.

Even before the formal declaration had been made, two major engagements occurred against heavy odds. On May 8, American and Mexican troops fought a battle on Palo Alto Prairie between Point Isabel and Matamoros. The Mexican army had a superior cavalry, but the combined determination of the American artillery and infantry forced the Mexicans to retreat. On May 9, near present-day Brownsville, American forces met the enemy at the Battle of Resaca de la Palma and forced them to retreat beyond the Rio Grande.

Taylor waited in the Brownsville area until July before crossing over the river into Mexico. American soldiers traveled upstream on boats to the Roma, Texas–Camargo, Mexico, area, then pushed on to Monterrey and Saltillo to conquer northern Mexico. Meanwhile, another American army under General Stephen Watts Kearny traveled from Fort Leavenworth, Kansas, to Santa Fe, which was in the territory claimed by the Republic of Texas, now the state of Texas. Santa Fe was taken without a fight. A detachment of Missourians under Colonel Alexander W. Doniphan went down the Rio Grande to present-day El Paso, then on to Chihuahua, and eventually joined Taylor's force in northern Mexico. A third American army under General John E. Wool went southward from San Antonio to Mexico. In late 1846 the scene of war shifted from northern to central Mexico with an invasion from Veracruz to Mexico City under the command of General Winfield Scott. In September, 1847, with the fall of the capital city, fighting ceased. In the resulting Treaty of Guadalupe Hidalgo, concluded on February 2, 1848, Mexico surrendered any claim to Texas and fixed the boundary at the Rio Grande. In addition, a large area stretching westward from Texas to the Pacific Ocean became American territory.

Approximately eight thousand Texans served in the American military during the conflict, which was a greater number than provided by any other state in proportion to population. Besides the Texas Rangers, a small group of mounted and infantry soldiers saw action. Even the governor of the state, J. Pinckney Henderson, went to war when he took a leave of absence from his office to command a division. With the conclusion of hostilities, the Texas population expanded with a rapid increase of settlers from the other states in the American Union.

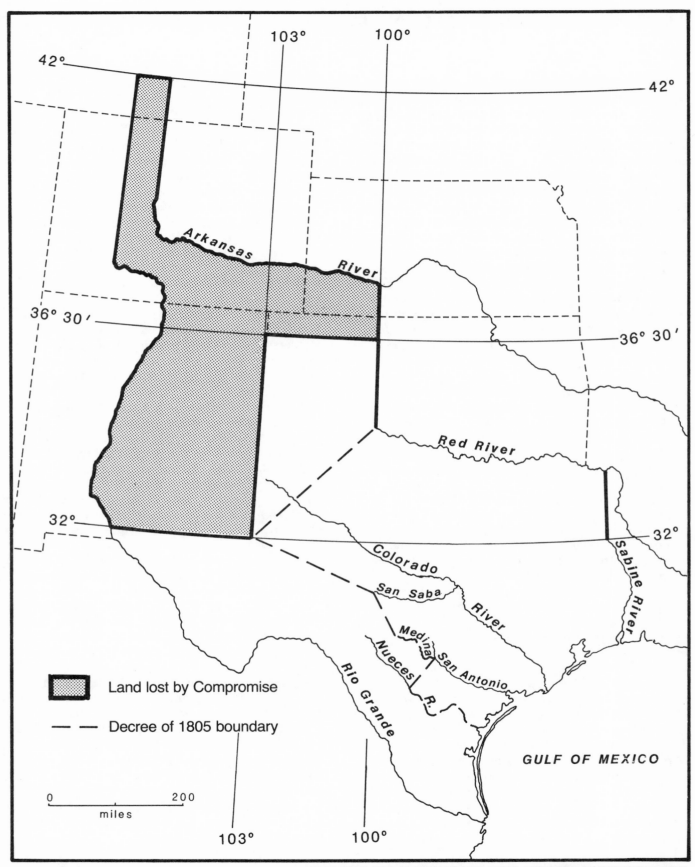

42°   42°

103°   100°

Arkansas   River

36° 30'   36° 30'

32°   32°

Red River

Colorado

San Saba   River

Medina
Nueces   San Antonio
R.
Rio Grande

Sabine River

GULF OF MEXICO

Land lost by Compromise

— — — Decree of 1805 boundary

0   200
miles

103°   100°

TEXAS BOUNDARIES TO THE COMPROMISE OF 1850

34. TEXAS BOUNDARIES TO THE COMPROMISE OF 1850

BY 1700, SPANISH SETTLEMENTS HAD EXTENDED as far north as the Rio Grande. Mission San Juan Bautista and Presidio del Rio Grande, opposite present-day Eagle Pass, Texas, served as the gateway to the mission attempts in central and eastern Texas during the eighteenth century. When the French threat from Louisiana evaporated upon the conclusion of the French and Indian War in 1763, Spain sent the Marqués de Rubí to inspect the northeastern frontier. Rubí's report, in which he made a distinction between a real versus an imaginary frontier, recommended a retreat of Spanish interests to the Rio Grande except for the settlements at San Antonio de Bexar and La Bahía (Goliad).

As settlements expanded in the northern provinces, Spanish authorities needed fixed boundaries between Coahuila, Nuevo Santander, and Texas. In 1805, the Spanish government issued a map with Texas bordered on the west by the Nueces, Medina, and San Saba rivers, thence northwesterly to the intersection of 103° west and 32° north, thence northeasterly to the intersection of the Red River and 100° west, thence down the Red.

After its independence from Spain, Mexico granted land for colonization. Settlement occurred to the north and east of the Nueces River. A disturbed relationship between Texans and the Mexican government eventually erupted in violence.

Representatives from Texas municipalities met in convention in November, 1835, to consider their plight. The Consultation of All Texans, as the meeting was known, sent an armed group to Bexar to oust the Mexican army from that place. As a result of that confrontation, the Texans took Bexar and secured a promise from the Mexican commander, Don Martín Perfecto de Cós, that he would withdraw his troops beyond the Rio Grande, which he did by January 1, 1836. Within a short time, however, forces commanded by Mexican President Antonio López de Santa Anna marched northward into Texas, took Bexar, San Patricio, Refugio, and Goliad, and continued eastward to a rendezvous with destiny at San Jacinto. Santa Anna's defeat and capture there placed the Mexican leader in a precarious position with the enraged Texans, who remembered the Alamo and Goliad massacres. In the resulting Treaties of Velasco on May 14, 1836, Santa Anna agreed to order his troops to withdraw beyond the Rio Grande in return for his freedom.

The question of an official western boundary for the Republic of Texas caused considerable debate in the Texas Congress. On December 19, 1836, the congress declared that the republic's boundaries would be from the mouth of the Sabine River running west along the Gulf of Mexico three leagues from land to the mouth of the Rio Grande, thence up that river to its source, thence north to the forty-second parallel. The line drawn by the United States and Spain in the Adams-Onís Treaty (1819) would be the northern and eastern limits. The measure encompassed large land areas that included settled portions of Tamaulipas, Coahuila, Chihuahua, and New Mexico.

The annexation agreement between Texas and the United States in 1845 accepted those boundaries. Following the American-Mexican War, 1846–48, Texas attempted to establish county government in the Santa Fe area. The American military, which occupied the area through conquest, refused to permit the Texas officials to carry out their plans when New Mexico residents declared they would prefer jurisdiction by the United States rather than by Texas. This controversy became incorporated in a national political debate.

In the Compromise of 1850, Texas accepted an adjusted boundary in return for $10 million in U.S. indemnity bonds bearing 5 percent interest and redeemable at the end of fourteen years, the interest payable half yearly at the treasury of the United States. The payment in bonds would offset the major portion of the Texas public debt incurred during the republic era. Congress deemed it as only fair to take that debt into account by paying Texas for relinquishing its far western lands. In the fall of 1850, in a special election, the people of Texas by a 75 percent majority favored accepting the terms. On November 25, Governor Peter H. Bell signed an act approved by a special session of the state legislature ratifying the adjustment. The western boundary then became a line from the mouth of the Rio Grande upstream to the thirty-second parallel, thence eastward to 103° west, thence northward along that meridian to the line of 36° 30′ north thence eastward along that parallel to the one hundredth meridian.

Camp Van Camp, 1854
•Fort Belknap, 1851
Camp Cooper, 1856 •

•Fort Worth, 1849

Fort Phantom Hill, 1851 •

Camp Colorado, 1857 •

•Fort Bliss, 1848

Fort Chadbourne, 1852 •
Camp Elizabeth, 1853 •

•Fort Graham, 1849

•Camp San Elizario, 1849

Camp J. E. Johnston, 1852 •

•Camp Colorado, 1855
•Fort Gates, 1849

•Fort Quitman, 1858

•Fort Stockton, 1859

Fort McKavett, 1852 •

Fort Mason, 1851

•Fort Croghan, 1849

•Fort Davis, 1854 •

Fort Lancaster, 1855 •

Fort Terrett, 1852 •

• Austin Depot,
1848

Fort Martin Scott, 1848 •

•Camp Verde, 1856

Camp Wood, 1857 •

San Antonio Depot, 1845

Camp Hudson, 1857 •
Fort Clark, 1852 •

Camp Sabinal, 1856 •
•Fort Lincoln, 1849

Fort Inge, 1849 •

Camp Eagle Pass, 1846 • Fort Duncan, 1849 •

Fort Merrill, 1850 •

Fort Ewell, 1852 •

•Camp Corpus Christi, 1850

•Fort McIntosh, 1849

Camp Harney, 1851 •
Fort Drum, 1852 •

Camp Ringgold, 1848 •

0   50   100 Miles
0   50   100 Kilometers

Fort Polk, 1846
Fort Brown, 1846

FEDERAL MILITARY POSTS BEFORE THE CIVIL WAR

© 1988 University of Oklahoma Press

35. FEDERAL MILITARY POSTS BEFORE THE CIVIL WAR

UPON ANNEXATION, Texas ceded to the United States all property and means pertaining to the public defense belonging to the Republic of Texas. The federal government assumed the responsibility of protecting the newly acquired domain. Shortly before the war with Mexico started, the government established Fort Polk at Point Isabel and Fort Brown at present Brownsville, plus an arsenal and depot at San Antonio. During the war, Camp Eagle Pass, at present-day Eagle Pass, served as a temporary post.

An article of agreement in the Treaty of Guadalupe Hidalgo that officially ended the American-Mexican War, 1846–48, stipulated that the United States would use force to restrain Indians ranging along the international boundary and to prevent them from entering Mexico to raid, plunder, and seek captives. The United States began a practice of establishing military posts to accomplish this commitment while protecting Texas frontier settlements. Fort Bliss at El Paso, Camp Ringgold at Rio Grande City, and Camp Drum at Zapata would control crossing of the Rio Grande. Camp Austin at Austin served as a military depot. Camp Corpus Christi for a time in the 1850s was the federal military headquarters and a depot for the military district of Texas. The post may have used the name Fort Marcy for a time.

A western line of forts along the cutting edge of settlement began in 1849 at Fort Inge near present-day Uvalde and extended to Fort Worth. Forts (with references to present-day local communities) along this chain were Martin Scott (near Fredericksburg), Croghan (at Burnet), Graham (near Hillsboro), Gates (near Gatesville), Lincoln (near Hondo), McIntosh (near Laredo), and Duncan (near Eagle Pass), with Camp San Elizario on the Rio Grande below El Paso.

Between 1850 and 1852, as the line of settlement moved westward, it became necessary to close many of these early-day outposts and establish new ones farther on to repeat the process of guarding a new frontier. Installations begun during this period include Forts Merrill (near Three Rivers), Belknap (at Belknap), Mason (near Mason), Phantom Hill (near Abilene), Ewell (near Cotulla), Terrett (between Junction and Sonora), McKavett (near Menard), Clark (at Brackettville), and Chadbourne (near Bronte), and Camps Joseph E. Johnston (near San Angelo), Elizabeth (near Sterling City), and Harney (in Zapata County).

Indian difficulties continued because of the reduction of game as more whites expanded their hunting ground to Indian country, the broad expanse the army had to cover, the inadequate number of troops for the job, and the obvious difficulty the infantry, walking beside its supply wagons, faced in trying to catch and punish Indian riders on swift ponies. In addition, the Indians had first-hand knowledge of the terrain, and the military was just learning it.

Roving bands continued to raid in Mexico, although they kept moving farther west to cross the Rio Grande. In order to abide by the terms of Article 14 of the Suspension of Hostilities agreement of February 29, 1848, at the conclusion of the American-Mexican War and to prevent a claims controversy, the U.S. War Department established new posts at trails, crossings, and waterholes. The American government had agreed to use military force "to prevent the incursions of savages into the Mexican territory." At the same time, during the middle and late 1850s, the government abandoned many of the earlier installations to meet current needs. This new policy of curtailing the Indians' movements led to the beginning of Forts Davis (at Fort Davis), Lancaster (near Ozona), Quitman (on the Rio Grande southwest of Sierra Blanca), and Stockton (in Fort Stockton). In addition, temporary outposts were established at Camps Cooper (between Albany and Throckmorton), Colorado (near Coleman), Verde (between Bandera and Kerrville as headquarters for the army's experiment with camels for transcontinental travel and campaign excursions, Hudson (near Del Rio), Wood (between Rocksprings and Uvalde), Sabinal (near Sabinal), and Van Camp (near Newcastle). A dual purpose for some of these posts was to provide security for transportation lines across Texas.

When differences between the sections resulted in the secession of Texas from the Union, the western forts were abandoned. In early 1861, General David E. Twiggs, commander of the Department of Texas with headquarters at San Antonio, surrendered Union military supplies and installations to Confederate Texas commanders after arranging for safe passage of his personnel to the Gulf Coast, where they would secure travel back east. His action brought to a close the first major phase of federal frontier protection through a military presence.

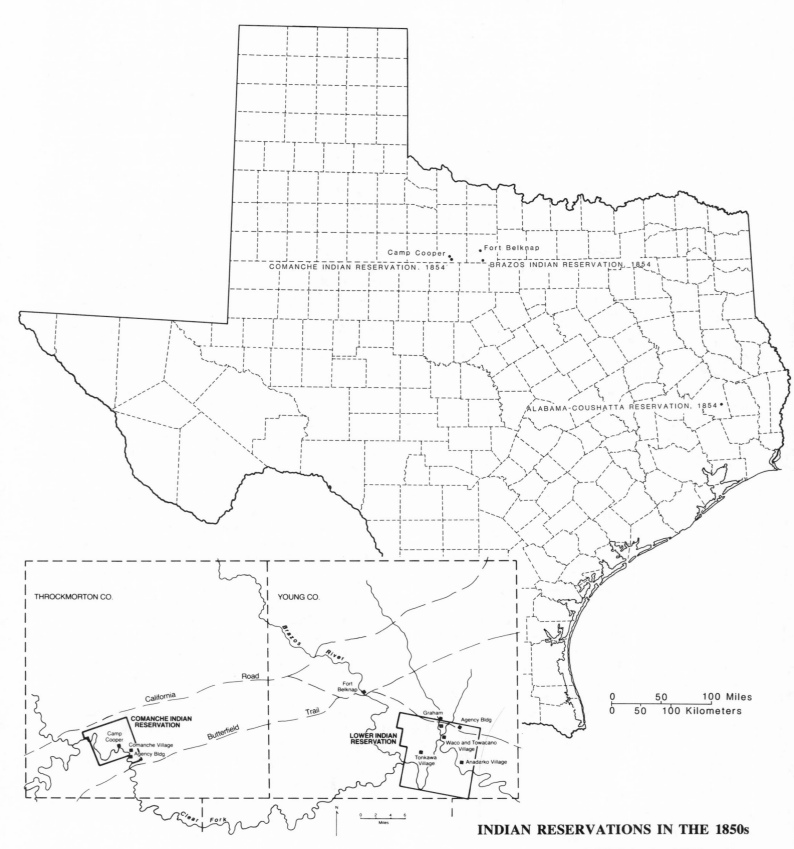

Camp Cooper •
• Fort Belknap
COMANCHE INDIAN RESERVATION, 1854
BRAZOS INDIAN RESERVATION, 1854

ALABAMA-COUSHATTA RESERVATION, 1854 •

THROCKMORTON CO.

YOUNG CO.

Brazos River

Road

Fort Belknap

California

Graham
Agency Bldg

COMANCHE INDIAN
RESERVATION

Trail

Camp Cooper

Butterfield

LOWER INDIAN
RESERVATION

Waco and Towacano
Village

Comanche Village

Agency Bldg

Tonkawa
Village

Anadarko Village

Clear Fork

N

0 2 4 6
Miles

0   50   100 Miles
0   50   100 Kilometers

INDIAN RESERVATIONS IN THE 1850s

© 1988 University of Oklahoma Press

36. INDIAN RESERVATIONS IN THE 1850s

TEXAS ENTERED THE UNION IN 1845 expecting the federal government either to take care of or to assist against marauding Indians. A chain of forts along the edge of western settlement established after annexation did little to ease the problem of too wide an expanse of territory with too few soldiers to guard it. Major Robert S. Neighbors, as special Indian agent in Texas, urged the federal government to purchase land in Texas as a place for the permanent settlement of Indians. Discussion in the legislative halls in Washington, D.C. and in Austin on how to control border and frontier problems did not relieve the situation even when Congress appropriated supplemental funds in 1852 for additional troop support.

Texas Indians objected to the steady westward expansion of Anglo-Americans. Whites were traveling across western Texas to the California gold fields, surveying a possible southern railroad route, locating headright certificates of land in territory claimed by the red man and gradually moving the line of settlement onto traditional hunting grounds. A conflict erupted when the native inhabitants resisted this pressure. Anglo settlers sought protection for their lives and property by demanding greater security even to the point of Indian removal from the state.

A hoped-for solution was reached in early 1854 when the Texas legislature granted to the United States jurisdiction over twelve leagues of vacant land for Indian colonization. Captain Randolph B. Marcy of the U.S. Army and Major Robert S. Neighbors, now the special supervising agent for Indians in Texas, located two reservations in West Texas. The Brazos Indian Reservation, situated on the Brazos River about twelve miles below Fort Belknap in present-day Young County, eventually occupied approximately 27,000 acres. Various numbers of Indians lived there, but probably never more than one thousand at any time. Indians from the Delaware, Caddo, Waco, Tawakoni, Anadarko, Ioni, Shawnee, and Tonkawa tribes unsuccessfully tried to convert from hunters to farmers there. The second site, approximately 18,000 acres about forty miles west of Fort Belknap on the Clear Fork of the Brazos in present Throckmorton County, was known variously as the Comanche Indian Reservation, the Clear Fork Reservation, and the Upper Reservation. Several hundred members of the Comanche tribe attempted to colonize there.

Trouble soon developed between the neighboring Anglo-Americans and the reservation Indians. Disappointing harvests because of untimely rain, poor cultural methods, and hordes of grasshoppers brought unexpected hardships to the reservations. Their inhabitants reverted to traditional hunting methods to secure food and by doing so sometimes crossed the reserve boundaries. In addition, depredations by other Indians or by white renegades were blamed on the reservation Indians. Uneasiness stalked the countryside. The climax came on December 27, 1858, when whites from Erath County attacked a hunting party of Indians who had strayed from the Brazos Reservation into neighboring Palo Pinto County. Citizens of frontier counties, fearing retaliation from the Indians, organized into armed companies. Additional army units marched to the area to keep the peace. In spite of pressure from Governor Hardin R. Runnels, the murderers were never brought to justice.

An additional attack by white neighbors under the leadership of John Robert Baylor on the lower reservation in April, 1859, convinced Major Neighbors peace could not be restored. Neighbors accompanied some local Indian leaders north of the Red River into Indian Territory to seek a safer haven. On August 1, 1859, the reservation Indians moved northward under a U.S. Army guard. Within two weeks they arrived at their new home on the Washita River near present Anadarko, Oklahoma. The reserved land provided for the Indians reverted to the state as stipulated in the original agreement. The state then granted the property to land certificate holders.

In contrast to the reservation policy failure in West Texas, another attempt was made during this period to place Indians on a reservation in East Texas. In 1854 the Texas legislature established a 1,280-acre reserve in Polk County for the Alabama and Coushatta tribes. Those Indians adjusted quite well to their surroundings in the developing southeastern Texas area. In 1927 the tract was expanded to include a total of 4,280 acres.

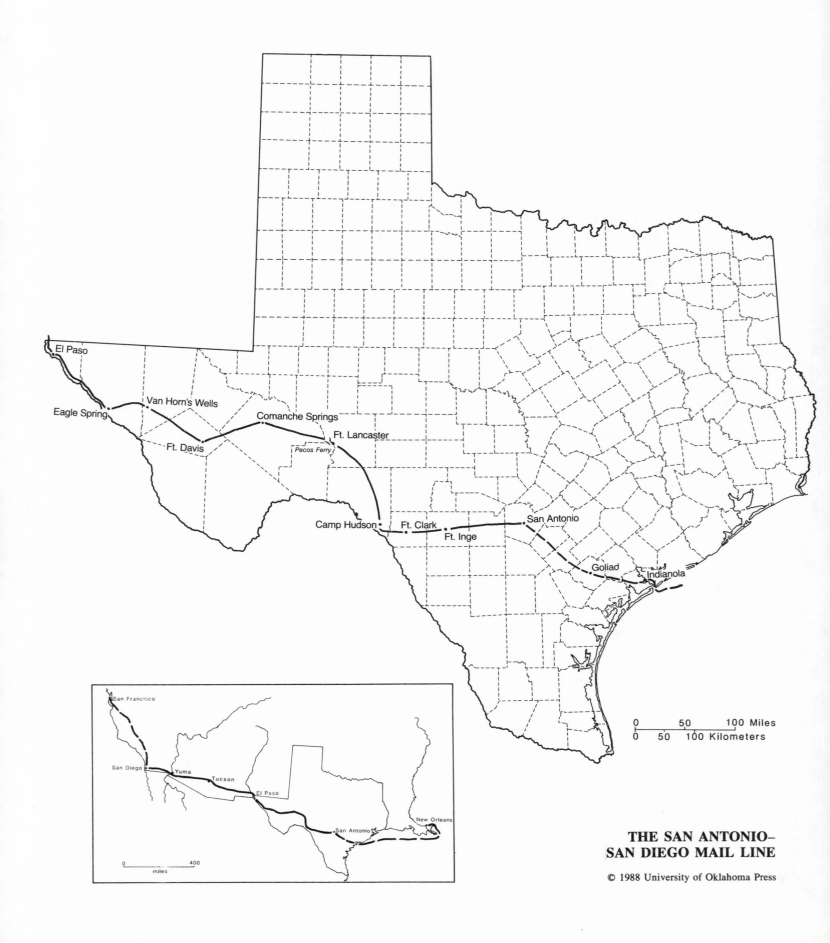

El Paso

Van Horn's Wells

Eagle Spring

Comanche Springs

Ft. Davis

Ft. Lancaster

Pecos Ferry

Camp Hudson

Ft. Clark

Ft. Inge

San Antonio

Goliad

Indianola

San Francisco

San Diego

Yuma

Tucson

El Paso

San Antonio

New Orleans

0   50   100 Miles
0   50   100 Kilometers

0   400
      miles

**THE SAN ANTONIO–
SAN DIEGO MAIL LINE**

© 1988 University of Oklahoma Press

37. THE SAN ANTONIO–SAN DIEGO MAIL LINE

REGULARLY SCHEDULED MAIL SERVICE between Texas and the west started in 1853 when George H. Giddings, a Texas merchant, began operating a monthly line from San Antonio to Santa Fe. This operation became the first link in a system that eventually evolved in service between New Orleans and San Francisco as the first transcontinental passenger and mail line in the United States. That extension came in March, 1857, when Congress authorized mail and passenger service between San Antonio, Texas, and San Diego, California.

On June 22, 1857, James E. Birch received a contract from the U.S. government for a semimonthly service at an annual compensation of $149,800. The subsidy later rose to $196,000 per year. The trip of 1,476 miles was to be made in thirty days or less. The first run took only twenty-one days; the average became twenty-seven days. Passengers paid $200 one-way between San Antonio and San Diego, or $100 to El Paso. Postage was three cents per one-half ounce for three thousand miles. That latter mileage figure came from Birch's system of linking mail service from New Orleans by ocean vessel to Indianola and by overland conveyances from Indianola to San Francisco via San Antonio, El Paso, Tucson, Fort Yuma, and San Diego.

At first the company employed any type of carrier available, but eventually it used mostly Concord coaches pulled by six mules. Pack mules were used at first to transport mail over the rugged terrain from Fort Yuma to San Diego, and the line was thus nick-named the "Jackass Mail." As service became better established, considerable funds were spent to construct stations at intervals of twenty-five to thirty miles and to improve roads. In addition to the normal problems of supplying food, forage, animals, and equipment to the way stations, the firm contended with Indian attacks, water scarcity, dust storms, floods, and snowstorms.

Birch had employed Giddings as an agent, a position Giddings held as he continued to operate his monthly San Antonio–Santa Fe mail service. When Birch died in September, 1857, his widow sold the company. In the political maneuvering that followed, Giddings received a contract from the government in March, 1858. The service then became known as the Giddings Line.

After the Butterfield Overland Mail began operations, the postmaster general on October 23, 1858, discontinued service on the Giddings Line between El Paso and Fort Yuma. The company compensated for the potential loss by starting a weekly service between San Antonio and El Paso and between Fort Yuma and San Diego. When in 1860 the government permitted the Butterfield Overland Mail to have solely the route from Fort Yuma to San Diego, the Giddings Line reduced its operation to the San Antonio–El Paso connection. The San Antonio–San Diego Mail Line terminated its business operations in August, 1861, when Giddings's contract expired. The ensuing conflict between the states caused the federal government to cancel any further services in southern states.

Colbert's Ferry
Gainesville
Sherman
Jacksboro
Bridgeport
Ft. Belknap
Pilot Point
Decatur
Denton
Ft. Richardson
Ft. Phantom Hill
Ft. Griffin
Ft. Bliss
Pope's Crossing
Franklin
Ft. Chadbourne
Ft. Quitman
Van Horn's Wells
Horsehead Crossing
Ft. Stockton
Ft. Davis

San Francisco
Los Angeles
Tipton
St. Louis
Ft. Smith
Ft. Yuma
Memphis
Little Rock
Franklin
Sherman

0   400
miles

0   50   100 Miles
0   50   100 Kilometers

BUTTERFIELD OVERLAND MAIL ROUTE, 1858–1861

© 1988 University of Oklahoma Press

38. BUTTERFIELD OVERLAND MAIL ROUTE, 1858–1861

AMERICA NEEDED A COMMUNICATION SYSTEM between the settled East and the frontier West. The U.S. Congress had earlier in the 1850s authorized railroad surveys to be conducted to find feasible routes for a transcontinental railroad, but sectional bickering about the location of the eastern terminus hopelessly delayed construction. In an effort to provide another way to meet the need for transcontinental transportation of passengers and mail, Congress in 1857 provided a $600,000 annual subsidy to the Overland Mail Company, a joint stock company organized by John Butterfield and associates. The firm collected additional revenue for express packages at varying costs depending on size and weight, which meant letters were carried at ten cents per half-ounce. Passengers traveled at fares of as much as $200 per person for the entire distance.

St. Louis, Missouri, and San Francisco, California, were the established mainline terminal points, with a branch line extending from Memphis, Tennessee, to Fort Smith, Arkansas. Since a railroad had already been built from St. Louis to Tipton, Missouri, 160 miles to the west, the actual starting point for the stages was at Tipton. The approximately 2,800 miles of this route had to be traversed in twenty-five days or less.

The first semiweekly run began on September 15, 1858, from each direction. Coaches from St. Louis and Memphis met at Fort Smith, and from there a single vehicle went through Indian Territory to cross the Red River at Colbert's Ferry north of Sherman, Texas.

Within Texas the Butterfield route touched such communities as Sherman, Gainesville, Jacksboro, Fort Belknap, Fort Phantom Hill, and Fort Chadbourne. The line then extended southwestward to the headwaters of the Middle Concho River to the west of present-day San Angelo and on to Horsehead Crossing on the Pecos River.

The route varied slightly at times. In the Trans-Pecos region, the road originally went up the Pecos River to the thirty-second parallel in the vicinity of Pope's Well. Turning westwardly, the trail went through Guadalupe Pass, jutted a distance northward to the New Mexico boundary, then dipped southwestward to Franklin, now El Paso, and to Fort Bliss. Later, the stages crossed the Pecos River at Horsehead Crossing and continued on to Fort Stockton, Fort Davis, Van Horn's Wells, Fort Quitman, and Franklin. From that point the trail extended through the southwestern desert to Tucson, Fort Yuma, Los Angeles, and San Francisco.

In North Texas, local citizens persuaded the company in 1860 to alter the route between Gainesville and Jacksboro to include Decatur and Bridgeport. In 1861, shortly before the termination of the experiment, the Butterfield Company redirected its line from Sherman to Pilot Point and Denton and then west to Decatur and Jacksboro.

A considerable investment was necessary to fund the extensive expenses for personnel, equipment, animals, forage, way stations, and corrals. In many places, the company constructed bridges, graded roads, sloped stream banks for easier crossing, dug wells, and provided extra protection against Indian attack. Local people and governments funded some of the work to encourage the route to be extended their way because of the obvious economic and transportation advantages to be derived.

The political conflict between the North and the South brought to a halt the operation of the southern overland or ox-bow route. In March, 1861, the federal government shifted the course of the Overland Mail Company's line to a central route from the Missouri River to California via Salt Lake City, thus ending the subsidized communication of Texans with outside areas.

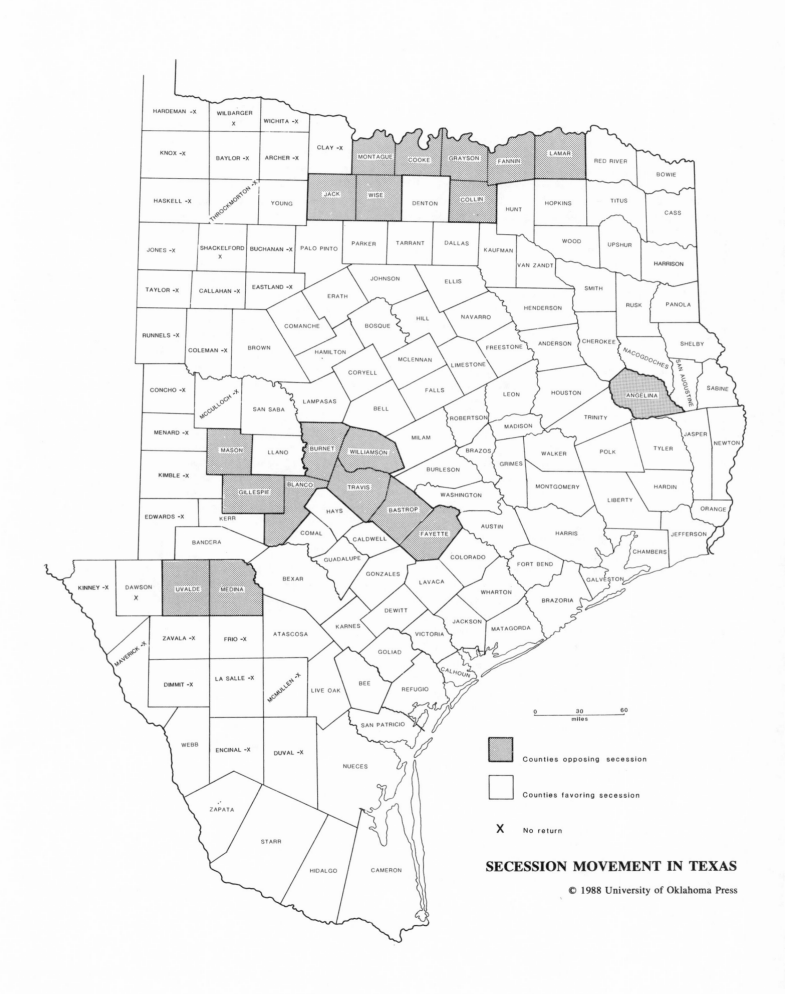

SECESSION MOVEMENT IN TEXAS

© 1988 University of Oklahoma Press

39. SECESSION MOVEMENT IN TEXAS

AFTER THE ELECTION of Abraham Lincoln to the presidency of the United States in November, 1860, political leaders in the southern states issued calls for conventions to consider secession from the Union. Governor Sam Houston refused to cooperate with the radicals, but when some prominent politicians began organizing the election of delegates to a secession convention, Governor Houston called a special session of the legislature to convene on January 21, 1861. The legislature recognized the Secession Convention and stipulated that an ordinance of secession must be submitted to the people at the ballot box. The convention assembled on January 28 and adopted an ordinance of secession on February 1. Texas became the seventh state to declare its ties to the Union to be severed.

A statewide election was held on Friday 23, 1861. A total of 60,826 citizens cast ballots, with the results being 46,129 for secession and 14,697 against secession. A 76 percent majority of Texas voters chose to leave the Union. In all, only 122 of the 154 counties in 1861 reported returns. Two organized counties, McCulloch and Presidio, were not heard from. In addition, Texas had 30 unorganized counties. Heavy slaveholding counties ran up a wide margin for the proposition, while major opposition seemed to have been centered in counties with a large German population or with an immigrant population from the border states.

The leaders of the secession movement immediately began the process of organizing a new state government. Sam Houston, a vocal Unionist, refused to take an oath of allegiance to the Confederate States of America, so the convention officials declared the office of governor to be vacant and appointed Lieutenant Governor Edward Clark as chief executive.

Election Returns, February 23, 1861, For and Against Secession

County	For	Against	County	For	Against	County	For	Against	County	For	Against
Anderson	870	15	DeWitt	472	49	Johnson	531	31	Red River	347	284
Angelina	139	184	Ellis	527	172	Karnes	153	1	Refugio	142	14
Atascosa	145	91	El Paso	871	2	Kaufman	461	155	Robertson	391	76
Austin	825	212	Erath	179	16	Kerr	76	57	Rusk	1376	135
Bandera	33	32	Falls	215	82	Lamar	553	663	Sabine	143	18
Bastrop	335	352	Fannin	471	656	Lampasas	85	75	San Augustine	243	22
Bee	139	16	Fayette	580	626	Lavacca	592	36	San Patricio	56	3
Bell	495	198	Fort Bend	486	none	Leon	534	82	San Saba	113	60
Bexar	827	709	Freestone	585	3	Liberty	422	10	Shelby	333	28
Blanco	86	170	Galveston	765	33	Limestone	525	9	Smith	1149	50
Bosque	233	81	Gillespie	16	398	Live Oak	141	9	Starr	180	2
Bowie	268	15	Goliad	291	25	Llano	134	72	Tarrant	462	127
Brazoria	527	2	Gonzales	802	80	McLennan	586	191	Titus	411	275
Brazos	215	44	Grayson	463	901	Madison	213	10	Travis	450	704
Brown	75	none	Grimes	907	9	Marion	467	none	Trinity	206	8
Burleson	422	84	Guadalupe	314	22	Mason	2	75	Tyler	417	4
Burnet	159	248	Hamilton	86	1	Matagorda	243	8	Upshur	957	57
Caldwell	434	188	Hardin	167	62	Medina	140	207	Uvalde	16	76
Calhoun	276	16	Harris	1084	144	Milam	468	135	Van Zandt	181	127
Cameron	600	37	Harrison	886	44	Montague	50	98	Victoria	313	88
Cass	423	32	Hays	166	115	Montgomery	318	98	Walker	490	61
Chambers	78	6	Henderson	400	49	Nacogdoches	317	94	Washington	1131	43
Cherokee	1106	38	Hidalgo	62	10	Navarro	621	38	Webb	70	none
Collin	405	948	Hill	376	63	Newton	178	3	Wilson	92	21
Colorado	584	330	Hopkins	697	315	Nueces	142	42	Wise	76	78
Comal	239	86	Houston	552	38	Orange	142	3	Wharton	249	2
Comanche	86	4	Hunt	416	339	Palo Pinto	107	none	Williamson	349	480
Cooke	137	221	Jack	14	76	Panola	557	5	Wood	451	191
Coryell	293	55	Jackson	147	77	Parker	535	61	Young	166	31
Dallas	741	237	Jasper	318	25	Polk	567	22	Zapata	212	none
Denton	331	256	Jefferson	256	15						

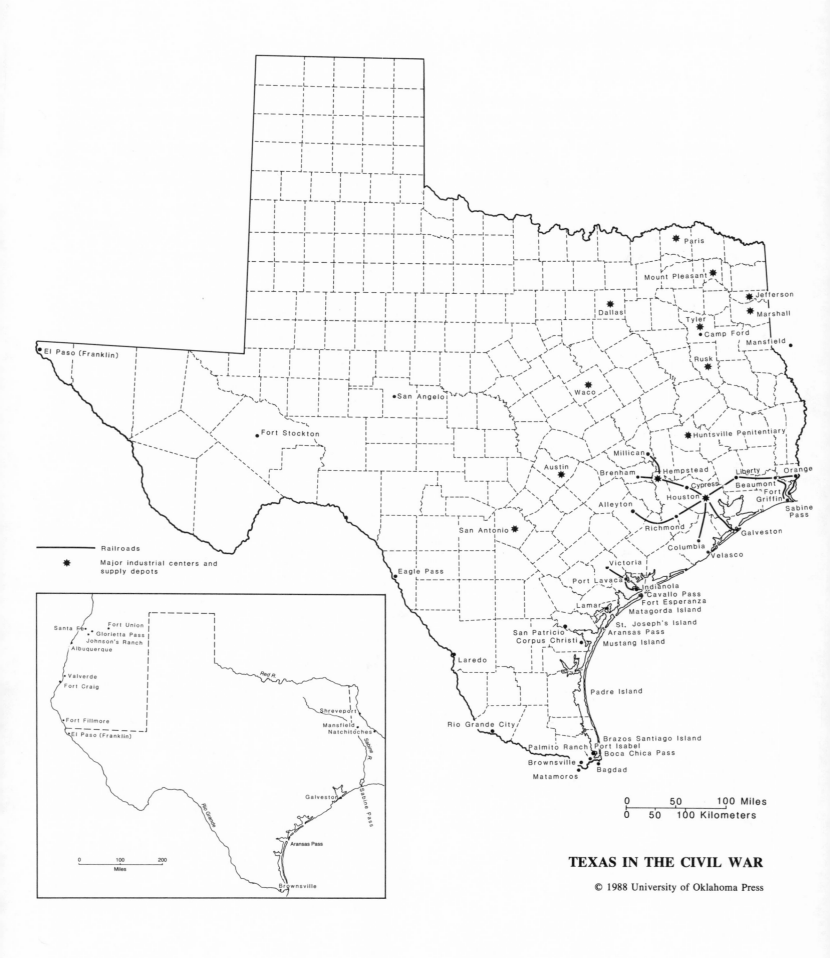

Railroads

✳ Major industrial centers and supply depots

El Paso (Franklin)

Paris
Mount Pleasant
Jefferson
Dallas
Tyler
Marshall
Camp Ford
Mansfield
Rusk
San Angelo
Waco
Fort Stockton
Huntsville Penitentiary
Millican
Austin
Brenham
Hempstead
Liberty
Orange
Cypress
Beaumont
Fort
Griffin
Houston
Alleyton
Sabine
Pass
San Antonio
Richmond
Galveston
Columbia
Velasco
Victoria
Eagle Pass
Port Lavaca
Indianola
Cavallo Pass
Fort Esperanza
Lamar
Matagorda Island
St. Joseph's Island
San Patricio
Aransas Pass
Corpus Christi
Mustang Island
Laredo
Padre Island
Rio Grande City
Brazos Santiago Island
Palmito Ranch Port Isabel
Boca Chica Pass
Brownsville
Bagdad
Matamoros

Santa Fe
Fort Union
Glorietta Pass
Johnson's Ranch
Albuquerque
Valverde
Fort Craig
Red R.
Shreveport
Fort Fillmore
Mansfield
Natchitoches
El Paso (Franklin)
Sabine R.
Rio Grande
Galveston
Sabine Pass
Aransas Pass
Brownsville

0   100   200
Miles

0   50   100 Miles
0   50   100 Kilometers

TEXAS IN THE CIVIL WAR

© 1988 University of Oklahoma Press

40. TEXAS IN THE CIVIL WAR

ILL-PREPARED FOR A MAJOR CONFRONTATION with the power of the federal government, Texas nevertheless joined with ten other southern states to form the Confederate States of America. Shortly after the Secession Convention met, military operations began. A Committee of Public Safety sent representatives to San Antonio to secure the surrender of all U.S. posts in Texas from General David E. Twiggs, commander of the federal army in Texas. General Twiggs capitulated on February 18, one day before he was to be relieved of command. He subsequently received a general's commission in the Confederate States Army.

Although the major arena of combat for the Civil War occurred in the southeastern states, Texas became the scene of several battles and skirmishes between vessels at sea and forces on land. A federal naval blockade effectively cut off Texas from the remainder of the Confederacy by water.

A military activity that involved Texans but reached a climax beyond the state's boundaries was the march of Sibley's Brigade. General Henry Hopkins Sibley organized a Confederate force at San Antonio in the summer of 1861, marched to El Paso, defeated a federal army at Valverde, took Albuquerque, and won the Battle of Glorieta Pass near Santa Fe in March, 1862, but suffered the destruction of wagons and supplies at Johnson's Ranch in nearby Apache Canyon. Shortage of rations and the threat of a combined federal force from Forts Union and Craig brought about the Confederate evacuation of New Mexico Territory.

Attempts by federal forces to invade and segment Texas resulted in a Confederate victory at Sabine Pass on September 8, 1863, when General Nathaniel P. Banks, with a fleet of twenty-two transport ships and five gunboats along with an invasion force of five thousand men, was repulsed by a small garrison, known as Fort Griffin, commanded by Lieutenant Dick Dowling. Dowling and his forty-seven men had previously established the exact range for their artillery pieces. Within forty-five minutes, Dowling's force sank two gunboats, rendered another helpless when its rudder was hit, drove away the remaining ships with the invasion troops aboard, and captured 315 enemy personnel. The Confederates suffered no losses in the encounter.

General Banks turned his attention to the extreme tip of Texas in November and took Brownsville. Texans had been using a route parallel to the Gulf Coast from the cotton-growing region of the state to Bagdad, a Mexican port on the Rio Grande below Matamoros, to transport their cotton to foreign buyers in exchange for war supplies. With the capture of Brownsville, the Texans had to alter their route through the interior to Laredo and even to Eagle Pass on their way to the Mexican port.

In the spring of 1864, federal forces attempted to enter Texas by coming up the Red River by way of Natchitoches and Shreveport and thence into East Texas to the vital Marshall-Jefferson region. General Banks pushed toward Texas while another Union army marched through Arkansas to converge with him at Shreveport. Confederate troops under the command of General Richard Taylor thwarted the federal plan by defeating Banks's army near Mansfield, Louisiana.

Battles with Indians and Confederate Army deserters repeatedly occurred on the northwestern frontier during the war years, since the withdrawal of federal troops and the inadequate numbers of Texas defenders made the frontier quite vulnerable. Skirmishes with Indians in West Texas, North Texas, and Indian Territory did little good in keeping the peace on the outer edges of settlement.

Throughout the period 1861–65, direct action between federal forces and Texan defenders continued along the Gulf coast, especially in the Matagorda Bay, Aransas Bay, Corpus Christi Bay, and Brownsville areas. Although the war ended officially with the surrender of General Robert E. Lee to General U.S. Grant on April 9, 1865, at Appomattox, Virginia, some time elapsed before the Texans learned the end had come. The final conflict of the Civil War occurred near Brownsville on May 13, 1865, at the Battle of Palmetto (Palmito) Ranch, which the Confederates won. The federal troops captured during the skirmish convinced Colonel John S. ("Rip") Ford that the war had already ended officially.

Approximately 75,000 Texas soldiers served in the war. Of that number some 50,000 to 60,000 wore the Confederate gray. Most of the engagements, particularly the bloodier skirmishes, happened far from Texas soil. The men in units such as Hood's Texas Brigade, Terry's Texas Rangers, Green's Brigade, Granbury's Brigade, and Ross's Cavalry Brigade acquired many honors and suffered heavy casualties. When the war ended, the surviving Texans began to pick up the pieces of their lives as they entered a new era of modern America.

• Fort Elliott, 1875

Camp Wichita, 1870 •

Fort Belknap, 1865 •   • Fort Richardson, 1866

Fort Griffin, 1867 •

Camp Kenny, 1874 •

• Fort Bliss, 1865

Camp Elizabeth, 1867 •   • Fort Chadbourne, 1865

Fort Hancock, 1882

Camp Charlotte, 1867 •   • Fort Concho, 1867

Fort Quitman, 1868   Camp Grierson, 1878

Fort Stockton, 1867   • Fort McKavett, 1868

Fort Davis, 1867 •   Fort Lancaster, 1868   • Fort Mason, 1866

• Fort Peña Colorado, 1880   Camp Austin, 1866 •

                          • Camp Verde, 1865

                  Camp Montel, 1870 •

Fort Hudson , 1867 •   Fort Clark   • Fort Inge, 1866   Fort Sam Houston, 1879 •
Camp San Felipe, 1876 •   1866

Fort Duncan, 1868 •

• Fort McIntosh, 1865

                          0   50   100 Miles
                          0   50   100 Kilometers

Fort Ringgold, 1865 •

• Fort Brown, 1869

MILITARY POSTS AFTER THE CIVIL WAR

41. MILITARY POSTS AFTER THE CIVIL WAR

AT THE CONCLUSION of the Civil War, the U.S. Department of War reestablished some forts that had been abandoned when the struggle started and established new ones as needed. As elsewhere in the former Confederacy, federal troops served as a check against civil disturbance and to uphold Republican state governments during the Reconstruction period. Unlike other Southern states, Texas faced serious security problems along its western and southwestern frontier. Bandits from Mexico crossed the Rio Grande with relative ease for a time until the Texas Rangers were reinstituted in the 1870s and their at times unorthodox but usually effective actions helped to restore order. Indians from present-day Oklahoma, West Texas, and New Mexico roamed at will, raiding small settlements and isolated ranches; foraging into Mexico for goods, livestock, and captives; and eluding the various federal military units.

Indians of the Great Plains depended upon the buffalo for their commissary. As the demand for buffalo hides increased, professional hunters diminished the number of the animals quickly and drastically. Buffalo hides, stronger and more resilient than horsehides or cowhides, were needed as industrial belting for the rapidly expanding number of factories back east, as leather goods, and as floor rugs and wall coverings in homes. Eventually the buffalo provided fertilizer from their bones and by-products. The efficiency of the hunters brought alarm to the Indians, who saw their food supply being threatened. Retaliation followed.

In order to cope with the disorder, the army sent out punitive expeditions from frontier outposts against particular bands or tribes. The heavier cavalry horses were no match in a chase with the smaller but speedier Spanish ponies ridden by Indians. The red warriors wisely never fought a pitched battle against the infantry which guarded waterholes, river crossings, main trails, and mountain passes. But widespread deployment of troops, winter campaigns when the Indians were most vulnerable and did not expect attack, and relentless pursuit broke the back of Indian resistance.

Peace came to the northwestern Texas area as a result of the Red River War in 1874–75, which forced the Comanches and Kiowas to retreat to reservation life. In the southwest and along the border, trouble occurred with the Kickapoo, Lipan Apache, and Mescalero Apache, who pillaged the ranch country south and west of San Antonio. Constant deployment of federal troops along the Rio Grande in Texas, in addition to extra legal punitive campaigns across the international border, made the Indians much more cautious. The army justified its excursions into Mexico as being in hot pursuit on a fresh trail, but Mexico strongly objected. In spite of ensuing diplomatic wrangling, the punishment produced desired results with the Kickapoo, Lipan, and Mescalero tribes.

Another division of the Apache people, the Chiricahua Apaches, shifted their movements to far west Texas from Arizona and New Mexico in the late 1870s. The army blocked river crossings, guarded waterholes, and sent units to harry the Indians in that great expanse of waterless desert and rough, barren terrain. Not until their great war chief, Victorio, was killed in Mexico by Mexican soldiers in 1880 did the Chiricahua threat in Texas diminish.

Soldiers stationed in Texas endured hardships of isolation and at times inadequate supplies, suffered exposure to hostile forces and the uncompromising elements, but earned the gratitude of Texans for bringing peace to the frontier. As the Indians began reservation life, cattlemen and sheepherders extended the line of settlement further west. As the Indian situation eased, the need for military outposts dimished and the government began their abandonment.

Listed below are the military installations in Texas that existed during the immediate post–Civil War period.

Installation	Location (present-day)	Installation	Location (present-day)	Installation	Location (present-day)
Camp Austin	in Austin	Fort Bliss	in El Paso	Fort Lancaster	near Ozona
Camp Charlotte	near Mertzon	Fort Brown	in Brownsville	Fort McIntosh	near Laredo
Camp Elizabeth	near Sterling City	Fort Chadbourne	near Bronte	Fort McKavett	near Menard
Camp Grierson	in Reagan County near Best	Fort Clark	at Brackettville	Fort Mason	near Mason
		Fort Concho	at San Angelo	Fort Peña Colorado	near Marathon
Camp Kenny	near Breckenridge	Fort Davis	in Fort Davis	Fort Quitman	southwest of Sierra Blanca on the Rio Grande
Camp Montel	at Montell in Uvalde County	Fort Duncan	near Eagle Pass		
		Fort Elliott	near Mobeetie	Fort Richardson	in Jacksboro
Camp San Felipe	at Del Rio	Fort Griffin	near Albany	Fort Ringgold	in Rio Grande City
Camp Verde	near Kerrville	Fort Hancock	in Fort Hancock	Fort Sam Houston	in San Antonio
Camp Wichita	near Buffalo Springs	Fort Hudson	near Del Rio	Fort Stockton	in Fort Stockton
Fort Belknap	near Graham	Fort Inge	near Uvalde		

LAST DAYS OF THE FREE INDIAN IN TEXAS

© 1988 University of Oklahoma Press

42. LAST DAYS OF THE FREE INDIAN IN TEXAS

AFTER THE CIVIL WAR ENDED, American stockmen, farmers, and buffalo hunters moved onto the Great Plains in increasing numbers. This westward extension exerted pressure on the Plains Indians, who saw their way of life eroding as white men took their land and exterminated their commissary, the buffalo. Resistance resulted.

In 1867 the federal government concentrated the Kiowa, Comanche, and Kiowa-Apache Indian tribes into the southwestern part of Indian Territory and promised supplementary hunting grounds in the Texas Panhandle. The government would distribute food and supplies through an agency while the Indians learned to "walk the white man's road" as farmers. These Indians did not adjust to their newly imposed life-styles. They conducted raids into settled areas of Texas for horses, plunder, and excitement.

In 1871, General William T. Sherman, the commanding general of the U.S. Army, barely escaped an attack by a Kiowa raiding party on Salt Creek near Jacksboro, Texas, while on an inspection tour of western forts. After General Sherman's group passed by, the Indians massacred the Warren wagon train crew en route to Fort Richardson. Sherman sent Colonel Ranald S. Mackenzie to trail the marauders while he continued his tour to Fort Sill. There he learned that a particular band of Kiowas had committed the atrocities. He arrested Satanta, Satank, and Big Tree and ordered them sent to Jacksboro to stand trial for murder in a Texas district court. This trial was the first case of Indians being tried in a white man's court in the United States. Satank was killed in an escape attempt, but the other two leaders were tried, found guilty, and imprisoned in the Texas state penitentiary in Huntsville. Governor E. J. Davis paroled Satanta and Big Tree in 1873 when easterners, whose ancestors had solved their Indian problems with flintlock and musket, brought political pressure to bear for the warriors' release because these "children of nature" were only doing what came naturally to them.

During the winter of 1873–74, and continuing into the spring and summer, Indian war parties ravaged Texas. An attack by a combined force of Kiowas, Comanches, and Cheyennes at Adobe Walls on June 27, 1874, failed when twenty-eight buffalo hunters with high-powered rifles repulsed a group of several hundred warriors. On July 12 a band of Kiowas ambushed a party of Texas Rangers at Lost Valley near the site of the Salt Creek Massacre of 1871. Other raids occurred.

General Philip Sheridan secured permission from General Sherman to launch an offensive against the Southern Plains Indians that would put a stop to this raiding. Sheridan's plan called for separate units to converge on the Indians' camps in the Texas Panhandle and western Indian Territory. Rather than attempting to exterminate the Indians, Sheridan's scheme was to destroy their camps, lodges, horses, and food supply and relentlessly pursue the hostiles until they became so weak from exhaustion that they would surrender. Friendly Indians had until August 4, 1874, to enroll at the Darlington Agency (Cheyenne and Arapaho) or at the Fort Sill Agency (Comanche, Kiowa, and Kiowa-Apache). Those who refused or missed the deadline would be regarded as hostile and would be treated as such by the army.

Units from Camp Supply, Indian Territory, under Colonel Nelson A. Miles, from Fort Sill under Lieutenant Colonel John W. Davidson, from Fort Union under Major William J. Price, from Fort Concho under Lieutenant Colonel Ranald S. Mackenzie, and from Fort Griffin under Lieutenant Colonel George P. Buell began movement by late summer. A number of skirmishes occurred in western Indian Territory and the Texas Panhandle with a few casualties but with much hardship on both the army and the Indians because of a hot, dry summer followed by an extremely bitter winter. Finally the hostiles were flushed from Palo Duro Canyon by Mackenzie and from other locations in the Panhandle by various commanders and were driven continually until all made their way to the reservations at Fort Sill and Darlington to surrender by June, 1875. The army confiscated all camp equipment, weapons, and horses, thus ensuring the end of Southern Indian warfare. Seventy-four leading tribal men of the war factions were arrested and sent to prison at Fort Marion at St. Augustine, Florida, to separate the "troublemakers" from the rest of the people. Satanta and Big Tree were returned to the Texas penitentiary for violating their parole. Sheridan's policy had succeeded. But it was starvation, not army bullets, that brought about the subjugation of the mighty Southern Plains Indians.

By 1875, no longer did a free Indian roam the southern Great Plains. With the demise of the red man and the destruction of the buffalo herd, Texans quickly carved out ranches in West Texas.

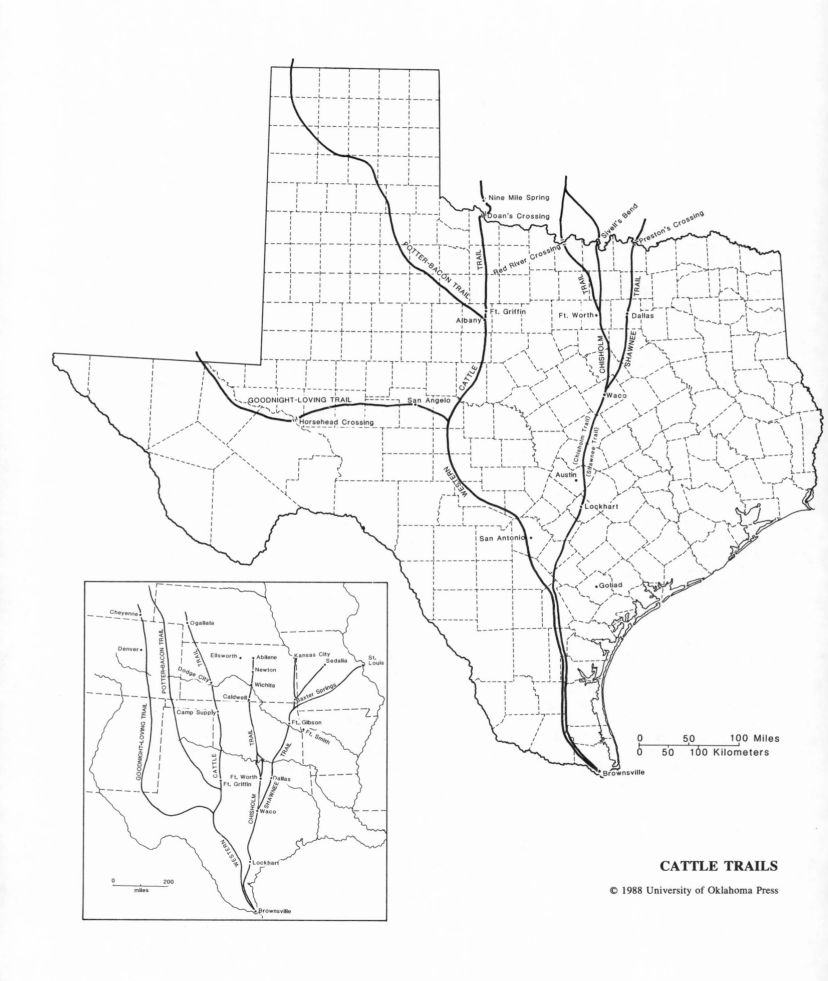

Nine Mile Spring
Doan's Crossing
Sivell's Bend
Preston's Crossing
Red River Crossing
POTTER-BACON TRAIL
CATTLE TRAIL
CHISHOLM TRAIL
SHAWNEE TRAIL
Ft. Griffin
Albany
Ft. Worth
Dallas
GOODNIGHT-LOVING TRAIL
San Angelo
Horsehead Crossing
Waco
(Chisholm Trail)
(Shawnee Trail)
Austin
WESTERN
Lockhart
San Antonio
Goliad
Brownsville

0   50   100 Miles
0   50   100 Kilometers

Cheyenne
Ogallala
Denver
Ellsworth
Abilene
Kansas City
Sedalia
St. Louis
POTTER-BACON TRAIL
TRAIL
Dodge City
Newton
Wichita
Caldwell
Baxter Springs
GOODNIGHT-LOVING TRAIL
Camp Supply
Ft. Gibson
CATTLE TRAIL
Ft. Smith
CHISHOLM TRAIL
SHAWNEE TRAIL
Ft. Worth
Dallas
Ft. Griffin
Waco
WESTERN
Lockhart
Brownsville

0   200
miles

CATTLE TRAILS

© 1988 University of Oklahoma Press

43. CATTLE TRAILS

FOLLOWING THE CIVIL WAR, a new economic enterprise opened for the American Southwest. As the subjugation of the Indians and the destruction of the great buffalo herds reached a climax in the late 1860s and 1870s, large areas of grassland became used by Americans in need of ways to recover from the devastation of the war years.

Spanish cattle and horses had been brought by Spanish explorers, missionaries, and settlers. As some of the animals escaped or were abandoned, they multiplied in numbers and prospered on the grass of the Gulf Coast prairies and the South Texas plains. Anglo-American pioneers had also brought cattle as they moved to Texas from the southeastern region; they too understood principles of livestock raising, which they adapted to their new surroundings. Texans attempted to market their livestock by shipping them on ocean-going vessels, by trailing them to the Dixie region, and by driving them to California in the early 1850s and to the Upper Midwest in the later 1850s, but without the success necessary to encourage men to continue the risk for a marginal profit at best.

After the Civil War, the demand for red meat in the triumphant North caused Texans to attempt again the marketing of cattle over the long trail. Such success greeted their efforts that soon many herds started north. From the southeastern, central, southern, and southwestern areas of Texas and from northern Mexico millions of cattle walked to railroad towns in Missouri, Kansas, and eventually North Texas. Such towns as Sedalia, Missouri; Baxter Springs, Abilene, Newton, Ellsworth, Wichita, and Dodge City, Kansas; and Fort Worth, Texas, became destinations at various times for the drovers with their herds as the railroads extended their lines westward.

Of those marketing centers, the best known in the literature of the Cattle Kingdom were Abilene and Dodge City. The Chisholm Trail, as the name became applied to a route used in Indian Territory by Jesse Chisholm, a part-blood Cherokee Indian, went from the southern part of Texas up along the division of the Central Texas Prairie and the Hill Country and continued on by the eastern edge of the Western Cross Timbers until it crossed the Red River north of present Nocona, Texas, into Indian Territory. From there the trail skirted the western edge of the Cross Timbers of Oklahoma and the eastern edge of the Great Plains, on through the prairie lands of present-day Oklahoma, and eventually to central Kansas. The main Chisholm Trail closely approximated present-day U.S. Highway 81 from southern Texas to central Kansas.

As settlement encroached on the path used by the cattlemen, and as railroads extended westward, the trail shifted westward in 1876. Texas drovers went through the Low or Rolling Plains west of the Western Cross Timbers, crossed the Red River at Doan's Crossing near present-day Vernon, Texas, and drove in a northerly direction along the western side of present Oklahoma until they reached the railroad town of Dodge City, which is near the intersection of the one hundredth meridian and the Arkansas River. The route of the Great Western or Dodge City Trail can be approximately traced through West Texas, Oklahoma, and Kansas by following U.S. Highway 283.

As Texas and Mexican cattle increased in demand not only by midwestern corn farmers as feeder stock for eventual slaughter but also by western ranchers, the Dodge City Trail was extended to Ogallala, Nebraska, and into the Dakotas, Wyoming, and Montana. Other trails also extended from Texas to the grasslands of the central and upper Great Plains to supply ranchers with brood stock. Drovers went over such routes as the Goodnight-Loving Trail and the Potter-Bacon Trail.

After the spring roundups, cattlemen separated the animals they proposed to sell at trail's end. Some ranchers had sufficient numbers for an entire herd while others consigned or sold their livestock to be driven northward. A trail drive usually consisted of approximately two thousand head of cattle and was conducted by about a dozen workers with approximately two hundred to three hundred horses for the risky journey and took up to three months to complete.

The long trails ceased as a marketing method in the mid-1880s when the open-range system changed to the enclosed-ranch system. Barbed-wire fences formed specific pastures, windmills and man-made ponds provided water in the enclosures, and imported British breeds made possible the upgrading to a more heavily muscled animal that soon sold by the pound instead of the head. As the railroads extended their lines into the big-ranch country, farmers who now had the means of transportation to get surplus commodities to market soon followed. An era much heralded later for its adventure soon came to an end. An even greater era, that of the modern livestock ranching enterprise, began.

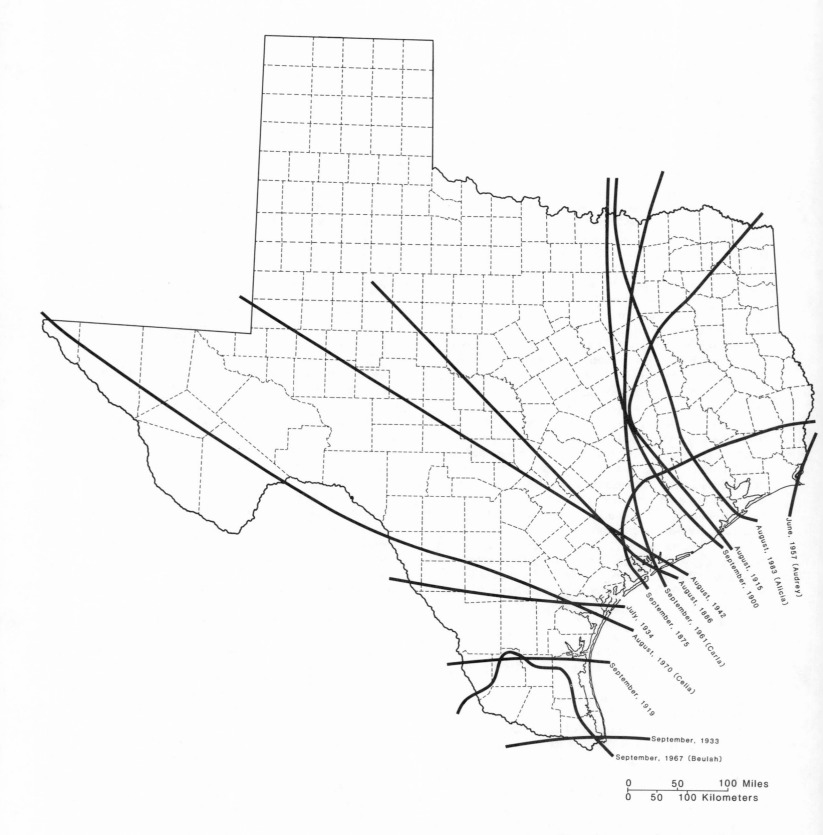

June, 1957 (Audrey)

August, 1983 (Alicia)

September, 1915

August, 1942

August, 1900

September, 1886

September, 1961 (Carla)

July, 1934

September, 1875

August, 1970 (Celia)

September, 1919

September, 1933

September, 1967 (Beulah)

| 0 | 50 | 100 Miles |
| 0 | 50 | 100 Kilometers |

HURRICANES AFFECTING TEXAS

© 1988 University of Oklahoma Press

44. HURRICANES AFFECTING TEXAS

WEATHER EXTREMES HAVE INFLUENCED TEXAS HISTORY since the beginning of record-keeping by the first Europeans to write about Texas. Along the Gulf Coast, the most destructive weather condition is the hurricane. Hurricanes, or tropical cyclones, frequently occur in August or September, although the hurricane season extends from June to October. Since 1870, when the U.S. Weather Service began keeping records, approximately seventy tropical storms of varying intensities have hit Texas. The weather disturbance must have sustained wind speeds of seventy-four miles per hour or greater to be classified as a hurricane.

The destructiveness of a hurricane results from excessive precipitation, causing flooding and collapsing roofs by its added weight; from forceful wave action during the storm; from strong and excessively gusty winds; and from tidal waves that result when accumulated water on land recedes forcefully after the strong wind reverses its direction once the eye of the storm has passed by. In addition, storm surges, (the piling up of water by high winds) and tornados spawned by converging weather patterns on the edge of hurricane storms contribute significantly to destruction in affected areas. Residential, industrial, and agricultural damage often results, often accompanied by loss of human life. Among the many hurricanes that have made a landfall along the Texas Gulf Coast since 1870, thirteen stand out because of their destructive force or their intensity.

On September 16, 1875, a hurricane crippled the town of Indianola, and another on August 19, 1886, destroyed the community. Rising waters of Matagorda Bay caused extensive flood damage and loss of lives.

The greatest natural disaster in the United States occurred at Galveston on September 8, 1900, when a storm slammed into that city with strong winds and high waters. The entire island was covered with one to five feet of water as the storm raged. After the eye of the hurricane passed over Galveston and the wind reversed directions, a tidal wave from four to six feet high rushed back toward the sea. Approximately six thousand people in Galveston and an additional two thousand elsewhere along the coast perished. Property damage of thirty million to forty million dollars resulted. Another major storm struck Galveston on August 16, 1915, with losses of life and property, but the recently constructed seawall reduced the destructive intensity of the storm surge.

Down the coast a severe hurricane came ashore below Corpus Christi on September 14, 1919. The brunt of the storm affected Corpus Christi the most, although damage occurred all along the coast. The residential North Beach area of Corpus Christi was devastated by a storm surge sixteen feet above normal sea level driven by wind speeds up to 110 miles per hour. A total of 284 persons died and $20.3 million in damage to property resulted.

Near Brownsville on September 4, 1933, an intense hurricane caused forty deaths and an estimated seventeen million dollars in property damage. The storm destroyed approximately 90 percent of the Lower Rio Grande Valley citrus crop.

Major storms struck near Seadrift in Calhoun County on July 25, 1934, and at Matagorda Bay on August 30, 1942. Storm surges and strong winds brought destruction to property, crops, and lives. Another big storm, Hurricane Audrey, struck Orange, Jefferson, Chambers, and Galveston counties on June 27, 1957, causing the loss of lives and property.

The largest tropical cyclone of record, Hurricane Carla, hit the Texas coast at Port O'Connor on September 11, 1961, and raked the coast from Corpus Christi to Port Arthur. A maximum wind velocity of 175 miles per hour was recorded at Port Lavaca, which had the highest storm surge, 18.5 feet. An orderly evacuation of residents greatly reduced the loss of life. Property and crop damage was estimated at three hundred million dollars.

On September 20, 1967, Hurricane Beulah made landfall near Brownsville. In addition to the wind and tidal forces, this storm is known for the great number of tornados it spawned and for the torrential rainfall at inland locations that flooded approximately 1.4 million acres.

On August 3, 1970, Hurricane Celia moved ashore at Portland in San Patricio County. The greatest property damage caused by the storm occured in Corpus Christi, where an estimated 90 percent of the downtown buildings were damaged or destroyed. Disaster preparedness and orderly evacuation greatly reduced the loss of life.

The greatest property damage caused by any hurricane was in 1983, when Alicia hit the Galveston-Houston area on August 18. The high-density region of Southeast Texas suffered an estimated $1.2 billion in property damages.

The tropical cyclone continues to be a major weather feature that affects Texas. With urban construction, industrial development, and population concentration along the Gulf Coast, a potential for disaster exists each time a great storm begins churning the Gulf waters with the storm center headed for Texas.

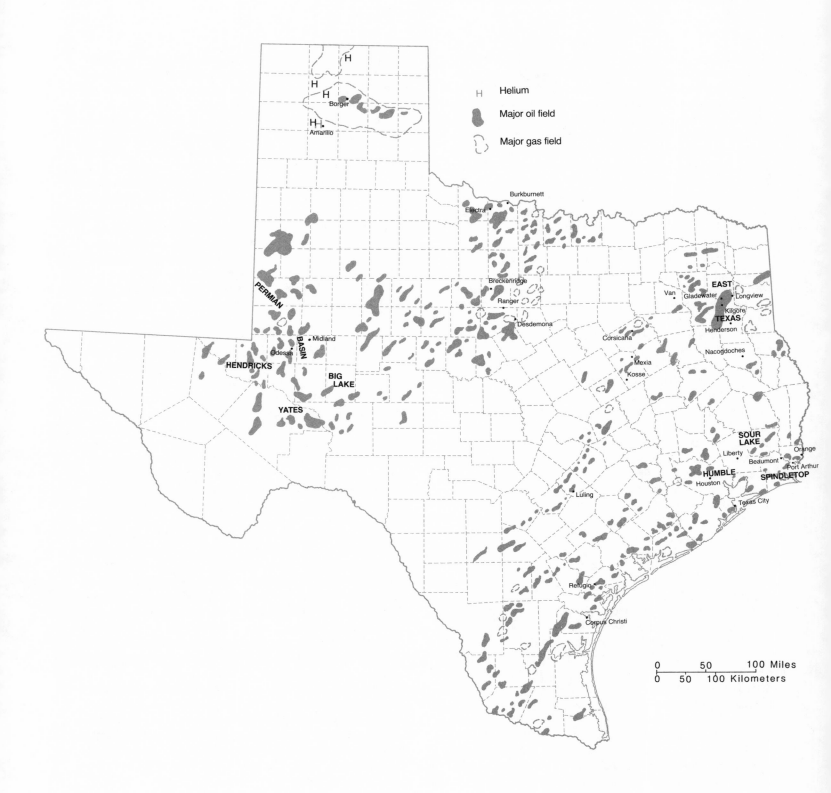

H Helium

Major oil field

Major gas field

Borger

Amarillo

H
H
H
H

PERMAN

Burkburnett

Electra

Breckenridge

Ranger

Desdemona

EAST

Van Gladewater Longview

Kilgore

TEXAS

Henderson

Corsicana

Nacogdoches

Mexia

Kosse

BASIN

Midland

Odessa

HENDRICKS

BIG
LAKE

YATES

SOUR
LAKE

Liberty   Orange

Beaumont Port Arthur

HUMBLE   SPINDLETOP

Houston

Luling   Texas City

Refugio

Corpus Christi

| 0 | | 50 | | 100 Miles |
| 0 | 50 | | 100 Kilometers | |

MAJOR OIL AND GAS DISCOVERIES

© 1988 University of Oklahoma Press

45. MAJOR OIL AND GAS DISCOVERIES

COMMERCIAL PRODUCTION OF CRUDE OIL in the United States dates from the Titusville, Pennsylvania, well drilled in 1859, and in Texas from the well at Melrose in Nacogdoches County in 1866. Discovery of other sources in Texas came at other places in the late nineteenth century, notably at Corsicana, but the blowing in of the Lucas well at Spindletop near Beaumont in 1901 changed the history of Texas and world industry. That well's gigantic flow caused a monumental boom to hit the Southwest as drilling, both in known productive fields and in areas where only dreams kept the wildcatters going, expanded throughout the Southwest.

Since Spindletop, the economic picture of Texas changed. Some Texas discoveries made world headlines because of the vast amount of crude petroleum tapped, with each new field seemingly outdoing the others before it. Each boom town created by the discoveries had a similar history: rapid influx of transient workers to turn sleepy towns into bustling cities, stock swindles as the unscrupulous fleeced a gullible public wishing to get rich quick, mud and more mud as tires from heavily laden wagons sliced the unimproved roads into quagmires during inclement weather, attraction of merchants of vice to peddle their wares to the public, and the consternation of original inhabitants about a situation they could not control and did not understand.

The big strikes came in regions where discovery wells attracted other drillers to the field to snap up leases. The first in north central Texas area occurred at Electra (1911), followed by Ranger (1917), Desdemona and Breckenridge (1918), and Burkburnett (1919). The central Texas area witnessed discoveries at Mexia (1920), Kosse (1921), Luling (1922), Corsicana (1923), and Darst (1929). Prospecting led to new fields along the Texas Gulf Coast after Spindletop, such as Sour Lake (1902), Humble (1905), Refugio (1920), Liberty (1925), and a second strike at Spindletop (1925).

The discovery of natural gas proved to be big news wherever the find came, especially in the Panhandle near Amarillo beginning in 1918. The entire region became an exciting scene of exploration and discovery for the next several years, with numerous wells producing huge amounts of oil and gas. Perhaps the most dramatic boom came at Borger in 1926, when the town increased in population from nothing to twenty thousand in a few months. The Panhandle region also became the nation's major producer of helium. As natural gas discoveries occurred in various Texas areas, nearby cities constructed pipelines to serve their citizens with this more efficient fuel for home heating and cooking.

Attention focused on West Texas beginning in 1923, when drillers found oil in the Permian Basin on University of Texas land. Geologists and wild-catters, roaming over the entire Permian Basin, brought in a great number of wells at various depths. The major finds in that area were the Big Lake (1923), Hendricks (1926), and Yates (1926) fields.

The largest field of them all was started in Rusk County in 1930 when the fabulous East Texas Field was brought in by independent drillers after the major oil companies bypassed it as unproductive. The East Texas Field finally consolidated around key wells near Henderson, Kilgore, Longview, and Gladewater.

An extremely heavy petroleum production in Texas and other states coming at a time when the Great Depression deflated the per-barrel price as well as retail consumption, plus the reduction of oil-flow pressure caused by excessive drilling in the same geologic formation, brought on the need for conservation. A national trend developed to institute production proration and spaced drilling. By these conservation measures the petroleum industry maintained the market price of crude for its own benefit then and to insure an orderly oil supply for the future. The Railroad Commission of Texas is the regulatory agency for the state's oil and gas industry.

Paved roads, improved scientific instruments to determine substrata deposits, sophisticated drilling equipment, more available commerical financing, and favorable tax laws have contributed to additional discoveries in Texas. None of them, however, attracted the widespread attention the wildcat wells commanded in earlier days.

Transport trucks, railroad cars, and pipelines carry crude petroleum from wells to refineries. Refineries exist in many sections of the state, but they are concentrated mostly in the areas of Beaumont–Orange–Port Arthur, Houston–Texas City, and Corpus Christi.

• Fort Bliss

Camp Bowie •

Camp MacArthur •

Camp Holland •

Fort D. A. Russell •

Camp Mabry •

Camp Logan •

Camp Stanley •
Camp Bullis •
Fort Sam Houston •
Camp Travis • Camp Kelly
Brooks Field

Fort Clark •

Fort Travis
Fort San Jacinto
Fort Crockett

Fort Duncan •

Fort McIntosh •

Fort Ringgold •

Fort Brown •

| 0 | 50 | 100 Miles |
| 0 | 50 | 100 Kilometers |

WORLD WAR I MILITARY INSTALLATIONS

46. WORLD WAR I MILITARY INSTALLATIONS

DURING THE NINETEENTH CENTURY, several military installations had been established in Texas by the federal government to protect the frontier against Indian raids from the west and northwest and against Mexican bandit raids across the Rio Grande. General peaceful conditions and the expansion of settlement had brought about deactivation of most of those outposts by the early twentieth century. When border conflict developed shortly before the outbreak of the First World War, National Guard units from several states were stationed in Texas along the Mexican-American boundary.

Upon American entry in World War I, regular army personnel and selective service recruits received training at existing and newly established posts. The effect on communities in regard to moral influence attracted considerable attention from the public. The influx of federal money in goods, services, and payrolls aided local economies. Many of the men trained in Texas saw combat in Europe as members of the American Expeditionary Force.

The following list indicates the names and locations of the federal military installations in Texas during World War I:

Military Post	Location
Brooks Field	San Antonio
Camp Bowie	Fort Worth
Camp Bullis	San Antonio
Camp Holland	Valentine
Camp Kelly	San Antonio
Camp Logan	Houston
Camp Mabry	Austin
Camp MacArthur	Waco
Camp Stanley	Boerne
Camp Travis	San Antonio
Fort Bliss	El Paso
Fort Brown	Brownsville
Fort Clark	Brackettville
Fort Crockett	Galveston
Fort D. A. Russell	Marfa
Fort Duncan	Eagle Pass
Fort McIntosh	Laredo
Fort Ringgold	Rio Grande City
Fort Sam Houston	San Antonio
Fort San Jacinto	Galveston
Fort Travis	Galveston

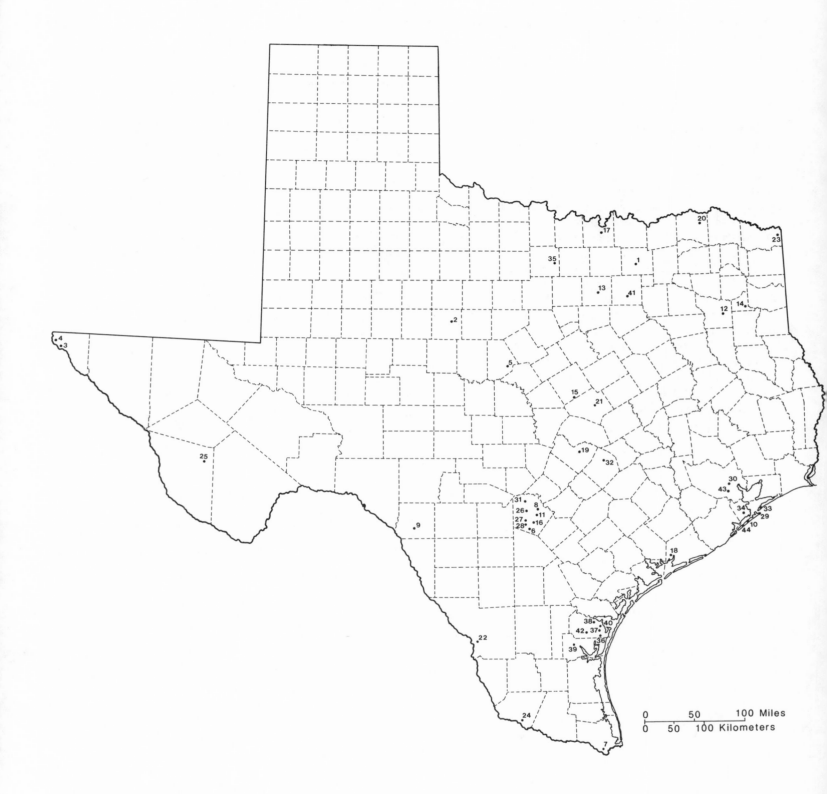

WORLD WAR II ARMY AND NAVY INSTALLATIONS

© 1988 University of Oklahoma Press

47. WORLD WAR II ARMY AND NAVY INSTALLATIONS

BEFORE AND DURING WORLD WAR II, the U.S. government established a significant number of training and defense installations in Texas. The broad expanse of the Texas landscape and favorable weather conditions for training purposes, the presence of major seaports on the Gulf of Mexico, and considerable political influence in Washington, D.C., made Texas a major location for permanent and temporary military posts, air fields, naval stations, and federal government hospitals.

In most cases, the sudden influx of defense personnel affected community housing and public services, but the rapid improvement of the local economy in the aftermath of the Great Depression reduced serious complaints by local citizens. Also, a patriotic zeal characteristic of Texans produced an understanding that even those who did not enter armed service must sacrifice to ensure a favorable conclusion to this greatest of world conflicts. Additional hardships came for all Americans through the shortage and rationing of most goods.

The following list indentifies the names and locations of military posts, naval stations, and federal hospitals:

Military Post	Location
1. Ashburn General Hospital	McKinney
2. Camp Barkeley	Abilene
3. William Beaumont General Hospital	El Paso
4. Fort Bliss	El Paso
5. Camp Bowie	Brownwood
6. Brooke General Hospital	San Antonio
7. Fort Brown	Brownsville
8. Camp Bullis	San Antonio
9. Fort Clark	Brackettville
10. Fort Crockett	Galveston
11. Camp Cushing	San Antonio
12. Camp Fannin	Tyler
13. Fort Worth Quartermaster Depot	Fort Worth
14. Harmon General Hospital	Longview
15. Camp Hood	Killeen
16. Fort Sam Houston	San Antonio
17. Camp Howze	Gainesville
18. Camp Hulen	Palacios
19. Camp Mabry	Austin
20. Camp Maxey	Paris
21. McCloskey General Hospital	Temple
22. Fort McIntosh	Laredo
23. Red River Ordnance Depot	Texarkana
24. Fort Ringgold	Rio Grande City
25. Fort D. A. Russell	Marfa
26. San Antonio Adjutant General Depot	San Antonio

Military Post	Location
27. San Antonio Army Service Forces Depot	San Antonio
28. San Antonio Arsenal	San Antonio
29. Fort San Jacinto	Galveston
30. San Jacinto Ordnance Depot	Houston
31. Camp Stanley	Boerne
32. Camp Swift	Bastrop
33. Fort Travis	Galveston
34. Camp Wallace	Galveston
35. Camp Wolters	Mineral Wells

Naval Air Station or Air Center

	Location
36. Air Training Center	Corpus Christi
37. Cabaniss Field	Corpus Christi
38. Cuddihy Field	Corpus Christi
39. Kingsville Field	Kingsville
40. Rodd Field	Corpus Christi
41. Dallas Naval Air Station	Dallas

Naval Hospital

	Location
42. Corpus Christi Naval Hospital	Corpus Christi
43. Houston Naval Hospital	Houston

Naval Training Center

	Location
44. United States Naval Training and Distribution Center	Galveston

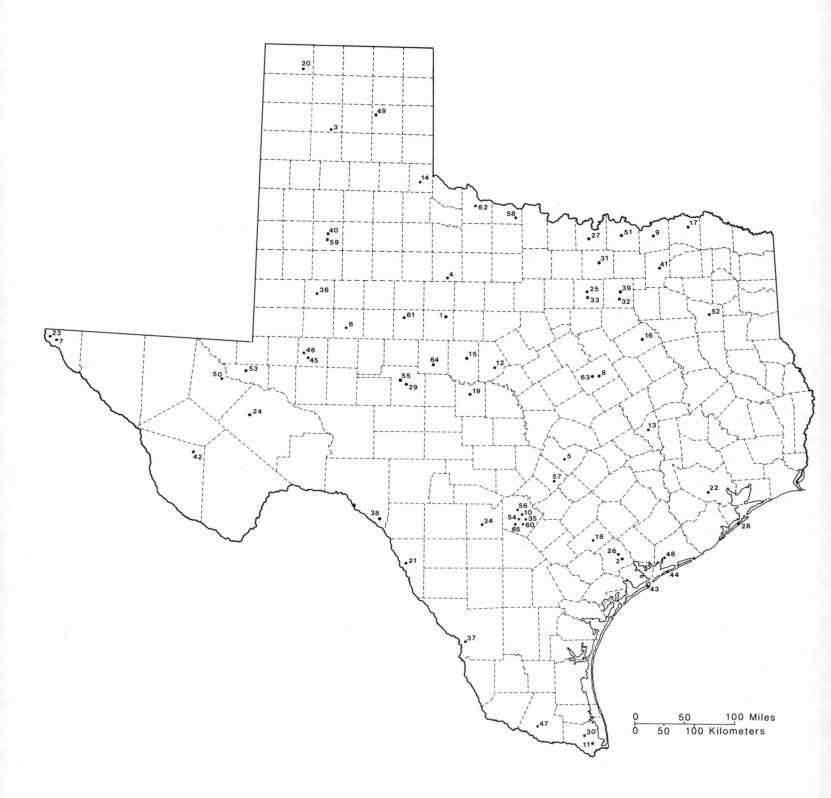

WORLD WAR II ARMY AIR FORCES STATIONS

© 1988 University of Oklahoma Press

48. WORLD WAR II ARMY AIR FORCES STATIONS

THE WIDE EXPANSE of relatively level terrain, coupled with a large number of clear weather days, enabled Texas to become a major location for the establishment of Army Air Forces stations. The federal government started new flying fields and contracted for the use of existing municipal facilities to meet the need for trained pilots, navigators, bombardiers, and maintenance personnel during World War II. These installations had an influence on local services and life-styles and brought about changes to communities much more quickly than would have occurred under traditional conditions.

When the conflict ended, the federal government made some of the fields a permanent part of the national defense system and transferred other properties to local governments. These acquisitions of improved air power facilities by municipalities and counties led to a marked increase in aviation for agriculture, business, commercial traffic, industry, and personal flying pleasure.

The following list provides the names and locations of Army Air Forces stations in Texas during World War II:

Army Air Forces Station	Location
1. Abilene Army Air Field	Abilene
2. Aloe Army Air Field	Victoria
3. Amarillo Army Air Field	Amarillo
4. Arledge Field	Stamford
5. Bergstrom Field	Austin
6. Big Spring Army Air Field	Big Spring
7. Biggs Field	El Paso
8. Blackland Army Air Field	Waco
9. Bonham Municipal Airport	Bonham
10. Brooks Field	San Antonio
11. Brownsville Municipal Airport	Brownsville
12. Brownwood Army Air Field	Brownwood
13. Bryan Army Air Field	Bryan
14. Childress Army Air Field	Childress
15. Coleman Flying School	Coleman
16. Corsicana Field	Corsicana
17. Cox Field	Paris
18. Cuero Municipal Airport	Cuero
19. Curtis Field	Brady
20. Dalhart Army Air Field	Dalhart
21. Eagle Pass Army Air Field	Eagle Pass

Army Air Forces Station	Location
22. Ellington Field	Houston
23. El Paso Municipal Airport	El Paso
24. Fort Stockton Field	Fort Stockton
25. Fort Worth Army Air Field	Fort Worth
26. Foster Field	Victoria
27. Gainesville Army Air Field	Gainesville
28. Galveston Army Air Field	Galveston
29. Goodfellow Field	San Angelo
30. Harlingen Army Air Field	Harlingen
31. Hartlee Field	Denton
32. Hensley Field	Dallas
33. Hicks Field	Fort Worth
34. Hondo Army Air Field	Hondo
35. Kelly Field	San Antonio
36. Lamesa Municipal Airport	Lamesa
37. Laredo Army Air Field	Laredo
38. Laughlin Field	Del Rio
39. Love Field	Dallas
40. Lubbock Army Air Field	Lubbock
41. Majors Field	Greenville
42. Marfa Army Air Field	Marfa
43. Matagorda Island Bombing and Gunnery Range	Victoria
44. Matagorda Peninsula Bombing Range	Victoria
45. Midland Army Air Field	Midland
46. Midland Municipal Airport	Midland
47. Moore Field	Mission
48. Palacios Army Air Field	Palacios
49. Pampa Army Air Field	Pampa
50. Pecos Army Air Field	Pecos
51. Perrin Field	Sherman
52. Pounds Field	Tyler
53. Pyote Army Air Field	Pyote
54. Randolph Field	San Antonio
55. San Angelo Army Air Field	San Angelo
56. San Antonio Municipal Airport	San Antonio
57. San Marcos Army Air Field	San Marcos
58. Sheppard Field	Wichita Falls
59. South Plains Army Air Field	Lubbock
60. Stinson Field	San Antonio
61. Sweetwater Municipal Airport	Sweetwater
62. Victory Field	Vernon
63. Waco Army Air Field	Waco
64. Bruce Field	Ballinger
65. San Antonio Aviation Cadet Center (Lackland Army Air Field, 1946)	San Antonio

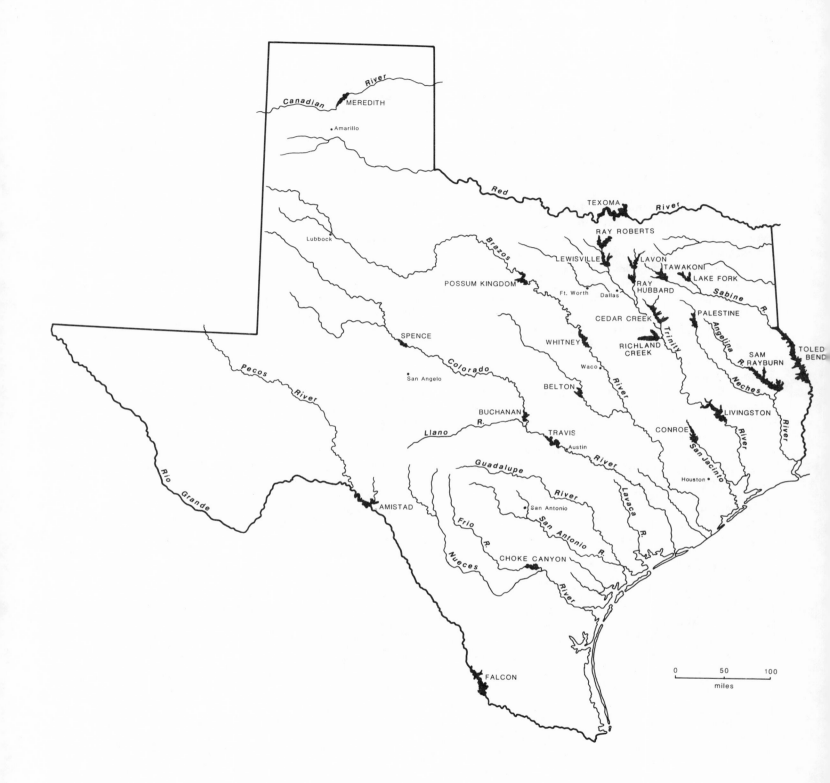

RIVERS AND RESERVOIRS

© 1988 University of Oklahoma Press

49. RIVERS AND RESERVOIRS

WITHIN THE VAST EXPANSE that is Texas, a large number of streams form that generally flow, in most instances, southeastward. The interconnecting branches, forks, and streams join at places depending upon local topography to form rivers. Each of the major rivers of Texas drains millions of acres of land.

The Sabine River heads in East Texas and becomes the Texas-Louisiana boundary on its way to Sabine Lake and the Gulf of Mexico. The Neches River begins in East Texas and also empties into Sabine Lake. Forming in north central Texas from several forks, the Trinity River flows to the Gulf by way of Galveston Bay. The Brazos River begins in New Mexico, winds through western and central Texas, and drains into the Gulf of Mexico in Brazoria County. The Colorado River is the longest river wholly in Texas. It starts in West Texas and empties into Matagorda Bay. The Guadalupe and San Antonio rivers have their beginnings in the Edwards Plateau and meet before entering San Antonio Bay. The Nueces River drains the Southwest Texas region on its way to Nueces Bay, Corpus Christi Bay, and the Gulf of Mexico in the Corpus Christi vicinity.

Rivers that form in the Coastal Plains and have a brief distance in their run to the Gulf waters are the San Jacinto (emptying into Galveston Bay), the San Bernard (Brazoria County), the Lavaca (Lavaca Bay), the Mission (Copano Bay), and the Aransas (Copano Bay).

Other streams flow through Texas or form a boundary of the state. The Pecos River begins in New Mexico and meets the Rio Grande in Val Verde County. The Rio Grande starts in Colorado, traverses New Mexico, and serves as the southwestern border between Texas and Mexico. It also is an international boundary from El Paso to the Gulf of Mexico near Brownsville. The Canadian River comes out of New Mexico, cuts across the Texas Panhandle, and becomes a part of the Arkansas River in Oklahoma. The Red River has several forks that begin in the Texas Panhandle and one with headwaters in New Mexico. The Red serves as the Oklahoma-Texas boundary from the one hundredth meridian eastward to Arkansas and then as the Arkansas-Texas boundary for a brief distance near Texarkana. After flowing through portions of Arkansas and Louisiana, the Red River becomes a part of the Mississippi River.

Because of the large discharge of water from the rivers' drainage basins, reservoirs of various sizes have been constructed to serve agricultural, municipal, industrial, recreational, reclamation, soil conservation, and flood control purposes. Twenty-four of the state's reservoirs have a conservation storage capacity of more than 400,000 acre-feet of water. They are listed below by name of reservoir and river along with their conservation surface area and conservation storage capacity.

Reservoir	Creek or River	Effluent River	Conservation Storage Area (acres)	Conservation Storage Capacity (acre-feet)
Amistad	Rio Grande		64,900	3,497,400
Belton	Leon	Brazos	12,300	457,300
Buchanan	Colorado		23,060	955,200
Cedar Creek	Cedar Creek	Trinity	33,750	679,200
Choke Canyon	Frio	Nueces	26,000	700,000
Conroe	San Jacinto		20,985	429,900
Falcon	Rio Grande		87,210	2,667,600
Lake Fork	Lake Fork	Sabine	27,690	635,200
Lavon	East Fork	Trinity	21,400	443,800
Lewisville	Elm Fork	Trinity	23,280	464,500
Livingston	Trinity		82,600	1,750,000
Meredith	Canadian		16,504	821,300
Palestine	Neches		25,560	411,300
Possum Kingdom	Brazos		17,700	569,380
Ray Hubbard	East Fork	Trinity	22,745	490,000
Ray Roberts	Elm Fork	Trinity	29,350	799,600
Richland Creek	Richland	Trinity	38,850	1,135,000
Sam Rayburn	Angelina	Neches	114,500	2,876,300
Spence	Colorado		14,950	484,800
Tawakoni	Sabine		36,700	936,200
Texoma	Red		89,000	2,722,000
Toledo Bend	Sabine		181,600	4,472,900
Travis	Colorado		18,930	1,144,100
Whitney	Brazos		23,560	622,800

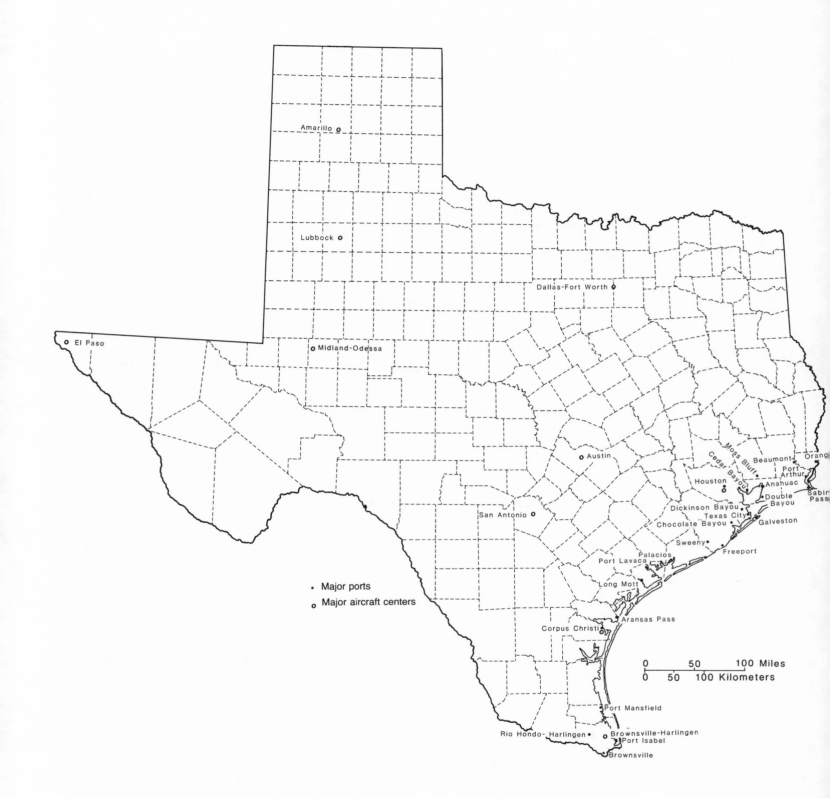

Amarillo o

Lubbock o

Dallas-Fort Worth o

El Paso o

Midland-Odessa o

Austin o

Moss Bluff
Cedar Bayou
Beaumont
Orang
Port
Arthur
Anahuac
Sabir
Pass
Houston
Double
Bayou
Dickinson Bayou
Texas City
Chocolate Bayou
Galveston
Sweeny
Freeport
Palacios
Port Lavaca
Long Mott

San Antonio o

• Major ports
o Major aircraft centers

Aransas Pass
Corpus Christi

Port Mansfield

Rio Hondo- Harlingen   o Brownsville-Harlingen
Port Isabel
Brownsville

| 0 | 50 | 100 Miles |
| 0 | 50 | 100 Kilometers |

SEA AND AIR PORTS

© 1988 University of Oklahoma Press

50. SEA AND AIR PORTS

FROM THE BEGINNING of Texas settlement to modern times, waterborne transportation has been most significant to the economic wellbeing of the region and its inhabitants. Early-day Texans imported products unavailable locally, such as processed food, agricultural implements, and manufactured goods, and exported surplus agricultural commodities. In modern times, even though the highway, railroad, and airway systems provide the major means for commerce transportation, Texas ports on the Gulf of Mexico continue to increase in tonnage handled.

The U.S. Congress, through appropriations in rivers and harbors acts since the 1870s, has aided waterborne commerce at Texas ports by dredging harbors, building protective jetties, providing turning basins, and constructing ship channels. In addition, the Intracoastal Canal, presently known as the Gulf Intracoastal Waterway, links South Texas with the major cities on the Atlantic Ocean in the U.S. Northeast. In Texas, the waterway extends approximately 423 miles through major channels and interior bays from Brownsville to Sabine Pass, with many tributary and feeder channels added.

Jetties have been built by the U.S. Army Corps of Engineers at Galveston (serving Galveston, Houston, Texas City, Anahuac, Moss Bluff, and Cedar Bayou), Sabine Pass (serving Port Arthur, Beaumont, Orange, and Sabine Pass), Aransas Pass (serving Corpus Christi, Harbor Island, Aransas Pass, Rockport, and Fulton), Freeport, Matagorda (serving Point Comfort, Palacios, and Port Lavaca), Brazos Island (serving Brownsville, Port Isabel, and Rio Hondo–Harlingen). Houston is the major port in Texas, Corpus Christi is second, and Beaumont is third in tonnage handled.

Major imports at Texas ports, in a variety of forms, are petrochemical products, building and construction supplies, motor vehicles, iron and aluminum ores, and foods. Major exports are petrochemical products and agricultual commodities.

The following listing of consolidated tonnage, in short tons, handled by Texas ports in 1981 indicates the relative size of the various ports:

Port	Tonnage
Anahuac	25,267
Aransas Pass	9,953
Beaumont	40,358,920
Brownsville	2,810,018
Cedar Bayou	231,485
Chocolate Bayou	4,301,199
Colorado River	403,016
Corpus Christi	41,980,354

Port	Tonnage
Dickinson Bayou	23,275
Double Bayou	26,136
Freeport	23,357,106
Galveston	11,268,337
Houston	110,966,741
Long Mott	2,930,820
Moss Bluff	196,402
Orange	484,942
Palacios	100,293
Port Arthur	26,037,529
Port Isabel	313,036
Port Lavaca	4,148,664
Port Mansfield	115,874
Rio Hondo–Harlingen	665,127
Sabine Pass	1,063,238
Sweeny	660,291
Texas City	27,852,242
Other Ports	848,517
1981 total of short tons handled	291,168,791

Lighter freight service, along with passenger traffic became possible with the development of municipal and regional airports. Aviation in Texas began during World War I, when local fields served as training grounds for American and Canadian pilots. In the 1920s mail and passenger service by airplane linked Texas with distant parts of the nation. During World War II a large number of air bases and practice landing fields were established in the state because of the favorable flying weather and the relatively level terrain. In the intervening years to the present time, air traffic centers handled commercial, business, industrial, agicultural, and private aviation needs.

When World War II ended, the federal government abandoned most of its temporary training bases and transferred ownership of them to municipalities. Improvements to existing facilities and construction of new airports have come through federal, state, county, and municipal funding. A tax on airplane fuel collected by federal agencies specifically for airport improvement has been paid by fuel purchasers who in turn benefit from those improvements.

In 1982, Texas had 14,484 landing facilities of all types, by far the largest number in any state. The top ten air traffic centers, based on aircraft departures performed and enplaned passengers, are Dallas–Fort Worth, Houston, San Antonio, Austin, El Paso, Lubbock, Midland-Odessa, Amarillo, Corpus Christi, and Brownsville–Harlingen–San Benito. Dallas–Fort Worth has more aircraft departures than all other Texas cities combined. Texas has four international airports, located at Dallas–Fort Worth, Houston, San Antonio, and El Paso.

AMTK — Amtrak
A&NR — Angelina and Neches River
ATSF — Atchison, Topeka and Santa Fe
BN — Burlington Northern
BRR — Belton Railroad
CRI&P — Chicago, Rock Island and Pacific
GH&H — Galveston, Houston and Henderson
GRR — Georgetown Railroad
KCS — Kansas City Southern
MKT — Missouri-Kansas-Texas
MP — Missouri Pacific
MC&SA — Moscow, Camden and San Augustine
OKT — Oklahoma, Kansas, Texas
PVS — Pecos Valley Southern
PC&N — Point Comfort and Northern
RS&S — Rockdale, Sandow and Southern
RS&P — Roscoe, Snyder and Pacific
SLSW — St. Louis Southwestern
SP — Southern Pacific
TC — Texas Central
TM — Texas Mexican
T&N — Texas and Northern
TNW — Texas North Western
TSE — Texas South Eastern
TS — Texas State
WMW&NW — Weatherford, Mineral Wells and Northwestern

TEXAS RAILROADS

© 1988 University of Oklahoma Press

51. TEXAS RAILROADS

RAILROAD CONSTRUCTION BEGAN IN TEXAS in 1852, although plans had been made and charters issued earlier. Limited local capital restrained the development of this all-important transportation means. By the time of the Civil War, a total of 403 miles of track linked various communities in the southeastern region of the state.

Following the Civil War, an infusion of outside capital, together with state land grants and support from communities and private individuals, brought about a rapid expansion in rail mileage. As the frontier receded westward, a network of rails brought life to old and new towns, provided a means for agricultural commodities to get to market, brought in much-needed consumer goods at comparatively affordable costs, and helped to win the wilderness to the plow and to civilzation. In relative short order, the railroad linked interior communities with the Gulf of Mexico, Louisiana, Arkansas, Indian Territory (later Oklahoma), and beyond to midwestern and northeastern markets. It also provided a means to quicken migration to the Texas frontier by people outside the state. The entire east-west length of the southern portion of Texas was on the main line of one of the four public-supported transcontinental railroads, the Southern Pacific, to provide direct linkage with California.

Troubled financial times and chronic mismanagement brought about bankruptcies, receiverships, mergers, and consolidations in the late nineteenth and early twentieth centuries. Eventually, major rail lines in Texas became a part of only a few national railway systems, namely the Burlington Northern, Missouri-Kansas-Texas (Katy), the Union Pacific–Missouri Pacific, the Southern Pacific, and the Atchison, Topeka and Santa Fe. Recently, the Frisco (St. Louis–San Francisco) became a part of the Burlington Northern system, and the Rock Island (Chicago, Rock Island and Pacific) has ceased to exist. Other railroad companies in operation in 1983 were the Angelina and Neches River; Belton; Galveston, Houston and Henderson; Georgetown;

Kansas City Southern; Moscow, Camden, and San Augustine; Pecos Valley Southern; Point Comfort and Northern; Rockdale, Sandow and Southern; Roscoe, Snyder and Pacific; St. Louis Southwestern, or "Cotton Belt"; Texas Central; Texas-Mexican; Texas and Northern; Texas North Western; Texas South Eastern; and Weatherford, Mineral Wells and Northwestern.

Railroad mileage increased from the first track constructed in 1852 until the greatest figure was reached in 1932 (17,078). Since then a steady decline has reduced the trackage to 12,341 miles in 1983.

Passenger service once touched almost every railroad community in the state. The advent of the automobile, commerical bus, and passenger airline eroded the number of passengers carried until the railroad companies ceased passenger operations. Amtrack, the National Railroad Passenger Corporation, in 1983 provided limited passenger train service to the following Texas communities: Alpine, Austin, Beaumont, Cleburne, Dallas, Del Rio, El Paso, Fort Worth, Houston, Longview, Marshall, McGregor, San Antonio, Sanderson, San Marcos, Taylor, Temple, and Texarkana.

Railroad Mileage in Texas, 1853–1983
(courtesy of the *Texas Almanac*)

Year	Mileage
1853	20
1860	403
1870	591
1880	3,025
1890	8,667
1900	9,838
1910	13,819
1920	16,049
1930	16,900
1932	17,078
1940	16,197
1950	15,555
1960	14,677
1970	13,545
1980	12,752
1983	12,341

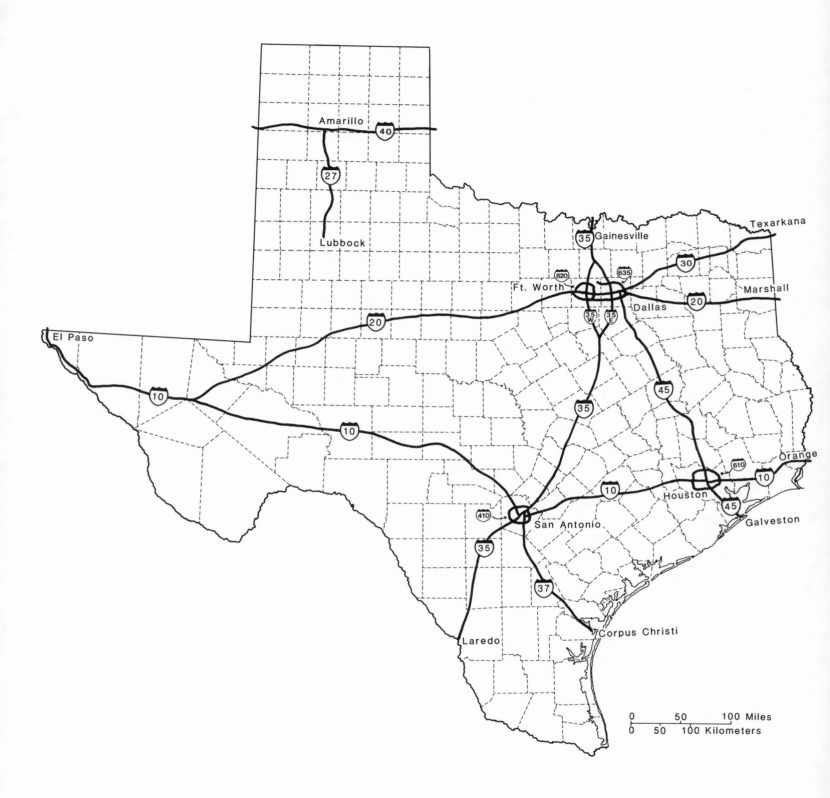

INTERSTATE HIGHWAY SYSTEM

© 1988 University of Oklahoma Press

52. INTERSTATE HIGHWAY SYSTEM

OVERLAND TRANSPORTATION in Texas has progressed from animal-drawn conveyances on makeshift roads alongside private property boundaries to the superhighway that cuts across country on wide-land roadbeds with limited access. Before 1917, all road work in Texas was left to county, community, and private initiative. In 1917, the legislature created the Texas Highway Department, the forty-fifth such state department, with duties of formulating policies and plans for a comprehensive system of roads in cooperation with county governments. The prevailing philosophy that the state should offer advice and have no control failed to produce improvement in the road system. Some counties voted bonds for road improvements, but as the less wealthy counties could not afford the necessary construction costs, some well-paved roads ended at a county line, with a dirt road ahead that was rough in dry weather and impassable during wet seasons.

In 1923, Governor Pat Neff unsuccessfully prevailed upon the legislature to provide road improvement funds, stating that no highway was better than its deepest mudhole. Finally, in 1925 the legislature granted to the Highway Department authority to construct and maintain a connected system of highways. The paved road milage has increased rapidly since that action. Additional programs for improved roads in Texas, other than designated state highways, are the U.S. highway system, which is now financed on a 50-50 matching basis by the national government, the farm-to-market road system begun in 1949 that has proved to be so valuable for farmers and ranchers living off the main highways, municipal- and county-funded streets and roads not in the state system, and the interstate highway system.

In 1944 the U.S. Congress established the Interstate and Defense Highway System as an improved means of public transportation and for civil defense purposes. Additional impetus was given by the Federal Aid Highway Act of 1956. Mass evacuations in times of crisis or natural disaster would be much more efficient with a multilane, limited-access roadway. For safety and convenience, and as a means of moving a high volume of traffic in a reasonable time, these expressways have proven their worth. After several amendments, the federal government now matches state funds on a 90-10 basis for new construction of freeways. In 1980, Texas had 70,605 miles of paved roads. Included in that number are 3,222 miles of interstate highways, approximately 1,000 miles of freeways not in the interstate system, plus approximately 1,300 miles of multilane divided roads.

Texas has connecting interstate roads that extend from distances beyond the state's boundaries to the east, north, and west, as well as expressways completely encompassed within the state. Interstate Highway I-10 enters from Louisiana at Orange and extends into New Mexico at El Paso. Highway I-20 runs from the Louisiana boundary near Marshall and converges with I-10 in Reeves County west of Pecos. Highway I-30 enters Texas at Texarkana and converges with I-20 west of Fort Worth. Interstate I-35 connects Laredo on the Mexican border with Oklahoma just north of Gainesville, and I-45 extends from Galveston to Dallas. The freeways wholly within the state are I-37 from Corpus Christi to San Antonio and I-27 from Lubbock to Amarillo. Some loops around urban areas carry the interstate designation, such as I-410 in San Antonio, I-635 in Dallas, I-820 in Fort Worth, and I-610 in Houston.

When one considers that the 1980 population for Texas was 14,228,383 and the 1980 motor vehicle registration was 11,989,419, it is readily apparent why Texans have such a great concern for improved highways.

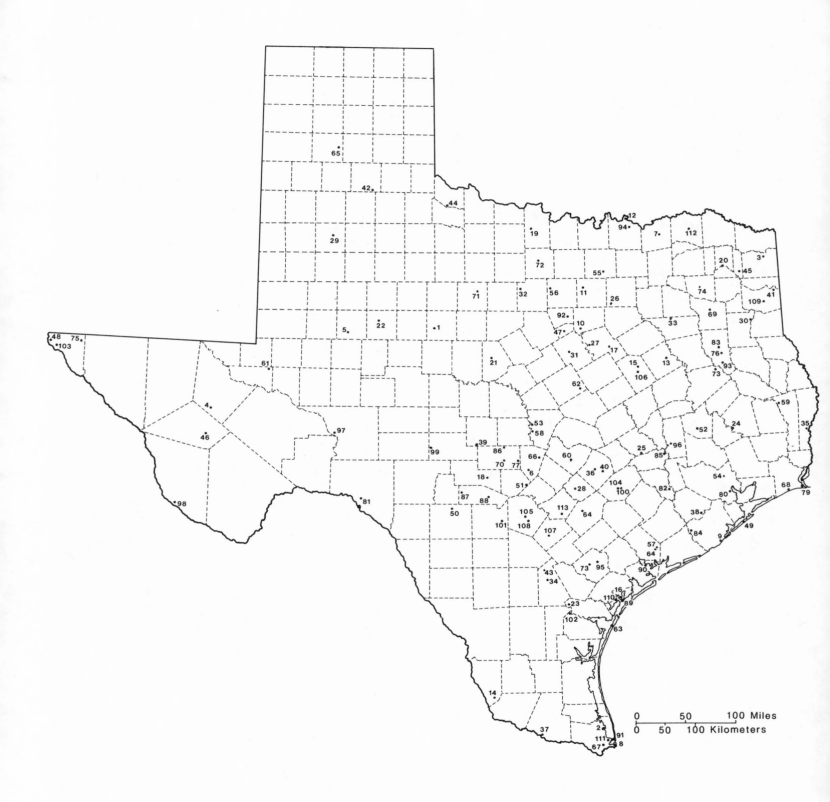

STATE PARKS

© 1988 University of Oklahoma Press

53. STATE PARKS

RECREATION ACTIVITIES traditionally have been a part of the Texas life-style. The state parks system of acquisition, development, and maintenance is a twentieth-century endeavor. In 1916, Isabella E. Neff, mother of later Governor Pat Morris Neff, donated a six-acre tract in Coryell County to the state. When her will was probated in 1921, no provisions existed to care for such property. In 1923 the legislature created a state parks board, and Mother Neff State Park became the first officially designated state park in Texas. From that time to November, 1982, the number of parks was increased to 113 as new areas became the property of the state through gift or purchase within seven categories: State Recreation Areas, State Parks, State Historical Parks, State Natural Areas, State Fishing Piers, State Historic Sites, and State Historic Structures. The Texas Parks and Wildlife Department oversees the management of the state parks system.

State Recreation Areas	Location	Acreage
1. Abilene	Buffalo Gap	621
2. Arroyo Colorado	Harlingen	687
3. Atlanta	Atlanta	1,475
4. Balmorhea	Toyahvale	46
5. Big Spring	Big Spring	370
6. Blanco	Blanco	105
7. Bonham	Bonham	261
8. Brazos Island	Brownsville	217
9. Bryan Beach	Freeport	878
10. Cleburne	Cleburne	529
11. Eagle Mountain Lake	Fort Worth	401
12. Eisenhower	Denison	457
13. Fairfield Lake	Fairfield	1,460
14. Falcon	Falcon	573
15. Fort Parker	Mexia	1,485
16. Goose Island	Rockport	307
17. Jeff Davis	Hillsboro	38
18. Kerrville	Kerrville	517
19. Lake Arrowhead	Wichita Falls	524
20. Lake Bob Sandlin	Mount Pleasant	258
21. Lake Brownwood	Brownwood	537
22. Lake Colorado City	Colorado City	500
23. Lake Corpus Christi	Mathis	365
24. Lake Livingston	Livingston	635
25. Lake Somerville	Somerville	5,200
26. Lakeview	Cedar Hill	1,827
27. Lake Whitney	Whitney	955
28. Lockhart	Lockhart	264
29. Mackenzie	Lubbock	542
30. Martin Creek Park Site	Longview	216
31. Meridian	Meridian	502
32. Possum Kingdom	Caddo	1,529
33. Purtis Creek Park Site	Tyler	1,533
34. Tips	Three Rivers	31
35. Village Creek Park Site	Fort Worth	942

State Parks	Location	Acreage
36. Bastrop	Bastrop	3,504
37. Bentsen. Rio Grande	Mission	588
38. Brazos Bend	Needville	4,897
39. South Llano River Park Site	Junction	2,630
40. Buescher	Smithville	1,017
41. Caddo Lake	Karnak	480
42. Caprock Canyons	Quitaque	13,655
43. Choke Canyon	Three Rivers	38,500
44. Copper Breaks	Crowell	1,889
45. Daingerfield	Daingerfield	551
46. Davis Mountains (Indian Lodge)	Fort Davis	1,869
47. Dinosaur Valley	Glen Rose	1,272
48. Franklin Mountains	El Paso	8,897
49. Galveston Island	Galveston	1,944
50. Garner	Concan	1,420
51. Guadalupe River	New Braunfels	1,900
52. Huntsville	Huntsville	2,083
53. Inks Lake	Burnet	1,201
54. Lake Houston	New Caney	4,705
55. Lake Lewisville	Lewisville	721
56. Lake Mineral Wells	Mineral Wells	2,853
57. Lake Texana	Edna	575
58. Longhorn Cavern	Burnet	639
59. Martin Dies, Jr.	Jasper	705
60. McKinney Falls	Austin	726
61. Monahans Sandhills	Monahans	3,840
62. Mother Neff	Moody	259
63. Mustang Island	Corpus Christi	3,704
64. Palmetto	Luling	264
65. Palo Duro Canyon	Canyon	16,402
66. Pedernales Falls	Johnson City	4,860
67. Resaca de la Palma Park Site	Brownsville	1,100
68. Sea Rim	Port Arthur	15,109
69. Tyler	Tyler	985

State Historical Parks	Location	Acreage
70. Admiral Nimitz	Fredericksburg	9.1
71. Fort Griffin	Albany	506
72. Fort Richardson	Jacksboro	389
73. Goliad	Goliad	184
74. Governor Hogg Shrine	Quitman	27
75. Hueco Tanks	El Paso	860
76. Jim Hogg	Rusk	177
77. Lyndon B. Johnson	Stonewall	718
78. Mission Tejas	Weches	118
79. Sabine Pass Battleground	Sabine Pass	56

State Historical Parks	Location	Acreage
80. San Jacinto Battleground	La Porte—Baytown	327
81. Seminole Canyon	Langtry	2,172
82. Stephen F. Austin	San Felipe	667
83. Texas State Railroad	Rusk	507
84. Varner-Hogg	West Columbia	66
85. Washington. on. the. Brazos	Washington	154

State Natural Areas	Location	Acreage
86. Enchanted Rock	Fredericksburg	1,643
87. Lost Maples	Vanderpool	2,174
88. Hill Country	Bandera	4,753

State Fishing Piers	Location	Acreage
89. Copano Bay	Fulton	5.9
90. Port Lavaca	Port Lavaca	1.8
91. Queen Isabella	Port Isabel	7.0

State Historic Sites	Location	Acreage
92. Acton	Granbury	0.006
93. Caddoan Mounds	Alto	70.1
94. Eisenhower Birthplace	Denison	2.8
95. Fannin Battleground	Goliad	13.0
96. Fanthorp Inn	Anderson	1.4
97. Fort Lancaster	Sheffield	81.6
98. Fort Leaton	Presidio	13.3
99. Fort McKavett	Fort McKavett	79.5
100. Kreische Complex	La Grange	35.9
101. Landmark Inn	Castroville	4.7
102. Lipantitlan	Corpus Christi	5.0
103. Magoffin Home	El Paso	1.5
104. Monument Hill	La Grange	3.9
105. José Antonio Navarro	San Antonio	0.3
106. Old Fort Parker	Groesbeck	11.1
107. Rancho de las Cabras	Floresville	99.1
108. San José Mission	San Antonio	22.8
109. Starr Mansion	Marshall	1.3

State Historical Structures	Location	Acreage
110. Fulton Mansion	Fulton	2.3
111. Port Isabel Lighthouse	Port Isabel	0.5
112. Sam Bell Maxey House	Paris	0.4
113. Sebastopol House	Seguin	2.2

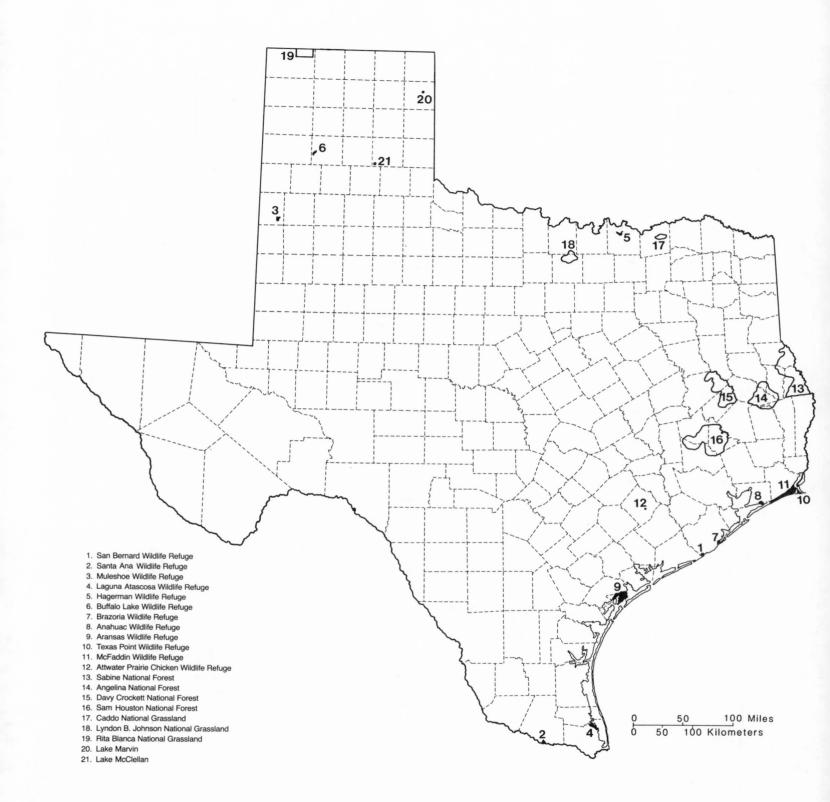

1. San Bernard Wildlife Refuge
2. Santa Ana Wildlife Refuge
3. Muleshoe Wildlife Refuge
4. Laguna Atascosa Wildlife Refuge
5. Hagerman Wildlife Refuge
6. Buffalo Lake Wildlife Refuge
7. Brazoria Wildlife Refuge
8. Anahuac Wildlife Refuge
9. Aransas Wildlife Refuge
10. Texas Point Wildlife Refuge
11. McFaddin Wildlife Refuge
12. Attwater Prairie Chicken Wildlife Refuge
13. Sabine National Forest
14. Angelina National Forest
15. Davy Crockett National Forest
16. Sam Houston National Forest
17. Caddo National Grassland
18. Lyndon B. Johnson National Grassland
19. Rita Blanca National Grassland
20. Lake Marvin
21. Lake McClellan

0   50   100 Miles
0 50 100 Kilometers

NATIONAL FORESTS, GRASSLANDS, AND WILDLIFE REFUGES

54. NATIONAL FORESTS, GRASSLANDS, AND WILDLIFE REFUGES

WHEN TEXAS ENTERED THE UNION in 1845, it retained its public lands. Property that became the possession of the federal government since then was purchased by the United States, donated by individuals, or presented by the state through appropriate legislation for a specific purpose. In each instance, property that came under public ownership by the U.S. government was acquired for public purposes.

In 1933 the Texas legislature authorized the purchase of tracts in East Texas for the creation of national forests. Acquisition began in 1934 under the authority of the Weeks Law of March 1, 1911, and on October 15, 1936, President Franklin D. Roosevelt proclaimed the establishment of four national forests in Texas. Their names relate to the history and geography of the state. The Sabine National Forest contains 184,767 acres in Jasper, Sabine, San Augustine, and Shelby counties. Angelina National Forest is made up of 154,537 acres in Angelina, Jasper, Nacogdoches, and San Augustine counties. Davy Crockett National Forest, with 161,748 acres, is in Houston and Trinity counties. Sam Houston National Forest has 158,411 acres in Montgomery, San Jacinto, and Walker counties.

Since the establishment of the national forests, management by the Forest Service has produced dense stands of marketable timber and regrowth of shrubs, wildflowers, and plants indigenous to the area. Tree farming techniques have been shared with neighboring private owners to enhance the economy of the region. Cattle grazing permits are granted to local ranchers for an annual fee. Within each national forest, scattered tracts as well as sizeable acreages exist within the official boundaries, interspersed with privately owned property of varied size.

In the region of the state with less precipitation, another land management program is administered by the federal government. Under the provisions of the Bankhead-Jones Farm Tenant Act of 1937, Congress authorized the Soil Conservation Service to purchase submarginal lands that had become unproductive for farming because of overcropping, recurrent drought, or severe erosion during the Dust Bowl era. The Soil Conservation Service developed a model of grassland agricultural management on the acquired properties for neighboring and regional property owners. The administration of the national grasslands was transfered to the Forest Service of the U.S. Department of Agriculture in 1953. In addition to land reclamation, programs in range, watershed, outdoor recreation, and fish and wildlife management have been developed. Limited grazing permits by annual fee have been granted to local residents.

Administration of the various units in the southwestern United States was consolidated in 1958 as the Panhandle National Grasslands, consisting of approximately 300,000 acres. Scattered tracts make up the individual projects. The Rita Blanca Grassland is in Dallam County, Texas, and Cimarron County, Oklahoma. Lake Marvin in Hemphill County and Lake McClellan in Gray County are associated administratively with the Black Kettle Grassland in Oklahoma. The Lyndon B. Johnson National Grassland, formerly the Cross Timbers National Grassland, is in Wise and Montague counties. The Caddo National Grassland is located in Fannin County.

Another conservation program administered by the federal government is the national wildlife refuge system. Particular tracts in Texas are associated with a farflung collection of lands and waters in the United States and neighboring countries to protect and also to preserve from extinction, in some cases, migratory birds and rare mammals. Although the program of wildlife refuges began nationally in 1903, acquisition of Texas property for this purpose began in 1935 at Muleshoe. Since then, eleven additional refuges have been established as integral parts of a system to benefit migratory and native wildlife, provide soil conservation and forestry programs, maintain recreational facilities, and promote wildlife education to the public. The twelve national wildlife refuges in Texas comprise approximately 231,000 acres. Their dates of establishment, location, and acreage are listed below.

National Wildlife Refuges in Texas

Refuge	County	Year Established	Size (acres)
Anahuac	Chambers	1963	9,836
Aransas	Aransas, Calhoun and Refugio	1937	54,829
Attwater Prairie Chicken	Colorado	1972	8,000
Brazoria	Brazoria	1966	10,321
Buffalo Lake	Randall	1937	7,677
Hagerman	Grayson	1946	11,429
Laguna Atascosa	Cameron and Willacy	1946	45,050
McFaddin	Jefferson	1980	42,956
Muleshoe	Bailey	1935	5,809
San Bernard	Brazoria and Matagorda	1968	24,455
Santa Ana	Hidalgo	1943	2,000
Texas Point	Jefferson	1979	8,952

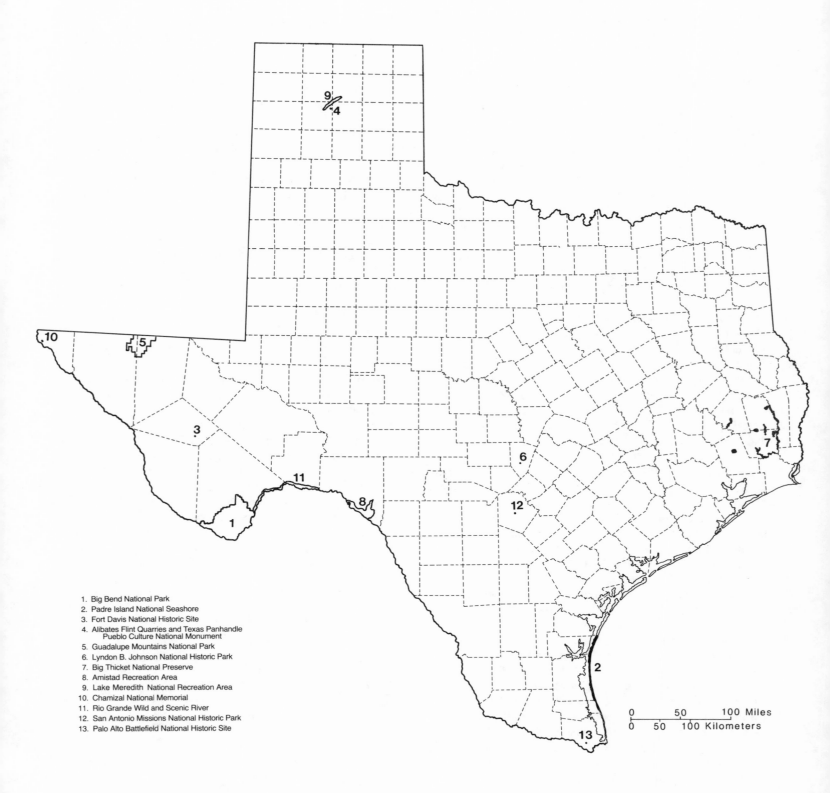

1. Big Bend National Park
2. Padre Island National Seashore
3. Fort Davis National Historic Site
4. Alibates Flint Quarries and Texas Panhandle
   Pueblo Culture National Monument
5. Guadalupe Mountains National Park
6. Lyndon B. Johnson National Historic Park
7. Big Thicket National Preserve
8. Amistad Recreation Area
9. Lake Meredith National Recreation Area
10. Chamizal National Memorial
11. Rio Grande Wild and Scenic River
12. San Antonio Missions National Historic Park
13. Palo Alto Battlefield National Historic Site

NATIONAL PARKS AND HISTORIC SITES

© 1988 University of Oklahoma Press

55. NATIONAL PARKS AND HISTORIC SITES

PRESERVATION OF SCENIC WONDERS and historical sites has been a general public concern in the United States. Americans have traditionally looked to the national government to protect areas deemed of special esthetic or historical value by removing them from private ownership and setting them aside for public use. These properties are administered by the National Parks Service in the Department of the Interior.

The first national park created in Texas was the Big Bend National Park, located in Brewster County. This 691,338.95-acre tract, established in 1944, was deemed worthy of preservation because of its wilderness features, scenic beauty, and unusual biological features.

To prevent private exploitation of the longest stretch of undeveloped seashore remaining in America, the U.S. Congress in 1962 created the Padre Island National Seashore on a barrier island off the Texas coast. That portion of Padre Island set aside for public use is in Kenedy, Kleberg, and Willacy counties and extends 67.5 miles.

The Fort Davis National Historic Site was established in 1963 in Jeff Davis County. Located on 454 acres, the site commemorates the military post that served to protect the Texas and Southwestern frontier during the Indian wars.

An accidental discovery of flint quarries in Potter County led to the designation in 1965 of the Alibates Flint Quarries and Texas Panhandle Pueblo Culture National Monument. A ridge three hundred feet wide and one mile long had been a source of flint for tools and weapons by ancient people. In the same vicinity two pueblos of later origin was discovered. The preserved site consists of 92.56 acres.

In 1966 the grandeur of scenic wonders unmatched elsewhere in Texas became the Guadalupe Mountains National Park. The park contains 77,500 acres in Hudspeth and Culberson counties. Guadalupe Park, the highest point in Texas at 8,751 feet, is located here.

The Lyndon B. Johnson National Historical Park was established in 1970 on 238 acres in Blanco and Gillespie counties. It commemorates the boyhood home and working ranch of the thirty-sixth president of the United States.

Perhaps the most controversial set-aside land in Texas for public preservation is the Big Thicket National Preserve. After years of intense discussion in public and private arenas, twelve units—eight tracts and four corridors—were established in 1974 on 84,550 acres in Polk, Hardin, Liberty, Tyler, Jasper, Orange, and Jefferson counties. The purpose of the Big Thicket National Preserve is to protect the rare biological treasures of the southeastern Texas region for future generations.

Facilities for camping and water-based activities have been established at the Amistad National Recreation Area in Val Verde County and the Lake Meredith National Recreation Area in Moore, Hutchinson, and Potter counties.

The Chamizal National Memorial in El Paso County commemorates the peaceful settlement in 1963 of a boundary dispute between Mexico and the United States along the Rio Grande. The basis for the controversy resulted a century earlier when that river changed its course, leaving part of Chihuahua in Texas and part of Texas in Chihuahua.

The Palo Alto Battlefield National Historic Site is located near Harlingen and Brownsville in Cameron County. General Zachary Taylor's forces first met a Mexican army at this location on May 8, 1846, to begin the American-Mexican War. American artillery, recently developed and used extensively for the first time in American military history, determined the outcome of this battle and became vitally important in other phases of that conflict.

A 191-mile stretch of the international border between Mexico and the United States has been designated the Rio Grande Wild and Scenic River. The strip extends through the canyons on the Rio Grande beginning at the Big Bend National Park and ending near Langtry.

A link with the Spanish period of Texas history is maintained by the existence of the San Antonio Missions National Historical Park. Four well-preserved and still active churches on the San Antonio River downstream from the central section of San Antonio provide a glimpse into Texas' Spanish past.

PUBLIC SENIOR COLLEGES AND UNIVERSITIES

© 1988 University of Oklahoma Press

56. PUBLIC SENIOR COLLEGES AND UNIVERSITIES

TEXANS HAVE LONG MAINTAINED an interest in public-financed higher education, but the absence of money for funding their dreams meant a considerable delay from initial expression to reality. In January, 1839, the Republic of Texas Congress set aside fifty leagues of land as an endowment fund for two universities of the first class, one for East Texas and one for West Texas. Later, under state government, the idea of a center of higher learning received attention again when in 1854 the legislature set aside $100,000 of the U.S. indemnity bonds obtained as a result of the Compromise of 1850 for a university, but once more educational desire came to nothing.

Funds secured by the state from the federal government through the Morrill Land Grant College Act of 1862 brought about the existence of the Agricultural and Mechanical College of Texas, now Texas A&M University, at College Station. Classes began in 1876. At the same time, the state opened a vocational agricultural school for blacks at Prairie View, but the school failed for lack of students. Since 1879, when the legislature changed the purpose of the school to general education, the school, now Prairie View

A&M University, has existed. The first college for teacher training began in 1879 in Huntsville (Sam Houston Normal Institute, now Sam Houston State University) in buildings obtained from Austin College, a Presbyterian institution, that had moved to Sherman to escape a yellow fever epidemic. Finally, in 1883 the long-desired state university opened its doors in Austin as the University of Texas. These four institutions comprised the extent of state-supported higher education by the end of the nineteenth century, teaching a total of 2,457 students.

Since 1900, a considerable number of schools have been established or taken over by the state after having begun as private or community colleges. To meet the demand for more extensive course offerings and to keep up with the times, many of the schools changed their names from normal schools to teachers' colleges to state universities. By 1987–88 a total of thirty-seven public universities had a combined enrollment of 368,775 students. The eight public medical schools and health sciences centers had an enrollment of 10,878 students.

Public Senior Colleges and Universities

1. Angelo State University	San Angelo
2. Corpus Christi State University	Corpus Christi
3. East Texas State University	Commerce
4. East Texas State University Center at Texarkana	Texarkana
5. Lamar University at Beaumont	Beaumont
6. Lamar University at Orange	Orange
7. Lamar University at Port Arthur	Port Arthur
8. Laredo State University	Laredo
9. Midwestern State University	Wichita Falls
10. Pan American University	Edinburg
11. Pan American University at Brownsville	Brownsville
12. Prairie View A&M University	Prairie View
13. Sam Houston State University	Huntsville
14. Southwest Texas State University	San Marcos
15. Stephen F. Austin State University	Nacogdoches
16. Sul Ross State University	Alpine
17. Tarleton State University	Stephenville
18. Texas A&I University	Kingsville
19. Texas A&M University	College Station
20. Texas A&M University at Galveston	Galveston
21. Texas Southern University	Houston
22. Texas Tech University	Lubbock
23. Texas Woman's University	Denton
24. University of Houston-Clear Lake	Houston
25. University of Houston-Downtown	Houston
26. University of Houston-University Park	Houston
27. University of Houston-Victoria	Victoria
28. University of North Texas	Denton
29. University of Texas at Arlington	Arlington
30. University of Texas at Austin	Austin
31. University of Texas at Dallas	Richardson
32. University of Texas at El Paso	El Paso
33. University of Texas of the Permian Basin	Odessa
34. University of Texas at San Antonio	San Antonio
35. University of Texas at Tyler	Tyler
36. Uvalde Study Center	Uvalde
37. West Texas State University	Canyon

Public Medical Schools and Heath Science Centers

38. Texas A&M University College of Medicine	College Station
39. Texas A&M College of Veterinary Medicine	College Station
40. Texas College of Osteopathic Medicine	Fort Worth
41. Texas Tech University Health Sciences Center	Lubbock
42. University of Texas Health Science Center at Houston	Houston
43. University of Texas Health Science Center at San Antonio	San Antonio
44. University of Texas Medical Branch at Galveston	Galveston
45. University of Texas Southwestern Medical Center at Dallas	Dallas

PUBLIC COMMUNITY COLLEGES

57. PUBLIC COMMUNITY COLLEGES

THE JUNIOR COLLEGE MOVEMENT in the United States has had a profound effect on educational achievements by the people. Although some private junior colleges operated in Texas in the late nineteenth and early twentieth centuries, a public junior college was not established in the state until 1922. As has been the experience in a number of cases, that school (now Midwestern State University in Wichita Falls) evolved into a four-year college.

Beginning as extensions of high schools supported by local school district taxes, junior colleges in 1929 were authorized by the legislature to create separate districts for tax purposes. In 1941, junior colleges became eligible for direct state aid and came under the jurisdiction of the Texas Education Agency. Supervision was changed in 1965 to the Texas Higher Education Coordinating Board.

The significant increase of public community junior colleges since World War II has provided educational opportunities for many people who could not have attended college otherwise because of work schedules, admission standards, or lack of geographical mobility. The convenience of location in communities has meant an increase in preprofessional courses, continuing education for adults, local places for high school graduates to begin their college studies, and an expansion of vocational and technical training which enhances the individual's job marketability and thereby serves society in general. In 1987–88, a total of 321,896 students were enrolled at the following forty-nine public community colleges with sixty-six campuses.

Public Community Colleges

1. Alamo Community College District — San Antonio
2. Alvin Community College — Alvin
3. Amarillo College — Amarillo
4. Angelina College — Lufkin
5. Austin Community College — Austin
6. Bee County College — Beeville
7. Blinn College — Brenham
8. Brazosport College — Lake Jackson
9. Central Texas College — Killeen
10. Cisco Junior College — Cisco
11. Clarendon College — Clarendon
12. College of the Mainland — Texas City
13. Collin County Community College District — McKinney
14. Cooke County College — Gainesville
15. Dallas County Community College District — Dallas
16. Del Mar College — Corpus Christi
17. El Paso Community College District — El Paso
18. Frank Phillips College — Borger
19. Galveston College — Galveston
20. Grayson County College — Denison
21. Hill College — Hillsboro
22. Houston Community College System — Houston
23. Howard County Junior College District — Big Spring
24. Kilgore College — Kilgore
25. Laredo Junior College — Laredo
26. Lee College — Baytown
27. McLennan Community College — Waco
28. Midland College — Midland
29. Navarro College — Corsicana
30. North Harris County College District — Houston
31. Northeast Texas Community College — Mt. Pleasant
32. Odessa College — Odessa
33. Panola Junior College — Carthage
34. Paris Junior College — Paris
35. Ranger Junior College — Ranger
36. San Jacinto College District — Pasadena
37. South Plains College — Levelland
38. Southwest Texas Junior College — Uvalde
39. Tarrant County Junior College District — Fort Worth
40. Temple Junior College — Temple
41. Texarkana College — Texarkana
42. Texas Southmost College — Brownsville
43. Trinity Valley Community College — Athens
44. Tyler Junior College — Tyler
45. Vernon Regional Junior College — Vernon
46. Victoria College — Victoria
47. Weatherford College — Weatherford
48. Western Texas College — Snyder
49. Wharton County Junior College — Wharton

INDEPENDENT COLLEGES AND UNIVERSITIES

58. INDEPENDENT COLLEGES AND UNIVERSITIES

IN THE DECADE FOLLOWING INDEPENDENCE, when much verbal support was given to promote educational activities on all levels, more learning was imparted at the family hearth than in schools. Religious denominations and interested communities applied for charters from the Congress of the Republic of Texas to organize academies, colleges, and universities to provide educational opportunities at home rather than sending their young people back east to school. In 1840, Rutersville College at Rutersville, near La Grange, became the first institution in Texas to offer courses resembling the higher learning of today. It later ceased operation, but its records were merged with other defunct colleges when Southwestern University at Georgetown began in 1873. The oldest college in continuous existence in Texas is Baylor University, which began in 1846 at Independence and later moved to Waco, where it merged with another school in 1887.

Through trial and error, consolidation, and dogged determination to establish an adequate financial base upon which to operate, and to provide a meaningful education for their people, private and denominational colleges and universities have flourished in Texas. By 1982–83, Texas had a total of thirty-nine independent senior colleges and universities with 79,201 students, four independent junior colleges with 1,270 students, and three independent medical, dental, and allied health schools with 1,673 students.

Independent Senior Colleges and Universities

1. Abilene Christian University	Abilene
2. Amber University	Garland
3. American Technological University	Killeen
4. Austin College	Sherman
5. Baylor University	Waco
6. Bishop College	Dallas
7. Concordia Lutheran College	Austin
8. Dallas Baptist University	Dallas
9. East Texas Baptist University	Marshall
10. Hardin-Simmons University	Abilene
11. Houston Baptist University	Houston
12. Howard Payne University	Brownwood
13. Huston-Tillotson University	Austin
14. Incarnate Word College	San Antonio
15. Jarvis Christian College	Hawkins
16. LeTourneau College	Longview
17. Lubbock Christian University	Lubbock
18. McMurry College	Abilene
19. Our Lady of the Lake University of San Antonio	San Antonio
20. Paul Quinn College	Waco
21. Rice University	Houston
22. St. Edward's University, Inc.	Austin
23. St. Mary's University of San Antonio	San Antonio
24. Schreiner College	Kerrville
25. Southern Methodist University	Dallas
26. Southwestern Adventist College	Keene
27. Southwestern Christian College	Terrell
28. Southwestern University	Georgetown
29. Texas Christian University	Fort Worth
30. Texas College	Tyler
31. Texas Lutheran College	Seguin
32. Texas Wesleyan College	Fort Worth
33. Trinity University	San Antonio
34. University of Dallas	Irving
35. University of Mary Hardin-Baylor	Belton
36. University of St. Thomas	Houston
37. Wayland Baptist Univeristy	Plainview
38. Wiley College	Marshall

Independent Junior Colleges

39. Jacksonville College	Jacksonville
40. Lon Morris College	Jacksonville
41. Southwestern Assemblies of God Junior College	Waxahachie

Independent Medical and Dental Schools

42. Baylor College of Dentistry	Dallas
43. Baylor College of Medicine	Houston

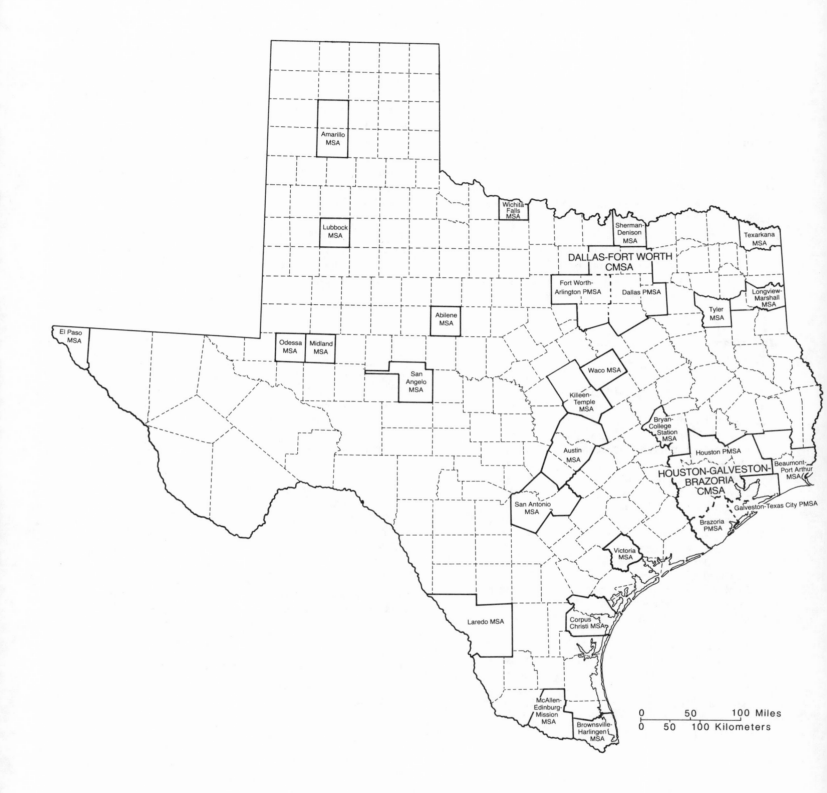

Amarillo
MSA

Wichita
Falls
MSA

Sherman-
Denison
MSA

Texarkana
MSA

DALLAS-FORT WORTH
CMSA

Lubbock
MSA

Fort Worth-
Arlington PMSA

Dallas PMSA

Longview-
Marshall
MSA

Tyler
MSA

Abilene
MSA

El Paso
MSA

Odessa
MSA

Midland
MSA

Waco MSA

San
Angelo
MSA

Killeen-
Temple
MSA

Bryan-
College
Station
MSA

Austin
MSA

Houston PMSA

HOUSTON-GALVESTON-
BRAZORIA
CMSA

Beaumont-
Port Arthur
MSA

San Antonio
MSA

Galveston-Texas City PMSA

Brazoria
PMSA

Victoria
MSA

Laredo MSA

Corpus
Christi MSA

McAllen-
Edinburg-
Mission
MSA

Brownsville-
Harlingen
MSA

0   50   100 Miles
0   50   100 Kilometers

METROPOLITAN STATISTICAL AREAS

59. METROPOLITAN STATISTICAL AREAS

TEXAS HAS BEEN RECOGNIZED as an urban state since the 1950 federal census revealed that more Texans lived in urban areas than in rural areas. As these urban communities developed, particular difficulties arose that had to be addressed with different procedures than previously required. Large concentrations of people brought on new problems that had to be considered concerning the distribution of goods and services, transportation, employment, health, suburban development, agricultural and manufacturing pursuits, and local social, cultural, and business conditions. In recent times communities in a geographical vicinity solved common problems by working together in a Standard Metropolitan Statistical Area (SMSA). In 1980, the Federal Committee on Metropolitan Statistical Areas made the most extensive changes in area standards since the federal government began designating metropolitan areas in 1948. The U.S. Office of Management and Budget adopted those recommended new definitions and made them effective as of June 30, 1983.

A city of at least 50,000 population, or an urbanized area of at least 50,000 with a total metropolitan population of at least 100,000, became recognized as a Metropolitan Statistical Area (MSA). All of a county is included in an MSA, and additional counties near a main city may be included if inclusive counties are essentially metropolitan in character and have an integrated economy.

In an area with more than one million population that meets certain other specified requirements, the term Consolidated Metropolitan Statistical Area (CMSA) applies. Within the CMSA major components receive the recognition of Primary Metropolitan Statistical Areas (PMSAs). Texas has twenty-three Metropolitan Statistical Areas, five Primary Metropolitan Statistical Areas, and two Consolidated Metropolitan Statistical Areas.

Increasingly, the state's population expansion has reflected a concentration in metropolitan areas, which indicates the historic trend toward urbanization. In 1980, approximately 80 percent of the Texas population resided in metropolitan statistical areas, as compared with 74 percent in 1970, 70 percent in 1960, and 62 percent in 1950. In 1980, approximately one-half of the state's inhabitants lived in the three largest metropolitan areas — Dallas–Fort Worth, Houston, and San Antonio.

Area Title	Area Type	Counties	Central Cities
Abilene	MSA	Taylor	Abilene
Amarillo	MSA	Potter and Randall	Amarillo
Austin	MSA	Hays, Travis, and Williamson	Austin
Beaumont–Port Arthur	MSA	Hardin, Jefferson, and Orange	Beaumont and Port Arthur
Brazoria	PMSA	Brazoria	(no central city)
Brownsville–Harlingen	MSA	Cameron	Brownsville and Harlingen
Bryan–College Station	MSA	Brazos	Bryan and College Station
Corpus Christi	MSA	Nueces and San Patricio	Corpus Christi
Dallas	PMSA	Collin, Dallas, Denton, Ellis, Kaufman, and Rockwall	Dallas, Denton, and Irving
El Paso	MSA	El Paso	El Paso
Fort Worth–Arlington	PMSA	Johnson, Parker, and Tarrant	Fort Worth and Arlington
Galveston–Texas City	PMSA	Galveston	Galveston and Texas City
Houston	PMSA	Fort Bend, Harris, Liberty, Montgomery, and Waller	Houston and Baytown
Killeen–Temple	MSA	Bell and Coryell	Killeen and Temple
Laredo	MSA	Webb	Laredo
Longview–Marshall	MSA	Gregg and Harrison	Longview and Marshall
Lubbock	MSA	Lubbock	Lubbock
McAllen–Edinburg–Mission	MSA	Hidalgo	McAllen, Edinburg, Mission
Midland	MSA	Midland	Midland
Odessa	MSA	Ector	Odessa
San Angelo	MSA	Tom Green	San Angelo
San Antonio	MSA	Bexar, Comal, and Guadalupe	San Antonio
Sherman–Denison	MSA	Grayson	Sherman and Denison
Texarkana, Texas–Texarkana, Ark.	MSA	Bowie (Texas) and Miller (Arkansas)	Texarkana, Texas, and Texarkana, Ark.
Tyler	MSA	Smith	Tyler
Victoria	MSA	Victoria	Victoria
Waco	MSA	McLennan	Waco
Wichita Falls	MSA	Wichita	Wichita Falls

The two Consolidated Metropolitan Statistical Areas are the Dallas–Fort Work CMSA, consisting of the Dallas PMSA and the Fort Worth–Arlington PMSA, and the Houston–Galveston–Brazoria CMSA, consisting of the Brazoria PMSA, the Galveston–Texas City PMSA, and the Houston PMSA.

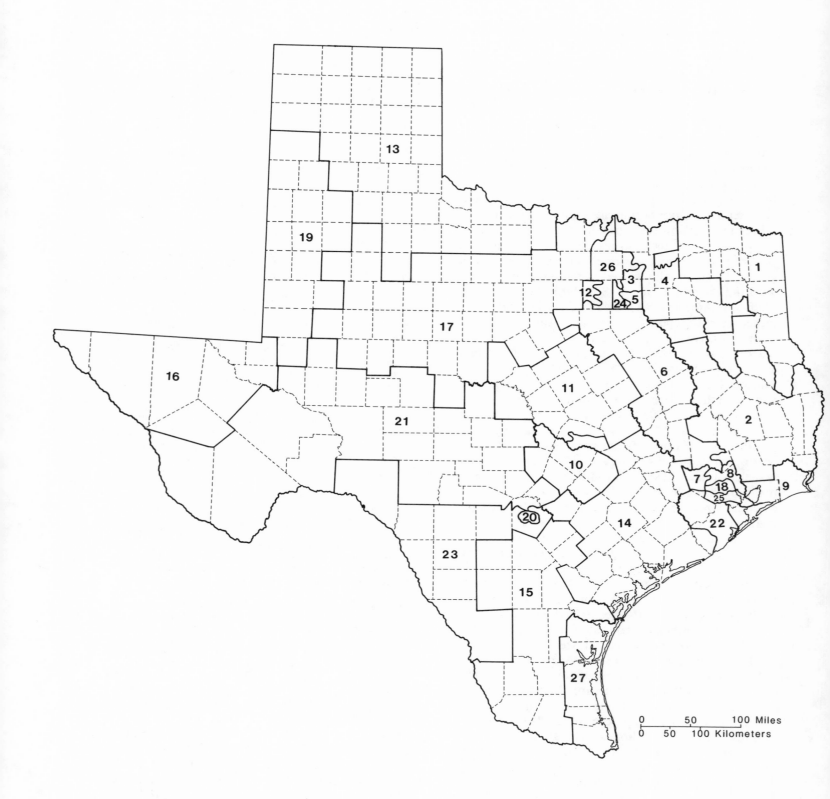

CONGRESSIONAL DISTRICTS

© 1988 University of Oklahoma Press

60. CONGRESSIONAL DISTRICTS

THE TEXAS DELEGATION to the U.S. House of Representatives increased through the years from the initial two members in 1846 to twenty-seven following the 1980 federal decennial census. Article I, section 2 of the Constitution of the United States specified that members of Congress shall serve two-year terms, with the exact number for each state apportioned after each federal decennial census. The population size of a district presumably should be in ratio to all others in a state, but at times state legislatures around the nation gerrymandered district boundaries into unusual patterns, protected favored Congress members by adding or deleting particular areas to insure reelection, or neglected to redistrict at all. Judicial attempts to force reapportionment based on balanced population figures in contiguous areas failed to achieve significant results until the 1960s.

In 1962 in the case of *Baker* vs. *Carr*, the U.S. Supreme Court handed down a decision that began massive intervention in the elective process by the judiciary in the drafting of local, state, and federal political boundaries. By this case, and as extended further by *Wesberry* vs. *Sanders* in 1964, districts were to be drawn so that a population balance would be achieved in contiguous areas. Thus began the "one man–one vote" doctrine so rigorously upheld by the courts. The reason given by the judicial branch for its new direction was to guarantee the Fourteenth Amendment rights of equal protection of the laws. The Texas legislature redistricted congressional districts in 1967 to conform to the one–vote policy.

In 1971, after the Texas legislature redrew congressional district boundaries, a lawsuit challenged the redistricting plan because of significant population variances among districts. A three-judge federal panel heard the case and, with direction from the Supreme Court, implemented in a new congressional district plan October, 1973.

The same process of federal intervention occurred after the 1980 federal census showed Texas was entitled to three additional seats. After the legislature drew up a plan for new district boundaries in 1981, the U.S. Department of Justice overturned it. Under the federal Voting Rights Act of 1965, which by now was extended to include Texas, the Justice Department reviewed all political boundary changes. When the governor refused to call a special legislative session, Republican legislators and minority groups challenged the redistricting plan in court because it did not establish a minority district. A three-judge federal panel intervened to redraw congressional boundaries that helped Hispanics in South Texas and Democrats in the Dallas–Fort Worth area. During the 1983 legislative session, Texas lawmakers accepted the court's plan with some adjustments that the Justice Department and a three-judge federal court subsequently approved. The current plan will stand until the 1990 census unless new legal challenges are instituted and are successful.

The following information presents the size of the Texas delegation in Congress as a result of each federal decennial census:

Membership of the Texas Delegation in Congress Following Each Federal Census

1846	1850	1860	1870	1880	1890	1900	1910	1920	1930	1940	1950	1960	1970	1980
2*	2	4	6	11	13	16	18	18	21	21	22	23	24	27

*The number of members of Congress permitted from Texas pending the results of the 1850 census report.

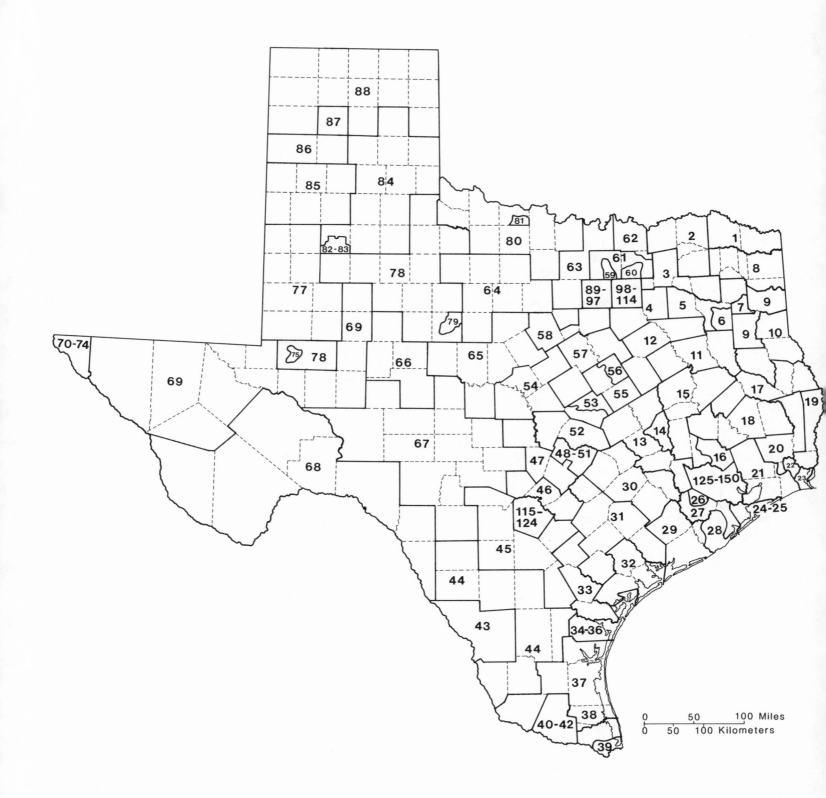

TEXAS STATE HOUSE OF REPRESENTATIVES DISTRICTS

© 1988 University of Oklahoma Press

61. TEXAS STATE HOUSE OF REPRESENTATIVES DISTRICTS

FROM THE INAUGURATION OF STATEHOOD, Texas constitutions provided for a two-house legislature. The House of Representatives has varied in authorized membership from a minimum of 45 to a maximum of 150. In the Constitution of 1845, districts were established for 66 members initially, but with a provision that the legislature could reapportion after each federal decennial census for no less than 45 or more than 90 members. After the Civil War, when Texas was readmitted to the Union, the Reconstruction Constitution of 1869 set the membership at 90.

The Convention of 1875, which drew up the current state constitution, provided for 93 members in the lower house serving two-year terms. Additional members could be added as the population increased, with a maximum number of 150 representatives. That maximum was reached in 1921.

Each constitution is a reflection of the times during which it is drafted. During the post-Reconstruction period, Texans reacted against the concept of stronger state government, as practiced under the Constitution of 1869, by desiring more local representation. If a single county had sufficient population, it could elect a house representative all its own. Counties too small for single representation could be consolidated to meet the population ratio for representation. Apportionment of more than one representative for a county was authorized if sufficient population warranted. A constitutional amendment approved by state voters in 1936 limited any one county, regardless of population, to a maximum of seven representatives.

After reapportionment in 1921, the legislature did not repeat the process until 1951 even though the constitution required the act be done every ten years. Redistricting came about in 1951, but only after Article III, Section 28, was ratified by Texas voters in November, 1948. The law, effective January 1, 1951, provided for a Legislative Redistricting Board in the event the legislature failed to reapportion its senatorial and representative districts after the publication of each U.S. census. Five members made up that board: the lieutenant governor, the speaker of the house, the attorney general, the comptroller of public accounts, and the commissioner of the General Land Office. The Legislative Redistricting Board was required by law to convene within ninety days after the regular session of the legislature adjourned and to complete its work within sixty days after assembling. If necessary, the state supreme court could compel the commission to perform its duties. Quite possibly, the threat of having the board do their work spurred the legislators to take action in 1951 and 1961.

Reapportionment cases decided by the U.S. Supreme Court in the 1960s, beginning with the *Baker* vs. *Carr* decision in 1962, affected political boundary making across the nation with the establishment of the one man–one vote doctrine. The Texas legislature redrew house boundaries in 1965 and again in 1967.

The first use of the Legislative Redistricting Board occurred in 1971 when the legislature reapportioned the house, and the state supreme court declared the plan unconstitutional. The board's plan created new single-member and multimember districts. In a multimember district candidates ran for places and voters in the entire district had one vote in each place. A majority that elected one person could possibly vote into office all candidates for places in that district of a particular ideology, thus giving a small group of voters considerable clout without regard to divergent interests in an urban community. When lawsuits challenged the board's action, a three-judge federal panel ruled that the plan violated the one man–one vote rule. The panel ordered the legislature to try again. Instead, the state appealed the case to the U.S. Supreme Court, which in 1973 supported the panel on the unconstitutionality of the multimember districts because of minority discrimination. The 1975 legislature provided for single-member districts in order to conform with federal law.

In 1981, when the legislature redistricted the state house, Republican legislators and minority groups challenged the plan in court. The state supreme court ruled against the redistricting act, which meant the Legislative Redistricting Board had to convene. The U.S. Department of Justice rejected the board's work. Under the federal Voting Rights Act, the Justice Department reviews revisions to political boundaries in certain states. A three-judge federal panel took up the issue and in 1982 drew district boundaries which the 1983 session of the legislature accepted with some modifications. The Justice Department subsequently approved the revised legislative plan.

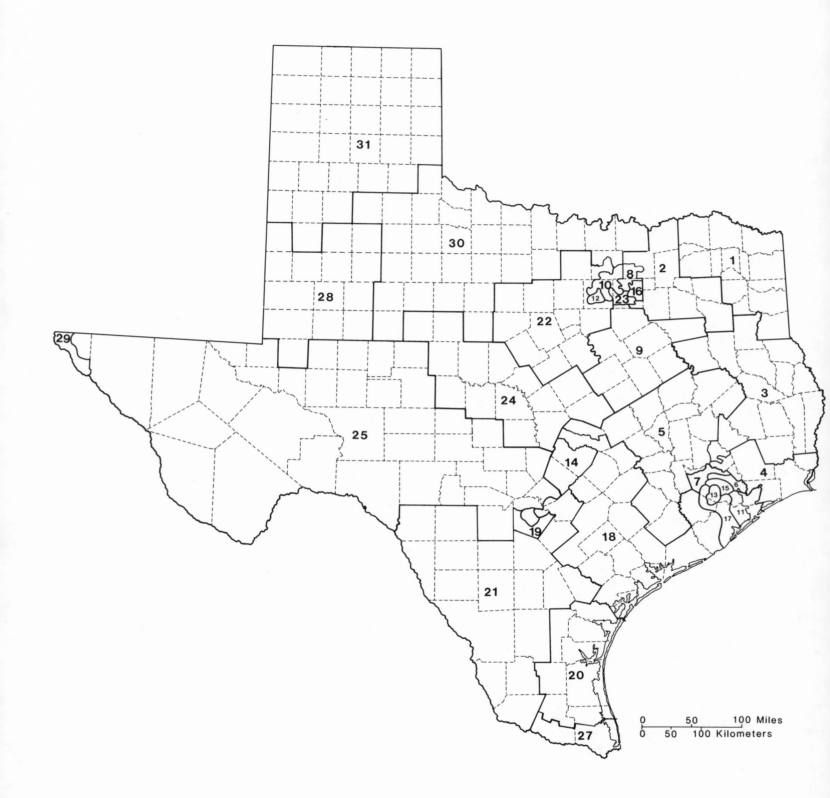

TEXAS STATE SENATE DISTRICTS

© 1988 University of Oklahoma Press

62. TEXAS STATE SENATE DISTRICTS

THE UPPER HOUSE of the Texas legislature, as provided by the Constitution of 1845, began with twenty members in specified districts for a four-year term. At the time of the first federal census after Texas statehood, 1850, the legislature could reapportion to have no fewer than nineteen or more than thirty-three districts. The Constitution of 1869 set the senate membership at thirty, with a six-year term. The present state charter, drafted in 1875 and effective since 1876, specified membership of the senate to be thirty-one with four-year terms each. Alternate rotation mandated in all the Texas constitutions provided for overlapping term expirations for the sake of continuity in the state senate.

The Constitution of 1876 specified the procedure for creating senatorial districts. Contiguous territories would be formed into districts "according to the number of qualified electors." During the first six decades of the twentieth century the term "qualified voters" was interpreted as persons who had paid a poll tax. A considerable variance existed in some districts between population and qualified voters. After the abolition in the 1960s of the poll tax as a requirement for voting, entities involved in senatorial redistricting relied on a formula mixing registered voters and total population.

Another restriction on districting included in the 1876 plan of government was the limitation of no more than one senator for a county. As the Texas population increased, some counties had their representation in the upper house greatly out of proportion to counties in rural areas.

Even though political redistricting was required by the state constitution after the publication of each U.S. census, the legislature sometimes failed to perform this responsibility. The senate redrew its boundaries in 1881, 1892, 1901, and 1921. No reapportionment was made between 1921 and 1951. Section 28 of Article III, adopted by the voters of Texas in 1948 to be in effect in 1951, provided for a Legislative Redistricting Board should the legislature fail to do its duty in the regular session after publication of census information. The law sets the membership of the board as the lieutenant governor, the speaker of the state House of Representatives, the attorney general, the comptroller of public accounts, and the commissioner of the General Land Office.

The senate redistricted itself in 1951 and 1961. In 1965 the lawmakers performed the task again to conform to recent U.S. Supreme Court decisions setting forth the one man–one vote rule first issued in *Baker* vs. *Carr* (1962). At that time the basis for determining constituencies shifted from "qualified electors" to total population in a district. The state restriction of no more than one senator for each county was changed.

When the senate failed to reapportion itself in 1971, the Legislative Redistricting Board performed the work, which soon met challenge in the courts. A three-judge federal court decided in favor of the board's plan. The U.S. Supreme Court upheld the lower court's ruling.

In 1981 the legislature approved a senate redistricting bill, but the governor vetoed the measure. The redistricting board drafted a plan of its own, which soon faced a court challenge. A three-judge federal panel redrew some senatorial district boundaries in early 1982. In 1983 the state legislature approved the federal court's plan with some modifications, and the new governor signed the bill. Immediately the Texas Republican party and several minority groups challenged the legislative act in court. In December, 1983, the panel of three federal judges approved the plan adopted by the legislature, thus establishing boundaries for Texas senate districts until 1991, barring intervening successful legal challenges.

Panhandle

South Plains   Nortex   Texoma   Ark-Tex

West Central Texas   North Central Texas

Permian   East Texas

Basin

Heart of Texas

Concho Valley   Central Texas   Deep East Texas

Brazos

West Texas   Valley

Capital Area

Middle Rio Grande Valley   Houston-Galveston   South East Texas

Alamo Area

Golden

Crescent

South Texas   Coastal Bend

Lower Rio Grande Valley

REGIONAL COUNCILS IN TEXAS

© 1988 University of Oklahoma Press

63. REGIONAL COUNCILS IN TEXAS

MOST LOCAL GOVERNMENTS have common problems such as transportation, aging needs, solid-waste disposal, water quality, and crime control that are not limited in their extent and impact to just a city or county. Recognizing the need for area planning to address these problems, the Fifty-ninth Texas Legislature in 1965 authorized the creation of regional councils. Two-thirds of the board membership in each council must be elected officials. An executive director is the chief administrator over each, and policy is set by a general board which meets semiannually. An executive committee of the board meets monthly.

Although the term "regional council" is generic for such a voluntary association of governments, the name most commonly used is "Council of Governments." Other names are "Planning Commission," "Development Council," "Planning Council," "Area Council," and "Association of Governments." Planning-region boundaries are set by the governor of Texas and are subject to review and adjustment at the end of each state biennium. Since the creation of the North Central Texas Council of Governments in 1966, an additional twenty-three regional councils have been recognized. The map on the facing page shows the location of planning districts as of 1988.

Regional-council membership is made up of city and county governments, school districts, soil and water conservation districts, and other special districts. Funding is provided by annual dues based on the type of political entity and population statistics, state funds, state-administered federal grants, and assistance fees for particular services rendered to local governments. As of January, 1982, 237 of the 254 Texas counties were associated with a regional council, and the total membership comprised 1,709 government entities, 237 counties, 906 cities, 270 school districts, 232 special districts, and 64 others.

The purpose of each regional council is to meet specific local needs through planning for the development of the area, coordination of programs to avoid duplications and to promote efficiency, reviewing and commenting on applications for federal financial assistance, service, and training. Major programs of current importance relate to technical assistance, review and comment, comprehensive planning, health, aging, alcoholism, criminal justice, economic development, manpower, planning and training, transportation, and areawide waste-treatment.

Population figures for the state of Texas are listed below, beginning with the federal census of 1850, the first such census taken after the admission of Texas into the Union.

Population of Texas, 1850–1980

Year	Population	Year	Population
1850	212,592	1920	4,663,228
1860	604,215	1930	5,824,715
1870	818,579	1940	6,414,824
1880	1,591,749	1950	7,711,194
1890	2,235,527	1960	9,579,677
1900	3,048,710	1970	11,198,655
1910	3,896,542	1980	14,229,191

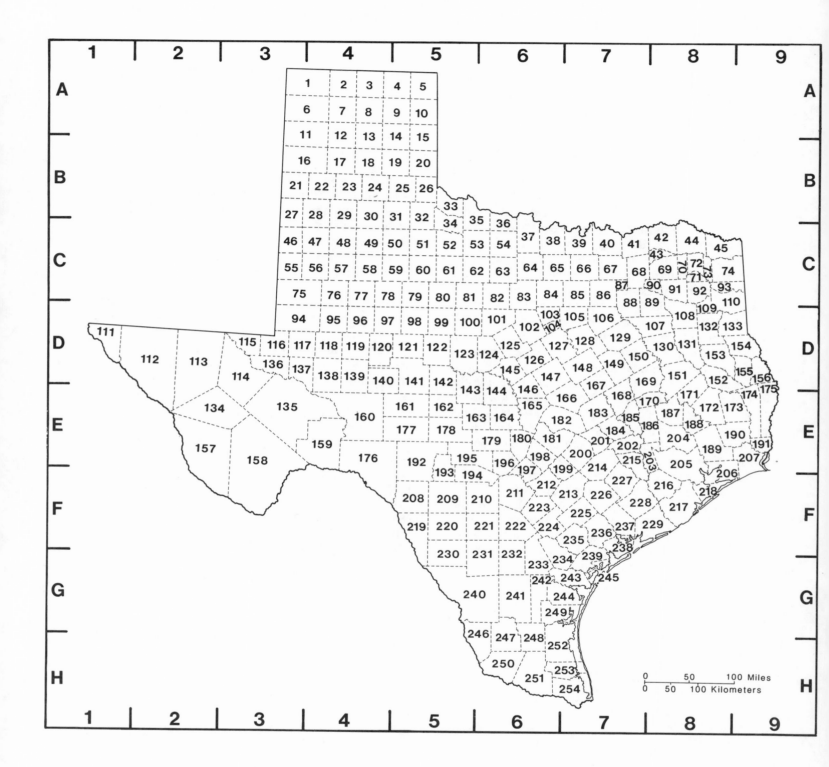

MODERN TEXAS

© 1988 University of Oklahoma Press

64. MODERN TEXAS

THE 1980 FEDERAL CENSUS REPORT indicated that a total of 14,229,191 people resided in Texas. The major concentrations occurred in the Upper Gulf Coast, Coastal Bend, and Lower Rio Grande Valley regions, Central Texas along Interstate Highway I-35, and particular counties of West Texas. Of the 254 counties in the state, only eleven had population counts exceeding 200,000. Those counties were Bexar, Cameron, Dallas, El Paso, Harris, Hidalgo, Jefferson, Lubbock, Nueces, Tarrant, and Travis. The state's population increased approximately 27 percent during the 1970s. For the larger period 1950–80, the gain exceeded 84 percent. In addition to the increase of births over deaths, Texas received an inflow of residents from the "frostbelt," as the northern and midwestern states were sometimes referred to, from neighboring states, and from south of the Rio Grande. A national trend developed whereby the "sunbelt" states, including Texas, attracted the relocation of industries and corporate offices that relied on local as well as introduced employees for a labor force. Federal defense installations and defense-related industries attracted new residents, also.

The economy of Texas has been enhanced over the decades through the development of local industry, the petroleum-chemical industry, educational institutions, state and federal agencies, small business, finance and insurance companies, improved transportation facilities, improved agricultural production, and agriculture-related industry. In addition to the continuing contributions of these endeavors, an advent in the 1980s of high-technology research and manufacturing favorably affected the economic scene in Texas.

Food and fiber production for in-state consumption and for export has been a major emphasis of the state's farms and ranches. Since World War II significant trends have developed in Texas agriculture. The main cultivation of cotton shifted from East Texas to the irrigated fields of West Texas, while the majority numbers of cattle on farms and ranches moved to the eastern part of the state. In addition to cattle raising in East Texas, other uses of the land are tree farming, poultry production, peanut growing, and dairying. Rice is grown commercially in the upper Gulf Coast area. In the Coastal Bend, Lower Rio Grande Valley, and South Texas regions, the primary agricultural pursuits, in addition to cattle raising, are cotton, grain sorghum, citrus fruit, and vegetable crops. Farms in the Blackland and Grand prairies and Cross Timbers produce cotton, wheat, grain sorghum, fruit, peanuts, and vegetables, in addition to raising beef and dairy cattle. Horse raising is becoming a major activity in the northern counties of the Central Texas prairies.

Cattle, sheep, and goats provide most of the farm income in West Texas's Edward Plateau. Only a small portion of the Basins and Ranges country is used for the agrarian purposes other than livestock raising. Notable exceptions are the irrigated lands around Presidio and Pecos, where cotton, grain sorghum, and vegetables are grown. On the Lower, or Rolling, Plains the cultivation of cotton, grain sorghum, and wheat are the major farm pursuits in addition to livestock ranching.

After World War II the extensive use of irrigation, agricultural chemicals, improved and hybrid seed, and transportation improvements transformed the High Plains into a major producing region for cotton, grain sorghum, wheat, and corn. What had been far-flung cattle ranches became highly productive farms. High Plains ranchers graze cattle on land unsuited to the cultivation of crops and on wheat pastures, but the greatest number by far are in the feedlots of the Texas Panhandle. Beginning in the 1950s huge feedlots began operations to finish cattle for slaughter near the centers of grain production.

As agriculture around the state became less labor-intensive with the widespread use of machines and chemicals, suitable labor became increasingly difficult to find because of better-paying jobs in urban areas. Which came first — a decreased labor supply or mechanization — is an open question. The number of farms decreased as the average acreage of farms increased. People left rural communities to seek more lucrative employment in urban areas. Land around developing cities became sites for housing subdivisions, roads, shopping centers, and industrial plants and no longer produced food and fiber for a rapidly expanding population. Improved seedstock of plants and animals and increased production on existing acreages, however, more than kept pace with the demand for Texas agricultural products.

Economic opportunities and a favorable climate contributed to the making of modern Texas. The continuing production of Texas farms and ranches, an expanding economic base of business and industry, a healthy financial status, an acute cultural awareness, and an increasing population all tend to make Texas a unique place in contemporary America.

Texas has 254 counties. The following alphabetical

listing, when used with the corresponding blocks of vertical numbers and horizontal letters, will aid in the location of particular counties:

No.	County	Location	County Seat	Population (1985 estimated)
130	Anderson	D–8	Palestine	46,400
94	Andrews	D–4	Andrews	16,500
152	Angelina	D–8	Lufkin	68,900
245	Aransas	G–7	Rockport	17,500
54	Archer	C–6	Archer City	7,900
18	Armstrong	B–4	Claude	1,900
222	Atascosa	F–6	Jourdanton	28,500
215	Austin	E–7	Bellville	20,800
27	Bailey	C–3	Muleshoe	8,300
194	Bandera	F–5	Bandera	8,900
200	Bastrop	E–7	Bastrop	25,000
53	Baylor	C–5	Seymour	4,900
234	Bee	G–6	Beeville	27,300
166	Bell	E–6	Belton	170,000
211	Bexar	F–6	San Antonio	1,134,900
180	Blanco	E–6	Johnson City	5,300
77	Borden	C–4	Gail	1,000
127	Bosque	D–6	Meridian	14,200
45	Bowie	C–8	Boston	80,500
217	Brazoria	F–8	Angleton	188,200
185	Brazos	E–7	Bryan	119,500
158	Brewster	E–3	Alpine	8,100
24	Briscoe	B–4	Silverton	2,300
248	Brooks	G–6	Falfurrias	9,300
124	Brown	D-6	Brownwood	35,100
184	Burleson	E–7	Caldwell	15,000
165	Burnet	E–6	Burnet	22,900
199	Caldwell	E–6	Lockhart	27,400
238	Calhoun	F–7	Port Lavaca	21,700
100	Callahan	D–5	Baird	12,600
254	Cameron	H–7	Brownsville	249,800
71	Camp	C–8	Pittsburg	10,000
13	Carson	B–4	Panhandle	6,900
74	Cass	C–8	Linden	30,600
22	Castro	B–4	Dimmitt	10,300
206	Chambers	F–8	Anahuac	19,400
131	Cherokee	D–8	Rusk	39,800
26	Childress	B–5	Childress	6,500
37	Clay	C–6	Henrietta	9.700
46	Cochran	C–3	Morton	4,600
121	Coke	D–5	Robert Lee	3,600
123	Coleman	D–5	Coleman	10,600
67	Collin	C–7	McKinney	196,900
20	Collingsworth	B–5	Wellington	4,100
227	Colorado	F–7	Columbus	20,100
197	Comal	F–6	New Braunfels	46,200
125	Comanche	D–6	Comanche	12,900
142	Concho	D–5	Paint Rock	2,800
39	Cooke	C–7	Gainesville	29,000
147	Coryell	D–6	Gatesville	57,200
32	Cottle	C–5	Paducah	2,700
137	Crane	D–4	Crane	5,200
160	Crockett	E–4	Ozona	4,700

No.	County	Location	County Seat	Population (1985 estimated)
49	Crosby	C–4	Crosbyton	8,400
113	Culberson	D–2	Van Horn	3,500
1	Dallam	A–3	Dalhart	6,600
86	Dallas	C–7	Dallas	1,781,700
76	Dawson	D–4	Lamesa	16,200
16	Deaf Smith	B–3	Hereford	20,400
43	Delta	C–8	Cooper	4,800
66	Denton	C–7	Denton	189,700
225	DeWitt	F–7	Cuero	20,200
50	Dickens	C–5	Dickens	3,100
230	Dimmitt	G–5	Carrizo Springs	11,900
19	Donley	B–5	Clarendon	4,100
241	Duval	G–6	San Diego	13,300
101	Eastland	D–6	Eastland	20,700
117	Ector	D–3	Odessa	134,700
192	Edwards	E–5	Rocksprings	2,100
106	Ellis	D–7	Waxahachie	73,300
111	El Paso	D–1	El Paso	545,000
102	Erath	D–6	Stephenville	25,000
167	Falls	D–7	Marlin	18,200
41	Fannin	C–7	Bonham	24,600
214	Fayette	E–7	La Grange	20,200
79	Fisher	C–5	Roby	5,600
30	Floyd	C–4	Floydada	9,100
34	Foard	C–5	Crowell	1,800
216	Fort Bend	F–8	Richmond	188,200
70	Franklin	C–8	Mount Vernon	7,200
150	Freestone	D–7	Fairfield	17,100
221	Frio	F–5	Pearsall	14,200
75	Gaines	C–3	Seminole	14,300
218	Galveston	F–8	Galveston	213,400
58	Garza	C–4	Post	5,500
179	Gillespie	E–6	Fredericksburg	15,000
119	Glasscock	D–4	Garden City	1,200
235	Goliad	F–6	Goliad	5,600
213	Gonzales	F–6	Gonzales	18,800
14	Gray	B–5	Pampa	27,100
40	Grayson	C–7	Sherman	96,700
109	Gregg	D–8	Longview	112,300
186	Grimes	E–7	Anderson	18,000
212	Guadalupe	F–6	Seguin	54,600
29	Hale	C–4	Plainview	37,500
25	Hall	B–5	Memphis	4,800
126	Hamilton	D–6	Hamilton	8,100
3	Hansford	A–4	Spearman	6,500
33	Hardeman	B–5	Quanah	6,400
190	Hardin	E–8	Kountze	43,400
205	Harris	E–8	Houston	2,794,700
110	Harrison	C–8	Marshall	57,900
6	Hartley	A–3	Channing	3,500
61	Haskell	C–5	Haskell	7,300
198	Hays	E–6	San Marcos	56,000
10	Hemphill	A–5	Canadian	5,500
107	Henderson	D–7	Athens	52,100
251	Hidalgo	H–6	Edinburg	352,200
128	Hill	D–7	Hillsboro	27,400
47	Hockley	C–4	Levelland	25,400

No.	County	Location	County Seat	Population (1985 estimated)
103	Hood	D–6	Granbury	25,600
69	Hopkins	C–8	Sulphur Springs	28,700
151	Houston	D–8	Crockett	22,700
96	Howard	D–4	Big Spring	36,300
112	Hudspeth	D–2	Sierra Blanca	2,600
68	Hunt	C–7	Greenville	65,200
8	Hutchinson	A–4	Stinnett	28,100
140	Irion	D–4	Mertzon	2,000
64	Jack	C–6	Jacksboro	7,700
237	Jackson	F–7	Edna	13,600
174	Jasper	E–9	Jasper	32,400
134	Jeff Davis	E–2	Fort Davis	1,700
207	Jefferson	E–9	Beaumont	254,700
247	Jim Hogg	H–6	Hebbronville	5,400
242	Jim Wells	G–6	Alice	40,300
105	Johnson	D–7	Cleburne	87,700
80	Jones	C–5	Anson	18,200
224	Karnes	F–6	Karnes City	13,400
88	Kaufman	D–7	Kaufman	49,300
196	Kendall	E–6	Boerne	14,000
252	Kenedy	H–6	Sarita	600
59	Kent	C–5	Jayton	1,300
195	Kerr	E–5	Kerrville	34,600
178	Kimble	E–6	Junction	4,300
51	King	C–5	Guthrie	400
208	Kinney	F–5	Brackettville	2,500
249	Kleberg	G–6	Kingsville	34,500
52	Knox	C–5	Benjamin	5,600
42	Lamar	C–8	Paris	44,700
28	Lamb	B–4	Littlefield	17,700
146	Lampasas	D–6	Lampasas	13,600
231	La Salle	G–6	Cotulla	5,800
226	Lavaca	F–7	Hallettsville	18,500
201	Lee	E–7	Giddings	13,200
169	Leon	D–7	Centerville	12,600
189	Liberty	E–8	Liberty	54,500
149	Limestone	D–7	Groesbeck	21,300
5	Lipscomb	A–5	Lipscomb	4,000
233	Live Oak	G–6	George West	9,500
164	Llano	E–6	Llano	12,100
115	Loving	D–3	Mentone	100
48	Lubbock	C–4	Lubbock	222,800
57	Lynn	C–4	Tahoka	7,800
143	McCulloch	E–5	Brady	9,000
148	McLennan	D–7	Waco	184,100
232	McMullen	G–6	Tilden	1,000
170	Madison	E–7	Madisonville	12,200
93	Marion	C–8	Jefferson	10,200
95	Martin	D–4	Stanton	5,300
163	Mason	E–5	Mason	3,600
229	Matagorda	F–7	Bay City	40,200
219	Maverick	F–5	Eagle Pass	34,200
210	Medina	F–5	Hondo	25,100
162	Menard	E–5	Menard	2,300
118	Midland	D–4	Midland	109,200
183	Milam	E–7	Cameron	23,700
145	Mills	D–6	Goldthwaite	4,500

No.	County	Location	County Seat	Population (1985 estimated)
97	Mitchell	D–4	Colorado City	9,000
38	Montague	C–6	Montague	18,500
204	Montgomery	E–8	Conroe	160,700
7	Moore	A–4	Dumas	17,400
73	Morris	C–8	Daingerfield	14,700
31	Motley	C–4	Matador	1,800
153	Nacogdoches	D–8	Nacogdoches	49,800
129	Navarro	D–7	Corsicana	39,100
175	Newton	E–9	Newton	13,400
98	Nolan	D–5	Sweetwater	17,600
244	Nueces	G–6	Corpus Christi	297,000
4	Ochiltree	A–5	Perryton	11,000
11	Oldham	B–3	Vega	2,300
191	Orange	E–9	Orange	83,200
83	Palo Pinto	C–6	Palo Pinto	26,300
133	Panola	D–8	Carthage	22,000
84	Parker	C–6	Weatherford	56,200
21	Parmer	B–4	Farwell	10,900
135	Pecos	E–3	Fort Stockton	17,300
172	Polk	E–8	Livingston	30,000
12	Potter	B–4	Amarillo	107,200
157	Presidio	E–2	Marfa	5,500
90	Rains	C–8	Emory	5,900
17	Randall	B–4	Canyon	85,600
139	Reagan	D–4	Big Lake	5,000
193	Real	E–5	Leakey	2,700
44	Red River	C–8	Clarksville	15,500
114	Reeves	D–3	Pecos	16,100
239	Refugio	F–7	Refugio	8,700
9	Roberts	A–5	Miami	1,000
168	Robertson	E–7	Franklin	15,900
87	Rockwall	C–7	Rockwall	20,800
122	Runnels	D–5	Ballinger	12,500
132	Rusk	D–8	Henderson	43,200
156	Sabine	D–9	Hemphill	9,800
155	San Augustine	D–9	San Augustine	8,800
188	San Jacinto	E–8	Coldspring	14,000
243	San Patricio	G–6	Sinton	61,800
144	San Saba	E–5	San Saba	5,700
161	Schleicher	E–5	Eldorado	3,200
78	Scurry	C–4	Snyder	19,800
81	Shackelford	C–5	Albany	4,000
154	Shelby	D–8	Center	23,900
2	Sherman	A–4	Stratford	3,100
108	Smith	D–8	Tyler	150,000
104	Somervell	D–6	Glen Rose	4,600
250	Starr	H–6	Rio Grande City	34,500
82	Stephens	C–6	Breckenridge	10,400
120	Sterling	D–4	Sterling City	1,600
60	Stonewall	C–5	Aspermont	2,500
177	Sutton	E–4	Sonora	5,400
23	Swisher	B–4	Tulia	8,800
85	Tarrant	C–6	Fort Worth	1,056,000
99	Taylor	D–5	Abilene	122,200
159	Terrell	E–4	Sanderson	1,500
56	Terry	C–4	Brownfield	15,400
62	Throckmorton	C–5	Throckmorton	2,300

No.	County	Location	County Seat	Population (1985 estimated)	No.	County	Location	County Seat	Population (1985 estimated)
72	Titus	C–8	Mount Pleasant	23,000	240	Webb	G–5	Laredo	118,100
141	Tom Green	E–5	San Angelo	96,700	228	Wharton	F–7	Wharton	41,500
181	Travis	E–6	Austin	533,200	15	Wheeler	B–5	Wheeler	7,300
171	Trinity	E–8	Groveton	11,800	36	Wichita	C–6	Wichita Falls	125,600
173	Tyler	E–8	Woodville	18,600	35	Wilbarger	C–5	Vernon	17,000
92	Upshur	C–8	Gilmer	32,700	253	Willacy	H–7	Raymondville	18,800
138	Upton	D–4	Rankin	5,600	182	Williamson	E–6	Georgetown	106,300
209	Uvalde	F–5	Uvalde	24,700	223	Wilson	F–6	Floresville	18,900
176	Val Verde	E–4	Del Rio	39,400	116	Winkler	D–3	Kermit	10,800
89	Van Zandt	D–7	Canton	37,300	65	Wise	C–6	Decatur	32,000
236	Victoria	F–7	Victoria	75,500	91	Wood	C–8	Quitman	28,200
187	Walker	E–8	Huntsville	51,700	55	Yoakum	C–3	Plains	9,600
203	Waller	E–7	Hempstead	23,500	63	Young	C–6	Graham	19,400
136	Ward	D–3	Monahans	15,900	246	Zapata	H–6	Zapata	8,500
202	Washington	E–7	Brenham	25,500	220	Zavala	F–5	Crystal City	12,000

REFERENCES

Map 1. Location Within the United States and in Relation to Mexico

Jordan, Terry G.; John L. Bean; and William M. Holmes. *Texas: A Geography.* Boulder: Westview Press, 1984.

Scott, Elton M. *Texas Today: A Geography.* Norman: Harlow Publishing Corp., 1963.

Texas Almanac and State Industrial Guide, 1970–1971. Dallas: A. H. Belo Corp., 1969.

U.S. News & World Report, December 16, 1963, p. 70.

Map 2. Longitude and Latitude

Kingston, Michael T. ed. *Texas Almanac and State Industrial Guide, 1984–1985.* Dallas: A. H. Belo Corp., 1983.

Scott, Elton M. *Texas Today: A Geography.* Norman, Okla.: Harlow Publishing Corp., 1963.

Wallace, Ernest, and David M. Vigness. *Documents of Texas History.* Austin: Steck Company, 1963.

Map 3. Geologic Age of Surface Materials

Renfro, H. B.; Dan E. Feray; and Philip B. King. *Geological Highway Map of Texas.* Tulsa: American Association of Petroleum Geologists, [ca. 1978].

Sellars, E. H.; W. S. Adkins; and F. B. Plummer. *The Geology of Texas.* Bulletin no. 3232. Austin: University of Texas, 1932.

Map 4. Physiographic Regions

Jordan, Terry G.; John L. Bean; and William M. Holmes. *Texas: A Geography.* Boulder: Westview Press, 1984.

Scott, Elton M. *Texas Today: A Geography.* Norman, Okla.: Harlow Publishing Corp., 1963.

U.S. Study Commission—Texas. *The Report of the U.S. Study Commission—Texas.* Austin: United States Study Commission on the Neches, Trinity, Brazos, Colorado, Guadalupe, San Antonio, Nueces, and San Jacinto River Basins and Intervening Areas, 1962. Part 2: Resources and Problems, Chapter 6.

Webb, Walter Prescott. *The Great Plains.* Boston: Ginn and Company, 1931.

Map 5. Precipitation

Bomar, George W. *Texas Weather.* Austin: University of Texas Press, 1983.

Griffiths, John F., and Robert Orton. *Agroclimatic Atlas of Texas.* Bulletin MP-888. College Station: Texas A&M University, Texas Agricultural Experiment Station, 1968.

Jordan, Terry G.; John L. Bean; and William M. Holmes. *Texas: A Geography.* Boulder: Westview Press, 1984.

Kingston, Michael T. ed. *The Texas Almanac and State Industrial Guide, 1984–1985.* Dallas: A. H. Belo Corp., 1983.

Larkin, Thomas J., and George W. Bomar. *Climatic Atlas of Texas.* No. LP-192. Austin: Texas Department of Water Resources, 1983.

Orton, Robert B. *Climates of the States: Texas.* Climatography of the United States, no. 60-41. Washington, D.C.: U.S. Department of Commerce, 1960; revised and reprinted, 1969.

U.S. Study Commission—Texas. *The Report of the U.S. Study Commission—Texas.* Austin: United States Study Commission on the Neches, Trinity, Brazos, Colorado, Guadalupe, San Antonio, Nueces, and San Jacinto River Basins and Intervening Areas, 1962. Part 2, Resources and Problems, plate 3.

Visher, Stephen Sargent. *Climatic Atlas of the United States.* Cambridge Mass.: Harvard University Press, 1954.

Map 6. Native Plant-Life Regions

Carter, W. T. *Soils of Texas.* Bulletin 431. College Station: Agricultural and Mechanical College of Texas, Texas Agricultural Experiment Station, 1931. Modification of map by William M. Holmes.

Cory, V. L., and H. B. Parks. *Catalogue of the Flora of Texas.* Bulletin 550. College Station: Agricultural and Mechanical College of Texas, Texas Agricultural Experiment Station, 1937.

Gould, F. W. *Texas Grasses, a Preliminary Checklist.* Bulletin MP-240. College Station: Agricultural and Mechanical College of Texas, Texas Agricultural Experiment Station, 1957.

———. *Texas Plants: A Checklist and Ecological Summary.* Bulletin MP-585. College Station: Agricultural and Mechanical College of Texas, Texas Agricultural Experiment Station, 1962.

Parks, H. B., and V. L. Cory. *Biological Survey of the East Texas Big Thicket Area.* College Station: Agricultural and Mechanical College of Texas, Texas Agricultural Experiment Station, 1936.

Tharp, Benjamin C. *Structure of Texas Vegetation East of the 98th Meridian.* Bulletin 2606. Austin: University of Texas, 1926.

———. *Texas Range Grasses.* Austin: University of Texas Press, 1952.

Winkler, C. H. *The Botany of Texas.* Bulletin 18. Austin: University of Texas, 1915.

Map 7. Texas Indians

Mayhall, Mildred P. *The Kiowas.* Norman: University of Oklahoma Press, 1962.

Morfi, Fray Juan Agustín. *History of Texas, 1673–1779.* Translated and edited by Carlos Eduardo Castañeda. Albuquerque: Quivira Society, 1935. Map in part 2, p. 426.

Newcomb, W. W., Jr. *The Indians of Texas.* Austin: University of Texas Press, 1961.

Wallace, Ernest, and E. Adamson Hoebel. *The Comanches: Lords of the South Plains.* Norman: University of Oklahoma Press, 1952.

Webb, Walter Prescott. *The Great Plains.* Boston: Ginn and Company, 1931.

Map 8. Cabeza de Vaca

Bancroft, Hubert Howe. *History of the North Mexican States and Texas.* 2 vols. San Francisco: A. L. Bancroft and Company, 1884.

Bandelier, Fanny, trans. *The Journey of |Alvar Núñez Cabeza de Vaca and His Companions from Florida to the Pacific, 1528–1536.* Edited by Ad. F. Bandelier. New York: Allerton Book Company, 1922.

Baskett, James Newton. "A Study of the Route of Cabeza de Vaca," *Quarterly of the Texas State Historical Association* 10, no. 3 (January, 1907): 246–79; 10, no. 4 (April, 1907): 308–40.

Bishop, Morris. *The Odyssey of Cabeza de Vaca.* New York: Century Company, 1933.

Bolton, Herbert Eugene. *Coronado: Knight of Pueblos and Plains.* Albuquerque: University of New Mexico Press, 1949.

Castañeda, Carlos E. *Our Catholic Heritage in Texas, 1519–1936.* Vol. 1, *The Mission Era: The Finding of Texas, 1519–1693.* Austin: Von Boeckmann–Jones Company, 1936; reprinted, New York: Arno Press, 1976.

Chipman, Donald E. "In Search of Cabeza de Vaca's Route across Texas: An Histographical Survey," *Southwestern Historical Quarterly,* 91, no. 2 (October, 1987): 127–48.

Coopwood, Bethel. "Route of Cabeza de Vaca," *Quarterly of the Texas State Historical Association* 3, no. 2 (October, 1899): 108–40; 3, no. 3 (January, 1900): 177–208.

Davenport, Harbert, and Joseph K. Wells. "First Europeans in Texas, 1528–36," *Southwestern Historical Quarterly,* 22, no. 2 (October, 1918): 111–42; 22, no. 3 (January, 1919): 205–59.

Hallenbeck, Cleve. *Alvar Núñez Cabeza de Vaca: The Journey and Route of the First Europeans to Cross the Continent of North America, 1534–1535.* Glendale, Calif.: Arthur H. Clark Company, 1940.

Ponton, Brownie, and Bates H. McFarland, "Alvar Núñez Cabeza de Vaca: A Preliminary Report of His Wanderings in Texas," *Quarterly of the Texas State Historical Association* 1, no. 3 (January, 1898): 166–86.

Map 9. The Coronado Expedition

Bolton, Herbert Eugene. *Coronado: Knight of Pueblos and Plains.* Albuquerque: University of New Mexico Press, 1949.

Castañeda, Carlos E. *Our Catholic Heritage in Texas, 1519–1936.* Vol. 1, *The Mission Era: The Finding of Texas, 1519–1693.* Austin: Von Boeckmann–Jones Company, 1936.

Castañeda, Pedro. *The Journey of Coronado.* Ann Arbor, Mich.: University Microfilms, 1966.

Donoghue, David. "The Route of the Coronado Expedition in Texas," *Southwestern Historical Quarterly* 32, no. 3 (January, 1929): 180–92.

Williams, J. W. "Coronado—From the Rio Grande to the Concho," *Southwestern Historical Quarterly,* 43, no. 2 (October, 1959): 190–220.

Winship, George Parker, trans. and ed. *The Journey of Coronado, 1540–1542.* New York: Allerton Book Company, 1922.

Map 10. The De Soto–Moscoso Expedition

Bolton, Herbert E. *Coronado: Knight of Pueblos and Plains.* Albuquerque: University of New Mexico Press, 1949.

———. *Spanish Borderlands: A Chronicle of Old Florida and the Southwest.* New Haven: Yale University Press, 1921.

Bourne, Edward Gaylord, ed. *Narratives of the Career of Hernando de Soto.* Vol. 1. Translated by Buckingham Smith. New York: Allerton Book Company, 1922.

Castañeda, Carlos E. *Our Catholic Heritage of Texas, 1519–1936.* Vol. 1, *The Mission Era: The Finding of Texas, 1519–1693.* Austin: Von Boeckmann–Jones Company, 1936.

Lewis, Theodore H., ed. "The Narrative of the Expedition of Hernando de Soto by the Gentleman of Elvas." *Spanish Explorers in the Southern United States, 1528–1543.* New York: Charles Scribner's Sons, 1925.

Strickland, Rex W. "Moscoso's Journey Through Texas," *Southwestern Historical Quarterly,* 46, no 2. (October, 1942): 109–37.

Williams, J. W. "Moscoso's Trail in Texas," *Southwestern Historical Quarterly* 46, no. 2 (October, 1942): 138–57.

Woldert, Albert, "The Expedition of Luis de Moscoso in Texas in 1542," *Southwestern Historical Quarterly* 46, no. 2 (October, 1942): 158–66.

Map 11. La Salle in Texas

Bolton, Herbert E. *The Location of La Salle's Colony on the Gulf of Mexico.* Houston: Union National Bank, 1929.

Castañeda, Carlos E. *Our Catholic Heritage in Texas, 1519–1936.* Vol. 1, *The Mission Era: The Finding of Texas, 1519–1693.* Austin: Von Boeckmann–Jones Company, 1936.

Cole, E. W. "La Salle in Texas," *Southwestern Historical Quarterly* 49, no. 4 (April, 1946): 473–500.

Dunn, William Edward. *Spanish and French Rivalry in the Gulf Region of the United States, 1678–1702: The Beginnings of Texas and Pensacola.* Bulletin no. 1705. Austin: University of Texas, 1917.

Parkman, Francis. *La Salle and the Discovery of the Great West.* Boston: Little, Brown and Company, 1901.

Weddle, Robert S., ed. *La Salle, the Mississippi, and the Gulf.* College Station: Texas A&M University Press, 1987.

Map 12. Spanish Missions

Bolton, Herbert Eugene. "The Mission as a Frontier Institution in the Spanish-American Colonies," *American Historical Review* 23, no. 1 (October, 1917): 42–61.

_____. *Texas in the Middle Eighteenth Century: Studies in Spanish Colonial History and Administration.* New York: Russell & Russell, 1962; first published in 1915 as Vol. 3 in the University of California Publications in History.

Castañeda, Carlos E. *Our Catholic Heritage in Texas, 1519–1936,* Vol. 2, *The Mission Era: The Winning of Texas, 1693–1731.* Austin: Von Boeckmann–Jones Company, 1936.

_____. *Our Catholic Heritage in Texas, 1519–1936,* Vol. 3, *The Mission Era: The Missions at Work, 1731–1761.* Austin: Von Boeckmann–Jones Company, 1938.

_____. *Our Catholic Heritage in Texas, 1519–1936.* Vol. 4, *The Mission Era: The Passing of the Missions, 1762–1782.* Austin: Von Boeckmann–Jones Company, 1939.

_____. *Our Catholic Heritage in Texas, 1519–1936.* Vol. 5, *The Mission Era: The End of the Spanish Regime, 1780–1810.* Austin: Von Boeckmann–Jones Company, 1942.

Eckhart, George B. "Spanish Missions of Texas, 1680–1800," *The Kiva* 32, no. 3 (February, 1967): 73–95.

Webb, Walter Prescott. *The Great Plains.* Boston: Ginn and Company, 1931.

Weddle, Robert S. *San Juan Bautista: Gateway to Spanish Texas.* Austin: University of Texas Press, 1968.

Map 13. San Antonio de Bexar

Bexar County Historical Commission, *Historical Markers in Bexar County.* San Antonio: Bexar County Historical Commission, 1981. Map.

Bolton, Herbert Eugene. "The Mission as a Frontier Institution in the Spanish-American Colonies," *American Historical Review* 23 no. 1 (October, 1917): 42–61.

_____. *Texas in the Middle Eighteenth Century: Studies in Spanish Colonial History and Administration.* New York: Russell & Russell, 1962; first published in 1915 as Vol. 3 in the University of California Publications in History.

Castañeda, Carlos E. *Our Catholic Heritage in Texas, 1519–1936.* Vol. 2, *The Mission Era: The Winning of Texas, 1693–1731.* Austin: Von Boeckmann–Jones Company, 1936.

_____. *Our Catholic Heritage in Texas, 1519–1936.* Vol. 4, *The Mission Era: The Passing of the Missions, 1762–1782.* Austin: Von Boeckmann–Jones Company, 1939.

_____. *Our Catholic Heritage in Texas, 1519–1936.* Vol. 5, *The Mission Era: The End of the Spanish Regime, 1780–1810.* Austin: Von Boeckmann–Jones Company, 1942.

_____. *Our Catholic Heritage in Texas, 1519–1936.* Vol. 6, *Transition Period: The Fight for Freedom, 1810–1836.* Austin: Von Boeckmann–Jones Company, 1950.

Houston, Andrew Jackson. *Military Maps of the Texas Revolution.* Houston, 1938. Located in the University of North Texas Library.

John, Elizabeth A. H. *Storms Brewed in Other Men's Worlds.* College Station: Texas A&M University Press, 1975.

Map 14. The Philip Nolan Expedition, 1800–1801

Lay, Bennett. *The Lives of Ellis P. Bean.* Austin: University of Texas Press, 1960.

Wilson, Maurine T. "Philip Nolan and His Activities in Texas." Master's thesis, University of Texas, 1932.

Yoakum, Henderson. *History of Texas from Its First Settlement in 1685 to Its Annexation to the United States in 1846.* Vol. 1. New York: Redfield, 1855; facsimile reproduction, Austin: Steck Company, 1935.

Map 15. The Neutral Ground Agreement

Haggard, J. Villasana. "The Neutral Ground Between Louisiana and Texas, 1806–1821," *Louisiana Historical Quarterly* 28, no. 4 (October, 1945): 1001–128.

Yoakum, Henderson. *History of Texas from Its First Settlement in 1685 to Its Annexation to the United States in 1846.* Vol. 1. New York: Redfield, 1855; facsimile reproduction, Austin: Steck Company, 1935.

Map 16. The Zebulon M. Pike Expedition in the Southwest, 1806–1807

Hollon, W. Eugene. *The Lost Pathfinder: Zebulon Montgomery Pike.* Norman: University of Oklahoma Press, 1949.

Jackson, Donald, ed. *The Journals of Zebulon Montgomery Pike with Letters and Related Documents.* 2 vols. Norman: University of Oklahoma Press, 1966.

Paullin, Charles O. *Atlas of the Historical Geography of the United States.* Edited by John K. Wright. Washington, D.C.: Carnegie Institution and American Geographical Society, 1932.

Map 17. The Gutiérrez-Magee Expedition, 1812–1813

Almaréz, Félix D., Jr. *Tragic Cavalier: Governor Manuel Salcedo of Texas, 1808–1813.* Austin: University of Texas Press, 1971.

Garrett, Julia Kathryn. *Green Flag Over Texas: A Story of the Last Years of Spain in Texas.* New York and Dallas: The Cordova Press, 1939.

Hatcher, Mattie Austin. *The Opening of Texas to Foreign Settlement, 1801–1821.* Bulletin no. 2714. Austin: University of Texas, 1927.

Warren, Harris Gaylord. *The Sword Was Their Passport: A History of American Filibustering in the Mexican Revolution.* Baton Rouge: Louisiana State University Press, 1943.

Map 18. Champ d'Asile, 1818

Castañeda, Carlos E. *Our Catholic Heritage in Texas, 1519–1936.* Vol. 6, *Transition Period: The Fight for Freedom, 1810–1836.* Austin: Von Boeckmann–Jones Company, 1950.

Ratchford, Fannie E., ed. *The Story of Champ d' Asile As Told by Two of the Colonists.* Translated by Donald Jackson. Dallas: Book Club of Texas, 1937; facsimile reproduction, Austin: Steck-Vaughn Company, 1969.

Warren, Harris Gaylord. *The Sword Was Their Passport: A History of American Filibustering in the Mexican Revolution.* Baton Rouge: Louisiana State University Press, 1943.

Map 19. Adams-Onís Treaty, 1819

Commager, Henry Steele. *Documents of American History.* 7th ed. Vol. 1. New York: Appleton-Century-Crofts, 1963.

Dangerfield, George. *The Awakening of American Nationalism, 1815–1828.* New York: Harper & Row, 1965.

Marshall, Thomas Maitland. *A History of the Western Boundaries of the Louisiana Purchase, 1819–1841.* Berkeley: University of California Press, 1914.

Paullin, Charles O. *Atlas of the Historical Geography of the United States.* Edited by John K. Wright. Washington, D.C.: Carnegie Institution and American Geographical Society, 1932.

Map 20. The James Long Expeditions, 1819–1822

Hatcher, Mattie Austin. *The Opening of Texas to Foreign Settlement, 1801–1821.* Bulletin no. 2714. Austin: University of Texas, 1927.

Warren, Harris Gaylord. *The Sword Was Their Passport: A History of American Filibustering in the Mexican Revolution.* Baton Rouge: Louisiana State University Press, 1943.

Yoakum, Henderson. *History of Texas from Its First Settlement in 1685 to Its Annexation to the United States in 1846.* Vol. 1. New York: Redfield, 1855; facsimile reproduction, Austin: Steck Company, 1935.

Map 21. Texas as a Part of Mexico in 1824

Castañeda, Carlos E. *Our Catholic Heritage in Texas, 1519–1936.* Vol. 6, *Transition Period: The Fight for Freedom, 1810–1836.* Austin: Von Boeckmann–Jones Company, 1950.

Millares, Jorge Hernandez, and Alejandro Carrillo Escribano. *Atlas Porrua de la Republica Mexicana.* Mexico City: Editorial Porrua, 1966. Modification by William M. Holmes.

Yoakum, Henderson. *History of Texas from its First Settlement in 1685 to Its Annexation to the United States in 1846.* Vol. 1. New York: Redfield, 1855; facsimile reproduction, Austin: Steck Company, 1935.

Map 22. Empresario Grants

Austin, Stephen F., comp. *Map of Texas with Parts of the Adjoining States.* Philadelphia: H. S. Tanner, 1835. Located in the University of Texas at Austin Archives.

Barker, Eugene C. *The Life of Stephen F. Austin, Founder of Texas, 1793–1836.* Nashville and Dallas: Cokesbury Press, 1925.

Freeman, J. D., comp. *[Colonization Grants in Texas].* Austin: Texas General Land Office, 1938. Located in the Texas General Land Office.

Henderson, Mary Virginia. "Minor Empresario Contracts for the Colonization of Texas, 1825–1834," *Southwestern Historical Quarterly* 31, no. 4 (April, 1928): 295–324; 31, no. 1 (July, 1928): 1–28.

Lukes, Edward A. *De Witt Colony of Texas.* Austin: Jenkins Publishing Company, 1976.

McLean, Malcolm D., compil. and ed. *Papers Concerning Robertson's Colony in Texas.* 13 vols. Vols. 1–3, Fort Worth: Texas Christian University Press, 1974–1976. Vols. 4–10, Arlington: University of Texas at Arlington Press, 1977–1987.

Oberste, William H. *Texas Irish Empresarios and Their Colonies.* Austin: Von Boeckmann–Jones Company, 1953.

Rather, Ethel Zively. "De Witt's Colony," *Quarterly of the Texas State Historical Association* 8, no. 2 (October, 1904): 95–192.

Map 23. The Fredonian Republic

Holt, Jordan. "The Edwards Empresarial Grant and the Fredonian Rebellion." Master's thesis, Stephen F. Austin State University, 1977.

Parsons, Edmund Morris. "The Fredonian Rebellion," *Texana* 5, no. 1 (Spring, 1967): 11–52.

Yoakum, Henderson. *History of Texas from Its First Settlement in 1685 to Its Annexation to the United States in 1846.* Vol. 2. New York: Redfield, 1855; facsimile reproduction, Austin: Steck Company, 1935.

Map 24. Texas in 1835

Almonte, Juan N. "Statistical Report of Texas," translated by C. E. Castañeda. *Southwestern Historical Quarterly* 28, no. 3 (January, 1925): 177–222.

Austin, Stephen F., comp. *Map of Texas with Parts of the Adjoining States.* Philadelphia: H. S. Tanner, 1835. Located in the University of Texas at Austin Archives.

Barker, Eugene C., *The Life of Stephen F. Austin, Founder of Texas, 1793–1836: A Chapter in the Westward Movement of the Anglo-American People.* Nashville: Cokesbury Press, 1925.

Binkley, William C. *The Texas Revolution.* Baton Rouge: Louisiana State University Press, 1952.

Castañeda, Carlos E. *Our Catholic Heritage in Texas, 1519–1936.* Vol. 6, *The Fight for Freedom, 1810–1836.* Austin: Von Boeckmann–Jones Company, 1950.

Yoakum, Henderson. *History of Texas from Its First Settlement in 1685 to Its Annexation to the United States in 1846.* 2 vols. New York: Redfield, 1855; reprinted, Austin: Steck Company, 1935.

Young, J. H. *New Map of Texas with the Contiguous American and Mexican States.* Philadelphia: S. Augustus Mitchell, 1836. Located in the University of Texas at Austin Archives.

Map 25. The Alamo

Bolton, Herbert Eugene. *Texas in the Middle Eighteenth Century: Studies in Spanish Colonial History and Administration.* New York: Russell & Russell, Inc., 1962; first published in 1915 as Vol. 3 in the University of California Publications in History.

Castañeda, Carlos E. *Our Catholic Heritage in Texas, 1519–1936.* Vol. 2, *The Mission Era: The Winning of Texas, 1693–1731.* Austin: Von Boeckmann–Jones Company, 1936.

_____. *Our Catholic Heritage in Texas, 1519–1936.* Vol. 3, *The Mission Era: The Missions At Work, 1731–1761.* Austin: Von Boeckmann–Jones Company, 1938.

_____. *Our Catholic Heritage in Texas, 1519–1936.* Vol. 4, *The Mission Era: The Passing of the Missions, 1762–1782.* Austin: Von Boeckmann–Jones Company, 1939.

_____. *Our Catholic Heritage in Texas, 1519–1936.* Vol. 5, *The Mission Era: The End of the Spanish Regime, 1780–1810.* Austin: Von Boeckmann–Jones Company, 1942.

_____. *Our Catholic Heritage in Texas, 1519–1936.* Vol. 6, *Transition Period: The Fight for Freedom, 1810–1836.* Austin: Von Boeckmann–Jones Company, Publishers, 1950.

de la Peña, José Enrique. *With Santa Anna in Texas: A Personal Narrative of the Revolution.* Translated and edited by Carmen Perry. College Station: Texas A&M University Press, 1975.

Houston, Andrew Jackson. *Military Maps of the Texas Revolution.* Houston; 1938. Located in the University of North Texas Library.

Labustida, Ygnacio de. *Plano de la Ciudad de San Antonio de Bejar y Fortificacion del Alamo.* San Antonio, March, 1836. Located in the University of Texas at Austin Archives.

Lord, Walter. *A Time to Stand.* New York: Harper & Brothers, 1961.

McDonald, Archie P. *Travis.* Austin: Jenkins Publishing Company, 1976.

Tinkle, Lon. *13 Days to Glory.* New York: McGraw-Hill Book Company, Inc., 1958; reprinted, College Station: Texas A&M University Press, 1986.

Yoakum, Henderson. *History of Texas from Its First Settlement in 1685 to Its Annexation to the United States in 1846.* 2 vols. New York: Redfield, 1855; fascimile reproduction, Austin: Steck Company, 1935.

Map 26. The Texas Revolution

Castañeda, Carlos E. *Our Catholic Heritage of Texas, 1519–1936.* Vol. 6, *Transition Period: The Fight for Freedom, 1810–1836.* Austin: Von Boeckmann–Jones Company, 1950.

_____, trans. *The Mexican Side of the Texas Revolution by the Chief Mexican Participants.* Dallas: P. L. Turner Company, 1928.

Harris, Dilue. "The Reminiscences of Mrs. Dilue Harris," *Southwestern Historical Quarterly* 4, no. 3 (January, 1901): 155–89.

Houston, Andrew Jackson. *Military Maps of the Texas Revolution.* Houston, 1938. Located in the University of North Texas Library.

Wallace, Ernest, and David M. Vigness. *Documents of Texas History.* Austin: Steck Company, 1963.

Map 27. The Goliad Massacre

Castañeda, Carlos E. *Our Catholic Heritage of Texas, 1519–1936,* Vol. 6, *Transition Period: The Fight for Freedom, 1810–1836.* Austin: Von Boeckmann–Jones Company, 1950.

Davenport, Harbert, "The Men of Goliad," *Southwestern Historical Quarterly* 43, no. 1 (July, 1939): 1–41.

Smith, Ruby Cumby. "James W. Fannin, Jr., in the Texas Revolution," *Southwestern Historical Quarterly* 23, no. 2 (October, 1919): 79–90; 23, no. 3 (January, 1920): 171–203; 23, no. 4 (April, 1920): 271–84.

Wortham, Louis J. *A History of Texas from Wilderness to Commonwealth.* Vol. 3. Fort Worth: Wortham-Molyneaux Company, 1924.

Yoakum, Henderson. *History of Texas from Its First Settlement in 1685 to Its Annexation to the United States in 1846.* Vol. 2. New York: Redfield, 1855; facsimile reproduction, Austin: Steck Company, 1935.

Map 28. The Battle of San Jacinto

Barker, Eugene C. "The San Jacinto Campaign," *The Quarterly of the Texas State Historical Association* 4, no. 4 (April, 1901): 237–345.

Castañeda, Carlos E., trans. *The Mexican Side of the Texas Revolution.* Dallas: P. L. Turner Company, 1928.

Houston, Andrew Jackson. *Military Maps of the Texas Revolution.* Houston, 1938. Located in the University of North Texas Library.

Pohl, James W., and Stephen L. Hardin, "The Military History of the Texas Revolution: An Overview," *Southwestern Historical Quarterly* 89, no. 3 (January, 1986): 269–308.

Tolbert, Frank X. *The Day of San Jacinto.* New York: McGraw-Hill Book Company, 1959.

Wortham, Louis J. *A History of Texas from Wilderness to Commonwealth.* Vol. 3. Fort Worth: Wortham-Molyneaux Company, 1924.

Yoakum, Henderson. *History of Texas from Its First Settlement in 1685 to Its Annexation to the United States in 1846.* Vol. 2. New York: Redfield, 1855; facsimile reproduction, Austin: Steck Company, 1935.

Map 29. Texas Capitals

Connor, Seymour V., et al. *Capitols of Texas.* Waco: Texian Press, 1970.

Winfrey, Dorman H. "The Archive Wars in Texas," *American Archivist* 23, no. 4 (October, 1960): 431–37.

Winkler, Ernest William. "The Seat of Government in Texas," *Quarterly of the Texas State Historical Association* 10, no. 2 (October, 1906): 140–71; 10, no. 3 (January, 1907): 185–245.

Map 30. Texas Counties, 1836 and 1845

Connor, Seymour V. "The Evolution of County Government in the Republic of Texas," *Southwestern Historical Quarterly* 55, no. 2 (October, 1951): 163–200.

Miller, Thomas Lloyd. *The Public Lands of Texas, 1519–1970.* Norman: University of Oklahoma Press, 1972.

Webb, Walter Prescott, and H. Bailey Carroll, eds. *The Handbook of Texas.* 2 vols. Austin: Texas State Historical Association, 1952.

White, Gifford, ed. *1840 Census of the Republic of Texas.* Austin: Pemberton Press, 1966.

Works Projects Administration, The Texas Statewide Records Project, Historical Records Survey Unit, Co-sponsored by the City of San Antonio. *Municipalities in the Republic of Texas, 1836.* N.p., May, 1940. Photocopy of map in possession of the author.

Young, James Hamilton. *Map of Texas.* Philadelphia: C. S. Williams, 1847. Located in the University of North Texas Library.

Map 31. Texan Santa Fe Expedition

Brinkley, W. C. *The Expansionist Movement in Texas, 1836–1850.* Berkeley: University of California Press, 1925.

Carroll, H. Bailey. *The Texan Santa Fe Trail.* Canyon: Panhandle-Plains Historical Society, 1951.

Falconer, Thomas. *Letters and Notes on the Texan Santa Fe Expedition, 1841–1842.* New York: Dauber & Pine Bookshops, 1930.

Kendall, George Wilkins. *Narrative of the Texan Santa Fe Expedition.* Chicago: Lakeside Press, R. R. Donnelley and Sons Company, 1929.

Marshall, Thomas Maitland. "The Commercial Aspects of the Texan Santa Fe Expedition," *Southwestern Historical Quarterly* 20, no. 3 (January, 1917): 242–59.

Siegel, Stanley. *Political History of the Texas Republic, 1836–1845.* Austin: University of Texas Press, 1956.

Yoakum, Henderson. *History of Texas from Its First Settlement in 1685 to Its Annexation to the United States in 1846.* Vol. 2. New York: Redfield, 1855; facsimile reproduction, Austin: Steck Company, 1935.

Map 32. The Snively Expedition

Carroll, H. Bailey. "Steward A. Miller and the Snively Expedition of 1843," *Southwestern Historical Quarterly* 54, no 3. (January, 1951): 261–86.

Yoakum, Henderson. *History of Texas from Its First Settlement in 1685 to Its Annexation to the United States in 1846.* Vol. 2. New York: Redfield, 1855; facsimile reproduction, Austin: Steck Company, 1935.

Map 33. The American-Mexican War, 1846–1848

Bauer, K. Jack. *The Mexican War, 1846–1848.* New York: Macmillan Publishing Company, Inc., 1974.

Bevans, Charles I., comp. *Treaties and Other International Agreements of the United States of America, 1776–1949.* Vol. 9, pp. 791–806, Treaty of Guadalupe Hidalgo, February 2, 1848. Department of State Publication 8615. Washington, D.C.: Government Printing Office, 1972.

Dillon, Lester R., Jr. *American Artillery in the Mexican War, 1846–1847.* Austin: Presidial Press, 1975.

Esposito, Vincent L., ed. *The West Point Atlas of American Wars.* Vol. 1, 1689–1900. New York: Frederick A. Praeger, 1959.

Singletary, Otis A. *The Mexican War.* Chicago: University of Chicago Press, 1960.

Singletary, Otis A. *The Mexican War.* Chicago: University of Chicago Press, 1960.

Smith, Justin H. *The War with Mexico.* 2 vols. New York: Macmillan Company, 1919.

Webb, Walter Prescott. *The Texas Rangers: A Century of Frontier Defense.* Boston: Houghton Mifflin, 1935.

Map 34. Texas Boundaries to the Compromise of 1850

Binkley, William Campbell. *The Expansionist Movement in Texas, 1836–1850.* Berkeley: University of California Press, 1925.

Commager, Henry Steele, ed. *Documents of American History.* 7th ed. Vol. 1. New York: Appleton-Century-Crofts, 1963.

Paullin, Charles O. *Atlas of the Historical Geography of the United States.* Edited by John K. Wright. Washington, D.C.: Carnegie Institution and American Geographical Society, 1932.

Yoakum, Henderson. *History of Texas from Its First Settlement in 1685 to Its Annexation to the United States in 1846.* Vol. 2. New York: Redfield, 1855; facsimile reproduction, Austin: Steck Company, 1935.

Map 35. Federal Military Posts Before the Civil War

Barrett, Arrie, "Federal Military Outposts in Texas, 1846–1861." Master's thesis, University of Texas, 1927.

Bevans, Charles I., comp. *Treaties and Other International Agreements of the United States of America, 1776–1949.* Department of State Publication 8615. Vol. 9, pp. 791–806, Treaty of Guadalupe Hidalgo, February 2, 1848; pp. 807–11, Suspension of Hostilities, February 29, 1848. Washington, D.C.: Government Printing Office, 1972.

U.S. Congress, Senate. "Map of the United States Exhibiting the Military Departments and Posts, 1860." *Senate Exec. Doc.* 52, 36th Cong., 1st sess. Separate map located in the University of Texas at Austin Archives.

Webb, Walter Prescott, and H. Bailey Carroll, eds. *The Handbook of Texas.* Vol. 1. Austin: Texas Historical Association, 1952.

Map 36. Indian Reservations in the 1850s

Harmon, George D. "The United States Indian Policy in Texas, 1845–1860," *Mississippi Valley Historical Review* 17, no. 3 (December, 1930): 377–403.

Koch, Lena Clara. "The Federal Indian Policy in Texas, 1845–1860," *Southwestern Historical Quarterly* 28, no. 4 (April, 1925): 259–86.

Neighbours, Kenneth Franklin. *Robert Simpson Neighbors and the Texas Frontier, 1836–1859.* Waco: Texian Press, 1975.

Webb, Walter Prescott, and H. Bailey Carroll, eds. *Handbook of Texas.* Vol. 1. Austin: Texas State Historical Association, 1952.

Map 37. The San Antonio–San Diego Mail Line

Austerman, Wayne R. *Sharps Rifles and Spanish Mules:*

The San Antonio–El Paso Mail, 1851–1881. College Station: Texas A&M University Press, 1985.

Conkling, Roscoe P., and Margaret B. Conkling. *The Butterfield Overland Mail, 1857–1869.* 3 vols. Glendale, Calif.: Arthur H. Clark Company, 1947.

Mahon, Emmie Giddings W., and Chester V. Kielman. "George H. Giddings and the San Antonio–San Diego Mail Line," *Southwestern Historical Quarterly* 61, no. 2 (October, 1957): 220–39.

Richardson's New Map of the State of Texas Including Part of Mexico, Compiled from Government Surveys and Other Authentic Documents. Philadelphia: Charles Desilver, 1859. Located in the Library of Congress Map Division.

Map 38. Butterfield Overland Mail Route, 1858–1861

Colton's New Map of the State of Texas. Compiled from J. De Cordova's large map. New York: J. H. Colton, 1861. Located in the Library of Congress Map Division.

Conkling, Roscoe P., and Margaret B. Conkling. *The Butterfield Overland Mail, 1857–1869.* 3 vols. Glendale, Calif.: Arthur H. Clark Company, 1947.

Gillespie, G.L., *Map of the States of Texas.* Compiled and drawn October 1865 and for stone, June, 1867, by Helmuth Holtz. Authorities, Pressler's *Map of Texas— Rebel Surveys—Military Map of Texas and New Mexico.* Located in the Library of Congress Map Division.

Johnson and Browning. *Johnson's New Map of the State of Texas.* Richmond, Va., 1861. Located in the Library of Congress Map Division.

Williams, J. W. *Old Texas Trails.* Edited and compiled by Kenneth F. Neighbours. Burnet, Texas: Eakin Press, 1979.

Winther, Oscar Osborn. *The Transportation Frontier: Trans-Mississippi West, 1865–1890.* New York: Holt, Rinehart and Winston, 1964.

Map 39. Secession Movement in Texas

Ashcraft, Allan C. *Texas in the Civil War.* Austin: Texas Civil War Centennial Commission, 1962.

Buenger, Walter L. *Secession and the Union in Texas.* Austin: University of Texas Press, 1984.

Winkler, Ernest William, ed. *Journal of the Secession Convention.* Austin: Austin Printing Company, 1912.

Map 40. Texas in the Civil War

Ashcraft, Allan C. *Texas in the Civil War.* Austin: Texas Civil War Centennial Commission, 1962.

Crow, James Burchell. "Confederate Military Operations in Texas, 1861–1865." Master's thesis, North Texas State University, 1957.

Fitzhugh, Lester N. "Saluria, Fort Esperanza, and Military Operations on the Texas Coast, 1861–1864, *Southwestern Historical Quarterly* 61, no. 1 (July, 1957): 60–100.

Hall, Martin Hardwick. *Sibley's New Mexico Campaign.* Austin: University of Texas Press, 1960.

Smith, David Paul. "Frontier Defense in Texas, 1861– 1865." Ph.D. diss., University of North Texas, 1987.

Wooten, Dudley G., ed. *A Comprehensive History of Texas.* Vol. 2. Dallas: William G. Scarff, 1898.

Map 41. Military Posts After the Civil War

Branda, Eldon Stephen, ed. *The Handbook of Texas: A Supplement.* Austin: Texas State Historical Association, 1976.

Hagan, William T. *American Indians.* Chicago: University of Chicago Press, 1961.

Utley, Robert M. *Frontier Regulars: The United States Army and the Indians, 1866–1890.* New York: Macmillan Publishing Company, 1973.

Webb, Walter Prescott, and H. Bailey Carroll, eds. *The Handbook of Texas.* Vol. 1. Austin: Texas State Historical Association, 1952.

Map 42. Last Days of the Free Indian in Texas

Andrist, Ralph K. *The Long Death: The Last Days of the Plains Indian.* New York: Macmillan Company, 1964.

Nye, Wilbur Sturtevant. *Carbine and Lance: The Story of Old Fort Sill.* Norman: University of Oklahoma Press, 1937.

Utley, Robert M. *Frontier Regulars: The United States Army and the Indian, 1866–1890.* New York: Macmillan Publishing Company, Inc., 1973.

Map 43. Cattle Trails

Atherton, Lewis. *The Cattle Kings.* Bloomington: Indiana University Press, 1961; reprinted, Lincoln: University of Nebraska Press, 1972.

Brayer, Garnet M., and Herbert O. Brayer, comps. *America's Cattle Trails.* Map. Denver: Western Range Cattle Industry Study and the American Pioneer Trails Association, 1949.

Dale, Edward Everett. *The Range Cattle Industry: Ranching on the Great Plains from 1865 to 1925.* Norman: University of Oklahoma Press, 1930, 1960.

Gard, Wayne. *The Chisholm Trail.* Norman: University of Oklahoma Press, 1954.

Jordan, Terry G. *Trails to Texas: Southern Roots of Western Cattle Ranching.* Lincoln: University of Nebraska Press, 1981.

Osgood, Ernest Staples. *The Day of the Cattleman.* Chicago: University of Chicago Press, 1929.

Potter, Jack. *Cattle Trails of the Old West.* Clayton, N.M.: Laura R. Krehbiel, 1935.

Skaggs, Jimmy M. *The Cattle-Trailing Industry: Between Supply and Demand, 1886–1890.* Lawrence: University Press of Kansas, 1973.

Webb, Walter Prescott. *The Great Plains.* Boston: Ginn and Company, 1931.

Map 44. Hurricanes Affecting Texas

Bomar, George W. *Texas Weather.* Austin: University of Texas Press, 1983.

Dallas Morning News, August 20, 1983, p. 23A; August 29, 1983, pp. 1A, 26A.

Henry, Walter K.; Dennis M. Driscoll; and J. Patrick McCormack. *Hurricanes on the Texas Coast*. Rev. ed. College Station: Texas A&M University, 1982.

Huff, Millicent, and H. Bailey Carroll, "Hurricane Carla at Galveston, 1961," *Southwestern Historical Quarterly* 65, no. 3 (January, 1962): 293–309.

Orton, Robert B. "Climates of the States: Texas." In *Climatography of the United States*. No. 60-41. Washington, D.C.: Department of Commerce, 1960; revised and reprinted, 1969.

Orton, Robert B., and Charles R. Condon. "Hurricane Celia, July 30–August 5." In *NOAA's Climatological Data, National Summary* 21, no. 8. Washington, D.C.: Department of Commerce, 1970.

Pass, Fred, ed. *Texas Almanac and State Industrial Guide, 1978–1979*. Dallas: A. H. Belo Corporation, 1977.

Weems, John Edward. *A Weekend in September*. College Station: Texas A&M University Press, 1980.

Map 45. Major Oil and Gas Discoveries

Rister, Carl Coke, *Oil! Titan of the Southwest*. Norman: University of Oklahoma Press, 1949.

Rundell, Walter, Jr. *Early Texas Oil: A Photographic History, 1866–1936*. College Station: Texas A&M University Press, 1977.

Texas Oil and Gas. Dallas: Texas Mid-Continent Oil & Gas Association, n.d.

Warner, C.A. "Texas and the Oil Industry," *Southwestern Historical Quarterly* 50, no. 1 (July, 1946): 1–24.

Map 46. World War I Military Installations

Branda, Eldon Stephen, ed. *The Handbook of Texas: A Supplement*. Austin: Texas State Historical Association, 1976.

Webb, Walter Prescott, and H. Bailey Carroll, eds. *The Handbook of Texas*. 2 vols. Austin: Texas State Historical Association, 1952.

Map 47. World War II Army and Navy Installations

Irvine, E. Eastman, ed. *The World Almanac and Book of Facts for 1945*. New York: New York World-Telegram, 1945.

Webb, Walter Prescott, and H. Bailey Carroll, eds. *The Handbook of Texas*. 2 vols. Austin: Texas State Historical Association, 1952.

Map 48. World War II Army Air Forces Stations

Irvine, E. Eastman, ed. *The World Almanac and Book of Facts for 1945*. New York: New York World-Telegram, 1945.

Webb, Walter Prescott, and H. Bailey Carroll, eds. *The Handbook of Texas*. 2 vols. Austin: Texas State Historical Association, 1952.

Map 49. Rivers and Reservoirs

Jordan, Terry G.; John L. Bean; and William M. Holmes. *Texas: A Geography*. Boulder: Westview Press, 1984.

Kingston, Michael T., ed. *Texas Almanac and State Industrial Guide, 1984–1985*. Dallas: A. H. Belo Corporation, 1983.

U.S. Study Commission—Texas. *The Report of the U.S. Study Commission—Texas*. Austin: United States Study Commission on the Neches, Trinity, Brazos, Colorado, Guadalupe, San Antonio, Nueces, and San Jacinto River Basins and Intervening Areas, 1962. Part 2: Resources and Problems.

Map 50. Sea and Air Ports

Kingston, Michael T., ed. *Texas Almanac and State Industrial Guide, 1984–1985*. Dallas: A. H. Belo Corporation, 1983.

Sharrer, Clyde G. "Aviation in Texas: An Address Delivered to the National Congress of Aviation Organizations," Kansas City, Mo., March 24, 1953. On file at the Texas Aeronautics Commission, Austin.

Map 51. Railroads

Kasparik, Ed, State Rail Planner, Railroad Commission of Texas, Austin, to A. Ray Stephens, April 18, 1984.

Kingston, Michael T., ed. *Texas Almanac and State Industrial Guide, 1984–1985*. Dallas: A. H. Belo Corporation, 1983.

Railroad Commission of Texas. *Texas Railroads*. Austin: Railroad Commission of Texas, 1982. Map of Texas Rail System.

Reed, St. Clair Griffin. *A History of the Texas Railroads and of Transportation Conditions under Spain and Mexico and the Republic and the State*. Houston: Saint Clair Publishing Company, 1941.

Zlatkovich, Charles P. *Texas Railroads: A Record of Construction and Abandonment*. Austin: Bureau of Business Research, University of Texas at Austin, and Texas State Historical Association, 1981.

Map 52. Interstate Highway System

Pass, Fred, ed. *Texas Almanac and State Industrial Guide, 1982-1983*. Dallas: A. H. Belo Corporation, 1981.

Texas Department of Highways and Public Transportation, Travel and Information Division. *The Texas Highway Department*. Austin: Texas Department of Highways and Public Transportation, 1973.

Map 53. State Parks

Branda, Eldon Stephen, ed. *The Handbook of Texas: A Supplement*. Austin: Texas State Historical Association, 1976.

Pass, Fred, ed. *Texas Almanac and State Industrial Guide, 1982–1983*. Dallas: A. H. Belo Corporation, 1981.

Texas Parks and Wildlife Department. *Texas State Park Information*. Brochure 4000-102. Austin: Texas Parks and Wildlife Department, 1982.

Texas State Department of Highways and Public Transportation. *Texas: Official Highway Travel Map*. Austin: Texas State Department of Highways and Public Transportation, [1983].

Webb, Walter, Prescott, and H. Bailey Carroll, eds. *The Handbook of Texas*. 2 vols. Austin: Texas State Historical Association, 1952.

Map 54. National Forests, Grasslands, and Wildlife Refuges

Fleetwood, Raymond J., Angleton, Texas, to A. Ray Stephens, April 27, 1971.

Kingston, Michael T., ed. *Texas Almanac and State Industrial Guide, 1984–1985*. Dallas: A. H. Belo Corporation, 1983.

Smith, James S., Refuge Supervisor, South Texas Refuge, to A. Ray Stephens, February 15, 1984.

U.S. Department of Agriculture. *National Forests in Texas*. Map F 79-R8. Lufkin: U.S. Department of Agriculture, Forest Service, Southern Region, 1968.

U.S. Department of Agriculture. *Panhandle National Grasslands, New Mexico, Texas, and Oklahoma*. Amarillo: U.S. Department of Agriculture, Forest Service, Southwestern Region, 1961.

U.S. Department of the Interior. *The National Wildlife Refuge System*. Leaflet RL 1A-R. Washington, D.C.: Department of the Interior, Fish and Wildlife Service, Bureau of Sport Fisheries and Wildlife, 1968.

Map 55. National Parks and Historic Sites

"An Act Authorizing the Establishment of a National Site at Fort Davis." *U.S. Statutes at Large* 75: 488–89, September 8, 1961.

"An Act to Authorize the Establishment of the Alibates Flint Quarries and Texas Panhandle Pueblo Culture National Monument." *U.S. Statutes at Large* 79: 587, August 31, 1965.

"An Act to Authorize for the Establishment of the Big Thicket National Preserve." *U.S. Statutes at Large* 88: 1254–57, October 11, 1974.

"An Act to Establish the Lyndon B. Johnson National Historic Site." *U.S. Statutes at Large* 83: 274, December 2, 1969; name changed to Lyndon B. Johnson National Historical Park, 94: 3540, December 28, 1980

"An Act to Provide for the Establishment of the Chamizal National Memorial." *U.S. Statutes at Large* 80: 232, June 30, 1966.

"An Act to Provide for the Establishment of the Big Bend National Park." *U.S. Statutes at Large* 49: 393–94, June 20, 1935.

"An Act to Provide for the Establishment of the Guadalupe Mountains National Park." *U.S. Statutes at Large* 80: 920–22, October 15, 1966.

"An Act to Provide for the Establishment of Padre Island National Seashore." *U.S. Statutes at Large* 76: 650–52, September 28, 1962.

"An Act to Provide for the Establishment of the San Antonio Missions National Historical Park." *U.S. Statutes at Large,* 92: 3635–39, November 10, 1978.

Kingston, Michael T., ed. *Texas Almanac and State Industrial Guide, 1984–1985*. Dallas: A. H. Belo Corporation, 1983.

Udall, Stuart. *The National Parks of America*. New York: G. P. Putnam's Sons, 1966.

U.S. Department of the Interior, National Park Service. *Big Thicket National Preserve, Texas*. Map no. 1983—318-578/194. Washington, D.C.: Government Printing Office, 1983.

Map 56. Public Senior Colleges and Universities

Branda, Eldon Stephen, ed. *The Handbook of Texas: A Supplement*. Austin: Texas State Historical Association, 1976.

Coordinating Board of the Texas College and University System. *Institutions of Higher Education in Texas, 1982–1983*. Austin: Coordinating Board of the Texas College and University System, [1983].

Webb, Walter Prescott, and H. Bailey Carroll, eds. *The Handbook of Texas*. 2 vols. Austin: Texas State Historical Association, 1952.

Map 57. Public Community Colleges

Branda, Eldon Stephen, ed. *The Handbook of Texas: A Supplement*. Austin: Texas State Historical Association, 1976.

Coordinating Board of the Texas College and University System. *The Institutions of Higher Education in Texas, 1982–1983*. Austin: Coordinating Board of the Texas College and University System, [1983].

Webb, Walter Prescott, and H. Bailey Carroll, eds. *The Handbook of Texas*. 2 vols. Austin: Texas State Historical Association, 1952.

Map 58. Independent Colleges and Universities

Branda, Eldon Stephen, ed. *The Handbook of Texas: A Supplement*. Austin: Texas State Historical Association, 1976.

Coordinating Board of the Texas College and University System, *The Institutions of Higher Education in Texas, 1982–1983*. Austin: Coordinating Board of the Texas College and University System, [1983].

Webb, Walter Prescott, and H. Bailey Carroll, eds. *The Handbook of Texas*. 2 vols. Austin: Texas State Historical Association, 1952.

Map 58. Independent Colleges and Universities

Branda, Eldon Stephen, ed. *The Handbook of Texas: A Supplement*. Austin: Texas State Historical Association, 1976.

Texas Higher Education Coordinating Board. *Institutions of Higher Education in Texas, 1987–1988*. Austin: Texas Higher Education Coordinating Board, [1987].

Webb, Walter Prescott, and H. Bailey Carroll, eds. *The Handbook of Texas*. 2 vols. Austin: Texas State Historical Association, 1952.

Map 59. Metropolitan Statistical Areas

Bradshaw, Benjamin S., and Dudley L. Poston. "Texas

Population in 1970: 1. Trends, 1950–1970," *Texas Business Review* 45, no. 5 (May, 1971): 1–13.

Federal Committee on Standard Metropolitan Statistical Areas. "The Metropolitan Statistical Area Classification: 1980 Official Standards and Related Documents," *Statistical Reporter,* December, 1979, pp. 33–45.

Labovitz, Sanford. "Population Projections for Texas Standard Metropolitan Statistical Areas, 1970," *Texas Business Review* 37, no. 3 (March, 1962); 1–5.

Lopez, Benito, Community Development Coordinator, State of Texas, Office of State-Federal Relations, Washington, D.C., to interested state and local officials, June 29, 1983.

"Metro Areas Revamped," *Texas Town and City* 70, no. 10 (October, 1983): 22–24.

Map 60. Congressional Districts

Biographical Directory of the American Congress, 1774–1971. Washington, D.C.: Government Printing Office, 1971.

Dallas Morning News, September 28, 1983, pp. 1A, 6A; January 31, 1984, pp. 1A, 6A.

Moxley, Warden, comp. *Congressional Districts in the 1970s.* 2d ed. Washington, D.C.: Congressional Quarterly, 1974.

Saffell, David C. "1980s Congressional Redistricting: Look Like Politics as Usual," *National Civic Review,* 72, no. 7 (July–August, 1983): 362–70, 381.

Senate Bill 480, "Apportionment of Congressional Districts . . . ," *General and Special Laws of the State of Texas,* 68th Legis., reg. sess., 1983, chap. 531, pp. 3086–98.

Texas Legislative Council. *Final County Population, 1980 Census: Texas Congressional Districts.* Austin: Texas Legislative Council, [1983]. Map based on Senate Bill 480 as passed.

Map 61. Texas State House of Representatives Districts

Anderson, James E.; Richard W. Murray; and Edward L. Farley. *Texas Politics: An Introduction.* 4th ed. New York: Harper & Row, 1984.

"Constitution of Texas." In Michael T. Kingston, ed., *Texas Almanac and State Industrial Guide, 1984–1985,* pp. 480–527. Dallas: A. H. Belo Corporation, 1983.

Jensen, James R. *Legislative Apportionment in Texas.* Social Studies Volume 2. Houston: Public Affairs Research Center, University of Houston, 1964.

Texas Almanac and State Industrial Guide, 1976–1977. Dallas: A. H. Belo Corporation, 1975.

Texas Legislative Council. *Texas Representative Districts Effective for 1982 Elections as Ordered by U.S. District Court, Northern District of Texas, Dallas Division, March 5, 1982.* Austin: Texas Legislative Council, May, 1982. Map.

Wallace, Ernest, and David M. Vigness, eds. *Documents of Texas History.* Austin: Steck Company, 1963.

Map 62. Texas State Senate Districts

Anderson, James E.; Richard W. Murray; and Edward L. Farley. *Texas Politics: An Introduction.* 4th ed. New York: Harper & Row, Publishers, 1984.

Dallas Morning News, May 29, 1983, p. 20A; December 25, 1983, p. 46A.

Jensen, James R. *Legislative Apportionment in Texas.* Social Studies Volume 2. Houston: Public Affairs Research Center, University of Houston, 1964.

Kingston, Michael T., ed. *Texas Almanac and State Industrial Guide, 1984–1985.* Dallas: A. H. Belo Corporation, 1983.

Legislative Redistricting Board of Texas. "Apportionment of the State of Texas into Senatorial Districts," October 15, 1971. Located in the Texas Legislative Reference Library, Austin, Texas.

Legislative Redistricting Board of Texas. "Minutes of the Legislative Redistricting Board of Texas," October 25–28, 1981. Located in the Texas Legislative Reference Library, Austin, Texas.

Texas Almanac and State Industrial Guide, 1970–1971. Dallas: A. H. Belo Corporation, 1969.

Texas Almanac and State Industrial Guide, 1976–1977. Dallas: A. H. Belo Corporation, 1975.

Texas Legislative Council. *Texas Senate Districts Effective for 1982 Elections as Ordered by U.S. District Court, Northern District of Texas, Dallas Division, March 5, 1982.* Austin: Texas Legislative Council, May 1982. Map. The map also indicates nine changes made by Senate Resolution 599 during the 1983 regular session.

Wallace, Ernest, and David M. Vigness, eds. *Documents of Texas History.* Austin: Steck Company, 1963.

Map 63. Regional Councils in Texas

Kingston, Michael T., ed. *Texas Almanac and State Industrial Guide, 1984–1985.* Dallas: A. H. Belo Corporation, 1983.

Texas Advisory Commission on Intergovernmental Relations. *Regional Councils in Texas: A Status Report and Directory, 1981.* Austin: Governor's Budget and Planning Office, 1982.

Map 64. Modern Texas

Dethloff, Henry C., and Irvin M. May, Jr., eds. *Southwestern Agriculture: Pre-Columbian to Modern.* College Station: Texas A&M University Press, 1982.

Kingston, Michael T., ed. *The Texas Almanac and State Industrial Guide, 1984–1985.* Dallas: A. H. Belo Corporation, 1987.

Texas Legislative Council. *Final County Population, 1980 Census.* Austin: Texas Legislative Council, November 15, 1982. Map.

INDEX